CLOCKSPEED

CLOCKSPEED

Winning Industry Control in the Age of Temporary Advantage

CHARLES H. FINE

PERSEUS BOOKS

Reading, Massachusetts

Library of Congress Catalog Card Number: 99-65117
ISBN 0-7382-0153-7

Perseus Books is a member of the Perseus Books Group

Cover design by Suzanne Heiser
Text design by Diane Sawyer
Set in 11-point Sabon by Sawyer Design Associates, Inc.

1 2 3 4 5 6 7 8 9-   -02 01 00 99

Perseus Books are available at special discounts for bulk purchases in the U.S. by corporations, institutions, and other organizations. For more information, please contact the Special Markets Department at HarperCollins Publishers, 10 East 53rd Street, New York, NY 10022, or call 212-207-7528.

Find Perseus Books on the World Wide Web at
http://www.perseusbooks.com

TO WENDY

Contents

ACKNOWLEDGMENTS

"If I have seen farther, it is by standing on the shoulders of giants."

—SIR ISAAC NEWTON[1]

I DON'T KNOW WHAT IT IS to see as far as Isaac Newton, but I do know what it is to have the benefit of standing on the shoulders of giants. I am deeply grateful to very many "giants" who have taught me over the years and supported my endeavors.

On the intellectual side, I am grateful to my teachers at Duke, Ken Baker and, especially, David Peterson, who was my mentor and role model for most of my formative undergraduate years. In graduate school at Stanford, I found giants under virtually every palm tree. I am very grateful for the quality and quantity of the education Stanford afforded me. I learned a great deal from Mike Harrison, Evan Porteus, Chuck Holloway, Joel Demski, Steve Wheelwright, Bob Wilson, and especially my dissertation advisor, David Kreps. Thank you.

At MIT, I found many more giants. I have benefited from an institution that is unparalleled in the expertise and opportunities for doing industrial research. I am grateful to many senior Sloan School colleagues who have supported my research efforts, especially Gabriel Bitran, Steve Graves, Arnoldo Hax, Tom Magnanti, and Lester Thurow. I cannot imagine a more supportive environment than what you created. Thank you.

What is particularly unique and enriching at MIT is

the research center structure that complements the academic department structure. MIT's research centers provide longevity and depth in relationships with industrial research partners around the world. Many of these centers and their industrial sponsors were instrumental in providing funding and research sites for my work. I am particularly indebted to Richard Lester and the Industrial Performance Center; Jim Rice, Yossi Sheffi, and Peter Metz at the Integrated Supply Chain Management Program; Dick Samuels and Pat Gercik at the MIT Japan Program; Ed Roberts and John Hauser at Sloan's International Center for Research in the Management of Technology; Kirk Bozdogan, Earll Murman, and Wes Harris at the Lean Aerospace Initiative; and Warren Seering at the Center for Innovation in Product Development.

Two additional research centers stand out particularly—giants among the giants. In 1993, Dan Roos invited me to serve as co-director of the International Motor Vehicle Program (IMVP). Following the success of *The Machine That Changed the World,* the opportunities to visit automotive industry sites and experts around the world were unparalleled. I learned an enormous amount both from Dan and from the opportunities that this unique program and its generous sponsors provided.

In 1988, Tom Magnanti and Kent Bowen launched what has been the most important program to me at MIT: the Leaders for Manufacturing (LFM) Program. I have had the opportunity to teach every LFM class through the class of 1998, and to be engaged in research projects at many of the partner companies, including Boeing, Chrysler, DEC, Eastman Kodak, Ford, General Motors, Hewlett-Packard, Intel, Johnson & Johnson, Motorola, Polaroid, United Technologies, and Bay Networks. Intel (Gene Meieran, Mike Splinter, David Marsing, Ken Thompson, Don Rose, and Randy Bollig) and Chrysler (Dennis Pawley, Don Lucas, and Jamie Bonini) were especially supportive of my research for this book in the early stages, for which I am very grateful. LFM also opened a window for me to MIT's engineering school, where I have learned much from Warren Seering, Kim Kimerling, John Kassakian, Tom Eagar, and numerous other colleagues.[2]

Complementing the industrial sponsors, I have benefited significantly from generous public sector support as well. Hirsh Cohen and Ralph Gomory at the Sloan Foundation have been extremely supportive of my work. In addition, ARPA's Agile Manufacturing initiative and Mantech at Wright Laboratories have both been instrumental in support of the learning within this project. Much thanks go to Mike McGrath, Kevin Lyons, Karen Richter, Mickey Hitchcock, and especially George Orzel.

Finally, I owe a great debt to colleagues who have worked with me directly (and indirectly) on the research represented here. First *without equal* is Dan Whitney. Dan's return to MIT in 1993 coincided with my entry into IMVP and the "agile projects." Our research and teaching collaborations shaped many of the ideas in this book; his insights are reflected in every chapter. In addition, teaching and research collaborations (and friendship) with Morris Cohen, Steven Eppinger, Karl Ulrich, Larry Wein, Rob Freund, Don Rosenfeld, John Sterman, Nelson Repenning, Anant Balakrishnan, Michael Cusumano, Bob Gibbons, and Lode Li taught me a great deal.

Certainly the richest renewable asset of MIT is its student body, which provides the opportunity to interact and work with the best and the brightest from around the world. Many have contributed to ideas in this book. I would like to thank my thesis students Gary Burchill, Maureen Lojo, Nitin Joglejar, Ed Anderson, Geoff Parker, Sharon Novak, Chris Couch, Betsy Adams, Charles Pieczulewski, Paul Gutwald, Angela Longo, Seth Taylor, Lance Mansfield, and literally dozens of LFM students whose field work informed me deeply. In addition, many students in the LFM classes of 1996, 1997, and 1998 sat through lectures and class discussions of early versions of material for this book and gave comments and criticism generously and usually gently.

Many colleagues and students read all or parts of this manuscript, providing countless suggestions that improved it. Among those most helpful were Dan Whitney, John Boardman, Nitin Joglekar, Jim Moore, Peter Senge, Steve Freeman, Sharon Novak, Geoffrey Parker, George Gilboy, and the entire LFM class of 1998.

Complementing the rich contributions from students, colleagues and mentors, are those of the support staff at MIT who provide support that goes into many dimensions far beyond office logistics. I am particularly grateful to Anna Piccolo and Gina Milton.

Crafting a wealth of research and ideas into a coherent book (my first) is a process whose length and complexity I underestimated severely. I owe a great debt to Donna Carpenter and the staff at Wordworks, Inc. in Boston—Christina Braun, Maurice Coyle, Fred Dillen, Erik Hansen, Susannah Ketchum, Martha Lawler, Toni Porcelli, Saul Wisnia, and G. Patton Wright—both for helping me think through how to structure a morass of ideas into a book and for editing (often repeatedly) my sometimes lifeless prose to create what I hope is a very readable manuscript. Also, my thanks to Diane Sawyer and her staff who prepared camera-ready copy for the book. Nick Philipson, my editor, and his colleagues at Perseus Books have been extremely helpful and supportive every step of the way. No less was the contribution of Helen Rees, who served as both my literary agent and the midwife for the book.

Complementing my debts to the intellectual giants, my debts on the spiritual side are no less great. My father (of blessed memory) and my mother taught me—by example—about love, honor, generosity, and respect. They also imbued in me the confidence to speak my mind and stand my ground. For these gifts I am forever grateful.

My parents-in-law, Harvey and Roslyn Wolfe, have accepted me as a son, and my brothers Pete and Bruce have always been by my side. Who could ask for more than that? My mentors R. Shmuel Posner, R. Reuven Cohn, and R. Gershon Segal each taught me a great deal about heritage, community, and being a mensch. I should only grow up to be as wise and good as they.

I am also grateful to Dr. Ned Hallowell, who helped me understand attention deficit disorder and provided the evidence that one could actually finish a book despite the constant tug of the distractions driven by ADD.[3] Through him I learned that ADD (and the novelty-seeking behavior that accompanies it) can actually be an advantage in a fast-clockspeed world.

My three sons, David, Stevie, and Jacob, have taught me more about life than I ever imagined possible. They have brought empirical meaning to the theories of chaos.

Finally, my greatest debts are to my wife, Wendy. Her acceptance of and commitment to me and my dreams were never earned, nor can they ever be compensated for. They are a gift for which I am thankful far beyond my ability to communicate. I can only offer in return my love.

Thank you, Wendy. This book's for you.

THE GENETICS OF BUSINESS:

LEARNING FROM THE FRUIT FLIES

1 EVOLUTION OR EXTINCTION

Competition in the Age of
Temporary Advantage

In the natural world, species evolve—that is, they
change to meet new challenges—or they die. The
same genetic imperative operates in business.

IN 1995, two Americans and a German won the Nobel Prize in medicine for their work on the process whereby embryos develop from a single cell into complex adults.[1] Their research shed light on how the various parts of the body develop from that single cell, which itself merges the genetic codes from two parents. The work was hailed as a breakthrough in explaining the formation of birth defects.[2] In pursuit of that goal, these three scientists spent years painstakingly examining hundreds of mutations in thousands of fruit flies *(Drosophila)*. They are not alone. Around the world, several thousand scientists devote their lives to the study of the seemingly insignificant fruit fly.[3]

Why fruit flies? That question changed the course of my research. Biologists study fruit flies because their genetic structure is similar to that of humans, because hundreds of them can be kept in a small milk bottle, and because, despite their genetic complexity, they evolve rapidly: They go from egghood to parenthood to death in under two weeks.[4]

Fruit flies enable a manifold increase in research productivity. In a 40-year career in genetics, a scientist studying humans can barely gather data from a single generation or two before he or she is forced by age to retire. The life span of the fecund fruit fly, however, is so short that scientists can study genetic changes in hundreds of generations during a decade.[5]

Fruit flies are what I call a *fast-clockspeed* species. That is, they have an extremely brief life cycle. Mammals, such as elephants and humans, live by much slower clockspeeds. They measure their lives in decades, not days. Even slower are the reptiles. The hardy sea turtle, whose life span can exceed a century, has evolved little since its terrestrial cousins, the dinosaurs, roamed the earth.

The Fruit Flies of Business

In the fall of 1995, I was four years into a seven-year research project on a challenging topic: the strategic impact of supply chain strategy on competitive advantage. But my work, focused primarily on the dinosaur-like metal-bending industries, was proceeding slowly—painfully so.

I had begun with a hypothesis contrary to the prevailing train of thought. Reengineering was then all the rage,[6] and business theorists sang the praises of outsourcing and downsizing. Corporate leaders were farming out their manufacturing—and engineering—in the relentless pursuit of cost reductions. I suspected, however, that this practice could seriously backfire, that the outsourcing company could lose capabilities essential to its future. So I began an investigation of the strategies behind the design of supply chains, those networks of companies from the final consumer downstream in the chain all the way upstream to the basic research and mineral extraction that support and supply a business. I wanted to learn how choices in supply chain design affected company performance.

I was making little headway in this research because the supply chains in the three industries I had chosen to explore—automobiles, machine tools, and semiconductor equipment—evolve rather slowly. Many of the customer-supplier relationships in Detroit dated back to the 1950s. The few companies left in the American machine-tool industry had stable, long-term arrangements with their heavy-industry customers.

Intel, the semiconductor company I had focused on, was growing its capacity at exponential rates by utilizing its innovative "copy exactly" manufacturing strategy, which emphasized maximum stability in its relationship with semiconductor equipment suppliers.[7] For all the supply chain dynamics on view, I might as well have been watching glaciers advance.

When I read of the Nobel Prizes in medicine for that research built around the study of fruit flies, I started thinking in a new direction: Instead of monitoring the supply chains of corporate slowpokes, why not speed things up by studying the industrial equivalents of fruit flies? If biologists could accelerate their research productivity one hundred-fold by studying *Drosophila*, could I speed up my research by finding and studying industrial fruit flies? Here was an intriguing possibility. But where could I find such specimens?

I looked again at Intel, the fastest evolving company in my study, and realized that I had been studying Intel's supply chain from the wrong end. The fruit flies were not Intel's equipment suppliers, who labored long and hard to develop robust technological solutions for multiple semiconductor generations. The fruit flies were Intel's *customers*—personal computer dynamos such as Compaq and Dell, whose products were outmoded within months of their launch and whose corporate lives seemed at risk on an almost daily basis.

From that insight came another, even more basic idea—that fruit fly companies might actually be able to serve the same function for a business researcher that the lowly *Drosophila* serves for geneticists. If so, it meant that lessons learned from observing the rapid evolution of supply chains in a Compaq or a Dell could be applied to benefit organizations in other industries.

The Clockspeed Concept

I began to look at other industries, seeking to understand their various rates of evolution. I came to think of these rates as industry *clockspeeds*. Each industry evolved at a different rate, depending in some way on its product clockspeed, process clockspeed, and organization clockspeed.

The information-entertainment industry, for instance, is one of the fastest-clockspeed fruit flies of the business world. Its products—motion pictures, for example—can have half-lives measured in hours, if not days. The biggest returns, for instance, often come from launching a successful product during the Christmas season when the number of viewers is greatest and when a movie can make an impression just before members of the Academy of Motion Picture Arts and Sciences nominate films for their annual award fest.[8] In December 1997 for example, the major U.S. movie studios and many of the most luminous American directors collectively launched almost $400 million worth of movies on a single Friday evening, with "their fates [to be] a settled issue by Saturday night," according to one commentator.[9]

Process clockspeeds in the information-entertainment industry are similarly breathtaking. We learn almost daily of new processes and services for delivering information content to the home, office, or mobile workstation. Organizational dynamics are turbulent as well. Relationships among such media giants as Disney, Viacom, Time Warner, Inc., and Rupert Murdoch's News Corporation are routinely negotiated, signed, sealed, and renegotiated in hardly more time than it takes a fruit fly to become a grandparent.

Somewhat slower, semiconductors have a clockspeed measured in years rather than months. An Intel microprocessor product family such as the Pentium II has a market life of two to four years. As for its process clockspeeds, each time Intel sinks a billion dollars into building yet another microprocessor superfactory, it expects much of that investment to be obsolete in little more than four years. That gives Intel a four-year window to recoup its outlay of billions of dollars in capital, plus achieve a return on that investment.

Moving at an even slower clockspeed, the automobile companies typically refresh their car and truck models every 4 to 8 years. In the process domain, they expect that a billion dollars invested in an engine or assembly plant will remain vibrant for 20 years or more.

At the slowest end of the clockspeed scale—up there with the sea turtles and the California redwoods—are the manufacturers of aircraft. The Boeing Company, for instance, measures its products' clockspeeds in decades. Mega-profits still flow from sales of its venerable 747 jumbo jet 30 years after its launch. The 747s produced in the 1990s rely on the same basic design and the same manufacturing plant that rolled out the first of these aircraft almost three decades ago. Elsewhere in the slow-clockspeed aircraft industry, Lockheed-Martin was working diligently in 1997 to design a warplane that was not expected to go into production before 2008.[10]

The First Lesson of the Fruit Flies

Observers often note that some industries—telecommunications, computers, and the like—undergo changes with astonishing rapidity, whereas others seem to mosey along at a leisurely pace, scarcely bothered by changes elsewhere in the business environment. This book, however, seeks to examine the experiences of companies in fast-clockspeed industries and draw from them lessons to apply to others, much as biologists learn about human beings from the research they conduct on fruit flies. In short, the insights that the corporate fruit flies offer can be illustrative and useful to *all* companies, even those with medium or slow clockspeeds.

Every student of industrial competition knows the story of one of the most information-rich fruit flies of the late twentieth century—namely, the computer industry. Specifically, this is the story of the famous—one might say, infamous—turning point that occurred when IBM made its fateful decision to outsource its personal computers' microprocessing needs to Intel and its operating system to Microsoft. Back in the early 1980s, when IBM launched its first personal computer (PC), the company pretty much *was* the entire computer industry. IBM had always prided itself on the technologically deep organization that designed and produced its super-sophisticated mainframe products. But the PC presented IBM with a special "three-dimensional" design challenge: The company needed to create a new product, a new process to manufacture it, and a new supply chain to feed that process and distribute the product.

The business and technical design IBM selected was a departure from the company's tradition of doing everything in-house, from product design and prototyping to manufacturing and distribution. To keep costs low and increase speed to market, IBM chose a modular product design, built around major components furnished by suppliers such as Intel and Microsoft.

By 1998, the personal computer had gone through seven microprocessor generations: 8088, 286, 386, 486, Pentium, Pentium-Pro, and Pentium II. Still a powerful, profitable, and influential company by the standards of the computer industry, IBM had nonetheless been far outdistanced by its two hand-picked suppliers, who had taken the lion's share of the profits and industry clout that flowed from IBM's standard-setting product. IBM's suppliers also won the allegiance of millions of customers who came to care far more about the supplier's logo—"Intel Inside" or "Windows 95"—than about the brand name of the company that assembled the components and shipped the final product. The power in the chain had shifted, as had the financial rewards.

IBM's decision to outsource its PCs' microprocessor and operating system determined the contours of the entire industry for years to come. In terms of its effect on IBM, the PC decision represents a powerful cautionary tale, a lesson from the sad experiences of a fruit fly company: When designing your supply chain, whatever your industry, beware of "Intel Inside."

That lesson applies equally well to slower clockspeed industries such as automobiles. The role of electronics subsystems, for example, has evolved in the automotive industry from the early years through the 1960s when the electrical systems—those controlling a vehicle's lights, radio, windshield wipers, starter motor, and so on—were little more than an afterthought. In those years, the core subsystem of the automobile was its steel body, which not only defined the car's styling, a critical factor in its market reception (Ford's Edsel comes to mind), but also determined the vehicle's structural integrity, ride, handling, and manufacturability. In contrast, the electrical components had little impact on design, manufacture, costs, or sales.

Today, the dollar value of a car's electronics is overtaking the value of its steel body, and the electronic system rivals the steel body as one of the most important subsystems: Car companies design their vehicles with a customer profile in mind, and virtually all the features that affect customers' perceptions of the vehicle are—or soon will be—mediated by electronics. Those features include acceleration, braking, steering, handling, and seating, as well as the communication, information, and entertainment systems.

Now consider the situation of Toyota, the third-largest automobile company in the world, and arguably the most formidable competitor in a no-longer-cozy oligopoly. Although the company maintains a virtually unassailable set of competitive advantages,[11] it has traditionally been far less vertically integrated in electronics than some of its competitors, including Ford and General Motors. In fact, Toyota has become dependent on one company—Denso (formerly Nippondenso)—for many of its electronic components and systems. The question arises whether Toyota will stay the course, risking the fate of IBM relative to Intel, or adjust its supply chain strategy and assert greater internal control over electronics.

The relatively slow clockspeed of the auto industry gives Toyota some time for deliberation and choice, but there may come a day when customers choose automobiles based on whether they say "Denso Inside" or "Bosch Inside" rather than by the name of the company that stamped and welded the sheet metal. As might be expected of the world's most benchmarked company, Toyota is not waiting around. It understands the dynamics of the fruit flies and has already begun increasing its investment in its own electronics capability.[12]

Boeing and Its Suppliers

To emphasize the contrast between fast- and slow-clockspeed industries, consider the Boeing Corporation's commercial aircraft business, which in recent decades has focused on the remarkable series of jets denoted the 747, 757, 767, and 777. Although Boeing has designed and built each one, suppliers from all over the world have made their contributions. By the late 1990s, outsourcing accounted for close to 50 percent of an airplane's total value. In fact, four Japanese aircraft manufacturers—Mitsubishi Heavy Industries, Kawasaki Heavy Industries, Ishikawajima-Harima Heavy Industries, and Fuji Heavy Industries—contribute approximately 40 percent of the value in airframes of widebody models, applying specialized skills and tooling that in many cases are unique in the world.

To understand the relationship between Boeing and these Japanese suppliers, you have to go back several decades to a time when the company made its first efforts to sell aircraft in Japan. In order to win sales to Japanese airlines, Boeing needed to give Japanese companies some of the manufacturing work involved. Boeing's managers accepted those terms, setting into motion a dynamic process that has led to an important interdependency.

Both sides of the partnership have been big winners. The Japanese bought scores of aircraft, helping Boeing to become the dominant commercial aircraft company in the world. At the same time, the Boeing relationship has enabled the Japanese manufacturers to improve their technological capabilities, thereby increasing their appeal to Boeing and other manufacturers worldwide.[13] Although Boeing depends greatly on its suppliers, the company's management believes that its systems-design and integration skills will prevent any supplier or set of suppliers from wresting away industry control.

In this turtle of an industry, upheavals and reversals of fortune do not take place overnight. Yet the examples of fruit fly industries in this book should raise a warning flag to Boeing that "Mitsubishi Inside" represents a clear if not present danger. Because of the slow clockspeeds typical of the aircraft industry, it is especially difficult to get executives in such industries to focus on the potential penalties for outsourcing key competencies—the results typically would not come to roost during the tenure of any currently active manager. This condition suggests that companies in slow-clockspeed industries should set clear guidelines as to who in the organization takes responsibility for monitoring those relationships, lest time lull the firms into a false sense of security.

Competition in the Age of Temporary Advantage

Part I of this book lays out the basic concepts and insights of business genetics. It focuses on case studies from fruit fly industries such as personal computers and information-entertainment. Beginning with the observations that industry clockspeeds vary and that faster learning may come from studying the fruit flies, chapter 2 draws out a number of rich lessons from the information-entertainment industry. Chapter 3 focuses on the implications of a single observation—that all advantage is temporary. No capability is unassailable, no lead is uncatchable, no kingdom is unbreachable. Indeed, the faster the clockspeed, the shorter the reign. Sustainable advantage is a slow-clockspeed concept; temporary advantage is a fast-clockspeed concept. And, clockspeeds are increasing almost everywhere.

By observing the fruit flies, we can see several patterns emerging in industry structure dynamics. Understanding these dynamic processes helps us develop principles to guide choices in the value chain—what I call supply chain design. In addition, by observing (in chapter 4) dynamic processes in the evolution of industry structures, we can develop insights to understand how an industry's future may unfold. Of course, no one has a crystal ball to gaze into the future. However, I believe that observing the fruit fly industries gives us the next best thing: an opportunity to see how one's future might play out based on the experiences of others—who happen to be traveling in a faster lane of traffic.

Part II of the book focuses on concepts to support the design of one's supply chain of capabilities.[14] In this age of temporary advantage, the *ultimate* core competency is the ability to choose capabilities well.[15] A company may have a core competence in product design, brand marketing, custom manufacturing, or high-volume distribution. Each of these may be important capabilities in its competitive environment. But the overriding competency is the ability to determine which of those capabilities are going to be the high-value-added capabilities and which will be the commodity abilities—and for how long. Lasting success will go neither to the company that manages to find a great business opportunity nor to the firm that develops the best proprietary technology. Rather, we will see (in chapter 5) that the greatest rewards go to the companies that can anticipate, time after time, which capabilities are worth investing in and which should be outsourced; which should be cultivated and which should be discarded; which will be the levers of value chain control and which will be controlled by others.

Observing the fruit flies leads us to another lesson: No company is an island. You may think of your company as a solitary, stand-alone entity served by subsidiary organizations, the collection of which is conveniently called the *supply chain*. That view, however, vastly underestimates the importance of the chain as a whole and fails to capture its true essence. Even the example of IBM, Intel, and Microsoft, briefly recounted above, illustrates how power and value can migrate up and down the chain. In fact, one sees in Bill Gates's search for Microsoft's encore to PC operating system dominance the instinct that future control of the information industry probably lies somewhere else in the chain. Winning with Windows is only a brief stop in a perpetually evolving competitive process.

Supply chain design is too important to leave to chance. Just as genetic engineering has begun to shortcut the process of species evolution, proactive chain design will shortcut and forever make obsolete the slow, incremental processes of industrial evolution. Chapter 6 examines this concept in greater detail. Analyzing fruit fly industries and individual companies enables us to see with greater clarity and accuracy the technology and market forces that will affect future needs. Understanding those needs makes it more likely that one can design superior capability chains.

Properly viewed, the company and its supply chain are joined at the hip, a single organic unit engaged in a joint enterprise. I propose (in chapter 7) that we view this extended enterprise as consisting of three strands: a chain of organizations, a chain of technologies, and a chain of capabilities. Strategic analysis must consider all three. Individual core capabilities, therefore, can be assessed only in the context of their capability chains.

Part III of the book focuses on implementation. Integrating new concepts into existing business processes can be harrowing. It sometimes requires tearing up the whole organizational chart.[16] But the principles proposed here do not demand that kind of radical organizational surgery.

Instead, I urge in chapters 8–11 that companies expand on a well-developed organizational process usually called concurrent engineering or integrated product development. Ultimately organizations should undertake what I call three-dimensional concurrent engineering (3-DCE), the simultaneous development of products, processes, and supply chains. In companies that now practice two-dimensional concurrent engineering (product and process only), supply chain development tends to be haphazard. Chain design decisions are not fully integrated into the development processes, and the strategic implications of supply chain design are typically not recognized in the same way as are those of the product decisions. Within the three dimensions of development, I propose (in chapter 8) analyzing strategic choices at the "architectural" level, assessing opportunities for crafting simultaneously product architectures, process architectures, and supply chain architectures.

Within 3-DCE lies the essence of supply chain design—the make/buy decision. Managers are called upon to determine which capabilities are core and which are ancillary. It is tempting to think that THE answer to the make/buy issue exists and is simple. Indeed, many business leaders advocate the buy-anything-you-can principle and articulate this position at every opportunity. Equally persuasive arguments exist for expanding widely the set of things considered as important competencies that can lead to a policy of make-as-much-as-you-can. Business situations rarely offer such either-or choices, and neither extreme strategy can stand the test of time and competition. Chapter 9, therefore, uses the clockspeed concept to expand our set of tools for evaluating and acting on critical make/buy decisions. Chapter 10 follows with instructions on how supply chain decisions can enhance other concurrent engineering methodologies. Chapter 11 offers two detailed case studies to illustrate the thinking and tools of 3-DCE—one each from medical information systems and communications satellite development. Chapter 12 revisits the PC industry in the late 1990s to observe the new insights from this robust industrial fruit fly and to sum up the ideas and methodologies presented.

The Epilogue concludes with ideas and illustrations on applying clockspeed ideas in the public sector—in university administration and regional economic development, as examples.

In the pages that follow, I offer not just a theory of industry clockspeed and business genetics, but a wealth of case histories that illustrate its principles. Moreover, I present concrete, practical tools of analysis and implementation. The objective throughout this book is to help managers and business leaders understand industrial evolutionary processes and to guide investment in evolving capability chains. As we will see, the dynamics of fruit fly evolution can lead to insights about how individual companies and entire industries evolve and adapt, as well as what dangers they face if they do not adapt quickly enough.

Myriad forces at work in the business world—economic, financial, political, social, environmental—make it impossible to prescribe a single solution for every problem. But it is neither impossible nor impractical to draw reasonable inferences about future behavior—that of companies, industries, and human beings—and to consider the implications of the increasing clockspeeds in the world in which we all live and do business. Some of those implications may surprise you. I hope that they will be useful in provoking ideas that will inspire new ways to think about designing and managing the extended enterprise.

2 WHAT FRUIT FLIES TEACH US ABOUT BUSINESS

The Insights of Clockspeed

Clockspeeds are to business genetics what lifecycles
are to human genetics.

IN CHAPTER 1, I argued that industries differ significantly in their clockspeeds. But how can these clockspeeds be measured? This is not a simple question. Some of the complexities have been relegated to the Appendix at the end of the book. However, we can begin by considering three submetrics: process clockspeed, product clockspeed, and organizational clockspeed.[1]

To measure process clockspeed in a manufacturing company, one needs to look at metrics such as capital equipment obsolescence rates. Intel's billion-dollar factory will be out of date in four years, whereas an auto company's will last twenty years or more. Ford Motor Company, for example, still operates many productive twenty-year-old plants with twenty-year-old equipment. Intel has no such relics in its portfolio. Neither Intel nor Ford is necessarily suboptimizing in this comparison; each merely operates in an industry with a different process clockspeed.

In the domain of product clockspeed, consider the commercial aircraft industry compared with MICE (multimedia information, communications, and electronics—

sometimes referred to as "infotainment"). Boeing's rate of (major) new product launches is slightly under two per decade (the 777 and the new 737 in the 1990s, the 757 and 767 in the 1980s, the 747 in the 1970s). Compare this rate with that of studios at the Walt Disney Company. In big-release children's animated movies, Disney seems to aim for one new product per year (*Beauty and the Beast, Lion King, Pocahontas, Hercules*, and so forth). As noted in chapter 1, a major movie studio may turn out dozens of new products per year, many of which will have their artistic and economic fate sealed in the first weekend after public release.[2] Although these products can have a long tail to their shelf life (*Snow White* is far older than the 747), Disney's product development teams must work on a cycle time geared to the time between new product introductions, a metric that suggests that MICE has a far faster product clockspeed than the commercial aircraft industry.

One tack for assessing organizational clockspeed is suggested by a 1997 article in the *New York Times*, which observed that in the 1990s, increased stockholder activism and impatient corporate boards seem to have led to an decrease in the average tenure of CEOs in large, publicly held companies.[3] Closely related, a research study at Stanford University measured organizational clockspeed by looking at the frequency of organizational restructurings.[4] That study found that industry sectors where the product clockspeed was higher tend also to have faster organizational clockspeeds.

Finally, one should consider clockspeed measurement for assets that are neither explicitly organizational nor technological. Two examples are distribution channels and brand names. Distribution channels such as the Sears catalog, the Wal-Mart department store, and Yahoo! advertising banners may vary significantly in the rates at which the assets can be constructed and at which they may decay. Similarly, the value of brand names such as Coca-Cola soft drinks or Tide detergent may have developed over decades and may be quite durable, whereas Saturn, Lexus, and Yugo automobiles each established a strong brand image in a fairly short period of time.

How Clockspeed Affects Decision Making

One of the most striking differences between the fruit flies and the sea turtles, the fast- and slow-clockspeed businesses, is the size of the time window for making decisions. The turtles have it—the luxury of enough time to look for and research all the options, the time to think and the time to debate. Then they have time to think again before they have to act.

In the 1970s, when Boeing began minting money with its 747 jumbo jet, a group of French, German, British, and Spanish businesses (with large government subsidies) decided to accelerate development at the Airbus consortium, a European venture to build and sell large commercial jet aircraft. The subsequent Boeing-Airbus competition has driven Lockheed and McDonnell Douglas out of the commercial aircraft business, leaving the field to two victors.[5]

Boeing has maintained the upper hand in this competition, and its jumbo jet monopoly is a good part of the reason why. For years now, Airbus and Boeing, separately and jointly, have talked about the possibility of a 600-seat super-jumbo that would surpass in a single stroke the 747 with its 400-plus seats. One problem: It might cost as much as $10 billion to develop and launch.

Boeing has no great incentive to spend that kind of money, unless Airbus commits. Airbus has been much more enthusiastic but fears that it could be financially crippled if each company actually built its own version of the super-jumbo in expectation of a market that never materializes.

In 1992, Boeing's proposal that the two organizations study the possibility of a joint super-jumbo project led to some discussions, but these ended in 1995. At that time, each company resumed its go-it-alone talk. The following year, Boeing bowed out, saying the potential market was too small and the super-jumbo was no longer being considered.[6] Airbus said it would seriously study the matter.

Meanwhile, time passes (albeit slowly), and Boeing's 747 still rules the jumbo roost. Boeing can shelve its super-jumbo plans, safe in its assumption that if it chooses to take another look two years later, all the same issues will still be in play. There seems little risk that Airbus, if it decides to move ahead on the plane, could sew up the market for the super-jumbo in that time. So with the confidence that comes with being on the slow side of the clockspeed dial, Boeing has the luxury of deciding not to decide—at least for now.

Of course, life is very different in the fast lane. For a fruit fly, to procrastinate is to die.

Netscape flashed onto the main screen of the computer world in 1994 like a bolt out of the blue. Who would have dreamed that the industry's next winning application would be access to the geek-bound World Wide Web? In a matter of months, Netscape gave away millions of copies of its Navigator browser and launched an initial public offering into Wall Street's stratosphere.

Microsoft's founder, chairman, and chief executive officer, William Gates III, wasn't amused. In 1995, he realized that Web browsers in general and Netscape's in particular had the potential to upset the dominance of his Windows franchise. In short order, Microsoft set its army of software engineers to revamping every one of the company's products to be Web-compatible. Beyond that, though, Microsoft's central mission was to develop a Web browser that could go head-to-head with Netscape's Navigator, which had captured nearly 100 percent of the market and was a darling of the industry and users around the globe.

Bill Gates also knew that to catch up, to gain market share for his Internet Explorer browser, his company would have to exercise its well-developed market muscle as well as its software development prowess. And his eye fell upon the largest single provider of on-line services to the marketplace, America Online (AOL).

At first AOL had resisted its users' desires to access the World Wide Web, insisting that its own offerings had everything an online customer could possibly desire. When the error of that position became clear, AOL cobbled together its own proprietary browser.

But Gates had other plans. To give his Internet Explorer immediate market penetration, he offered AOL a chunk of cash and a coveted button of its own on the Windows desktop—if AOL would make Explorer its exclusive browser. For Microsoft, the deal meant Explorer would become browser of choice overnight for AOL's millions of customers. For AOL, it meant that all 100 million Windows users would be able to access AOL with a single click of the mouse.

AOL's leaders had a decision to make. If they got into bed with Microsoft, they would surely realize a boost in their membership rolls—and collect some much-needed cash. On the other hand, by bolstering Internet Explorer (and thereby helping in the efforts to eliminate Netscape), they might further tighten Microsoft's stranglehold on the industry, thereby signing their own future death warrant by bringing closer the day when the public prefers Internet access directly from a Windows desktop without bothering to go through AOL first. Instead of choosing Microsoft, a potential enemy, AOL could offer Netscape's Navigator to its users, strengthening Netscape and stepping firmly into the "Stop Microsoft" camp.

Unlike Boeing and the sea turtles, AOL and its fast-clockspeed neighbors don't have the luxury of procrastinating on such decisions. Before there is barely a moment to stop and think, the time is up. In the end, for better or worse, AOL took the Microsoft deal, a decision quickly made. In the fast-clockspeed environment of the fruit flies, delay is tantamount to idling in the pit while the competition goes roaring by.

Commerce at the Speed of Light

Consider again one of the swiftest of all fruit flies, the so-called info-tainment industry, created from the convergence of the multimedia, information, communications, and electronics (MICE) industries. One might say that this industry runs at light speed, since it is driven in part by the capacity of fiber-optic communication systems to transmit information and entertainment at the speed of light.[7]

Figure 2.1 represents the MICE industry's overall function as developing and delivering information content for consumption by final customers. Information content is represented at the far right of the diagram. Video/audio entertainment such as movies, sports, news, art; print media such as newspapers, magazines, and books; communication services including voice and video telephony as well as e-mail; educational courses; shopping opportunities; and a wide panoply of offerings on the Internet—from chat groups to library services—constitute part of the wide range of content accessible to consumers. This information content can be shipped to customers across a range of different "pipeline" technologies, including copper and fiber-optic phone lines, cable TV networks, retail stores for buying or renting CDs, tapes, or print media, and a host of airwave technologies including traditional broadcast TV, cellular systems, and microwave/satellite systems. These pipelines can deliver the content to a range of different types of "reception boxes," including televisions (with or without VCRs), personal computers, telephones, pagers, and a multitude of hybrids just beginning to hit the market. Customers then consume the information content off the "box" of their choice, often with support of "box software" developed somewhat independently of the hardware box.

Can you find any dominant modes of supply chain design strategy in this industry? A few of the interesting plays include Disney's 1995 purchase of ABC broadcasting, Microsoft's 1996 partnership with

NBC broadcasting (MSNBC), and its 1997 billion-dollar investment in Comcast,[8] the fourth-largest cable TV operator in the United States. Other plays include Time Warner's ownership of magazines and cable companies, Viacom's ownership of cable TV, Blockbuster video, and Paramount studios, and myriad telephone service providers who now offer Internet access. In fact, the late 1990s seems to be a period of aggressive investment in vertical integration throughout the MICE supply chain.[9]

I believe that the common strategies behind all of this activity may

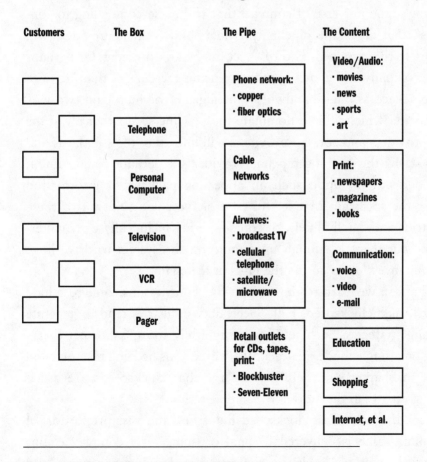

Figure 2.1. The MICE Industry Supply Chain

be characterized as hedging. Hedging against what? Perhaps many of the players believe that somewhere in this huge and dense industrial thicket is a pot of gold—not a literal one, of course, but an opportunity for some well-placed company or entrepreneur to reap Microsoft-like profits. The hedging comes about because few players can predict with confidence which sector (content, pipeline, or box) is most likely to provide this pot of gold, let alone pick which individuals or companies have the best chance.

Perhaps in the domain of the reception box, some company will hit upon the right hybrid appliance (perhaps with a user-friendly interface to browse the universe of content) that will be so compelling to consumers that all of the pipeline providers and content providers will line up to the standards and rules set by the box provider. Or perhaps some company will come up with a pipeline technology that provides universal access, high-bandwidth, intelligent switching, and two-way interaction which will so dominate the pipeline sector that all of the box providers and content providers will line up to the standards and rules set by the winning pipeline provider. Or perhaps some content provider will hit upon such an appealing package of information across the spectrum that it will control the chain. Not all of these scenarios are equally likely, of course—either technically or commercially—but there is enough uncertainty in the system to drive huge hedging investments across the links in the chain.

What can we learn from this fruit fly? Four lessons come to mind.

First, high-clockspeed, high-uncertainty industries tend to generate hedging strategies. Such settings are typically too risky to bet everything on a single mode of attack. We will see this hedging phenomenon again in chapter 4, where we observe that clockspeeds are accelerating rapidly in the automotive supplier sector.

Second, even in fast-clockspeed industries, the vast proportion of economic value is delivered to final consumers via complex chains comprising many individual organizations, technologies, services, and capabilities. One strategy for making money is to try to control the entire chain, an approach illustrated with significant aggressiveness by Disney and Microsoft, for example.

Third, the high-opportunity strategy may not stay constant between being a component supplier and being a chain dominator. Microsoft cleaned up as a component supplier from the mid-1980s to the mid-1990s. It then shifted strategies to attempt to be a chain dominator by playing in increasingly many segments of the chain. This dynamic process will be revisited in more detail in chapter 4.

Fourth, even if you exert little control over the chain, you can make money by supplying a critical component. The information-entertainment industry relies on both the semiconductor industry and the telecommunications industry, each of which has experienced component performance improvements at "killer technology" rates. (A "killer technology" is one that delivers enhanced systems performance of a factor of at least a hundredfold per decade.[10])

In the domain of component supply, most companies have to choose some variant of a niche strategy. One may seek to succeed in low-margin, high-volume components, such as DRAMs (dynamic random access memories) in computers. Or one may seek out low-volume, high-margin niches, such as high-capacity telecommunications switches. In some instances, however, one may find the happy circumstance of a component business that offers both high volumes and high margins.

Two examples illustrate this point. For over a decade from the mid-1980s to the late 1990s, Intel Corporation, provider of microprocessors for the personal computer, reaped high margins on high volumes despite exerting very little control in the overall MICE chain. Similarly, in the late 1990s, despite negligible chain control, Lucent Technologies and Corning Glass, the primary U.S. suppliers of fiber-optic cable, also reaped high margins on high volumes as the entire world raced to wire itself up for the Internet age. These three companies demonstrate that niches of prolonged competitive advantage for component suppliers may sometimes be found even in fast-clockspeed industries. Chapter 6 will shed more light on how component suppliers, because of their position upstream in the chain, may sometimes bear less of the brunt of hyper-fast clockspeeds in their industry segments.

Clockspeed Drivers: Technology and Competition

What whips up the winds of creative destruction in fast-clockspeed industries?[11] I believe there are two primary drivers: technological innovation and competitive intensity. When an industry is subjected to an important innovation, that industry typically feels a significant uptick in the overall clockspeed. The jet engine with its effects on the transportation industry provides one example. The effect of genomics on pharmaceuticals, discussed at some length in chapter 5, provides another.

Consider again the MICE industry. The killer technologies mentioned above—semiconductors and fiber optics—have had a combined impact of propelling the clockspeeds of the industry into the stratosphere. Performance of integrated circuits shows dramatic growth—in transistors per chip, transistors per unit cost, and data processing speed—during that period.[12] Similarly, for almost a century, transmission technology crept along at a growth rate of approximately tenfold in performance per decade as a result of incrementally improving electromechanical, electronic, and microwave technology. In the late 1970s the adoption of fiber-optic systems became widespread, and the slope of change jumped to "killer" rates.[13]

These two technologies have come together in the information transmission industry and serve as a "backbone" technology for virtually every other industry. As a result the clockspeeds of all industries have been propelled upward, leading to both the perception and the reality of dizzying acceleration in clockspeeds in practically every form of economic activity on the planet.

Even in a world of relative technological stability, increased competitive intensity can trigger an uptick in industry clockspeeds. In the 1950s and 1960s, Detroit's Big Four—General Motors, Ford, Chrysler, and American Motors—ran a sleepy industry that lagged (or perhaps ignored) their European counterparts in the adoption of new technologies and their Japanese counterparts in the adoption of new production methods. Complacency was rampant, yet profitability continued apace largely because the Big Four were the only show in town. When the Volkswagen Beetle began to make inroads in the early 1970s, Detroit responded with hardly a shrug; after all, the profit margins were low in the small-car market.

The Middle East oil embargo of 1973, however, changed the game forever. The gas-guzzlers produced by Detroit suddenly went out of favor with the American public, who clamored for small cars. Japanese automakers seized upon the opportunity to show their small, high-quality domestic vehicles to North American consumers and began carving out portions of the U.S. market. That presence has vastly changed the practices and strategies of the large domestic automakers. Detroit has fought its way back to prominence, but certainly not dominance, in an industry that bears little resemblance to what it was prior to the early 1970s. Competition has accelerated product and process development and led to some acquisitions (for example, Daimler-Benz and Chrysler), as companies continue to seek ways to reduce costs, improve technology, increase market leverage, and enhance product marketing.

For example, when Jeep had the only mass-market sport utility vehicle on the road, the public accepted its styling and features for years, and few changes were made to the basic design. Now, several new sport utility models enter the market each year, and consumers can choose from a dozen or more. Thus, no brand (Jeep included) can afford to rest on its laurels. All makers feel pressure to bring out new models and features with breathless—some would say distressing—

frequency. In short, as a result of increased competition, the clock-speed of the automotive industry, particularly in the United States, has soared.

These observations shed some light on why the 1990s have been perceived to be an era of unprecedented clockspeed acceleration across the industrial spectrum. Historically, technological innovations had local effects. Of course, the coming of the railroads in the United States and many other innovations had far-reaching impacts. But innovations usually did not hit simultaneously every industry in every corner of the globe. Every innovation in information and communication technologies hits everywhere at once.

Increases in competitive intensity have tended to be local as well. One industry might feel the competition ratchet up, but such effects would not usually strike all industries at once. Political and economic conditions in the 1990s, however, have changed the response rate. On the political front, trade barriers have fallen dramatically in the 1990s, increasing the globalization of virtually all industries at one time. Furthermore, the information technologies have reinforced the globalization by facilitating access to global markets.

Technology and competition, simultaneously and universally, have driven us to an economy with unprecedented rapid clockspeeds. The first consequence of this phenomenon is the marginalization of the concept of sustainable advantage. If there ever was such a thing, competitive advantage in perpetuity is dead and buried. All advantage is temporary, and the faster the clockspeed, the more temporary the advantage. To understand better these complex relationships, in the next chapter we examine two cases from two very different generations—Kodak and Microsoft—and ask what is to be learned from each about the future of competitive advantage.

3 SURVIVAL OF THE FITTEST

The Temporary Nature of Advantage

The faster an industry evolves—that is, the faster its clock-speed—the more temporary a company's advantage. The key is to choose the right advantage—again and again.

BEFORE THE DAWN OF THE INDUSTRIAL Revolution, two varieties of Gypsy moths could be seen fluttering about the English countryside. One was a mixture of black and white, what you might call pepper and salt; the other was all black. In the struggle for survival, the pepper-and-salt moth was clearly the fitter of the two species and by far the more populous. It easily blended into the mottled birch bark on which it roosted, making it an elusive target for predator birds. Black moths, on the other hand, were easier to spot.

Then in the nineteenth century, coal-burning factories and locomotives drastically altered the environment. Soot covered the birch trunks. Now the black moth was all but invisible, and because it escaped the notice of predators, its numbers soared. The pepper-and-salt moth, on the other hand, became an endangered species.[1]

Had the pepper-and-salt Gypsy moths been capable of thinking about it, they surely would have pronounced themselves more satisfied with their pre–Industrial Revolution circumstances and confident about their future. "What could go wrong?" they might have asked.

It's a question that many of us ask. In human experience, as in all of nature, competitive advantage is temporary: The Roman empire; sports dynasties such as the Dallas Cowboys, the Boston Celtics, and the New York Yankees; Henry Ford's Model T; IBM and Sears, Roebuck—they have all had their day in the sun. No doubt, they all thought that sun would never set.

But history provides one absolute: All competitive advantage is temporary. That is true whether your business is large or small, diversified or focused, publicly or privately owned, Asian, European, or American, high-tech, low-tech, or no tech at all. It is a tough pill to swallow—so tough, in fact, that many executives have run their companies into the ground trying to disprove it.

Now business genetics provides another absolute, a dictum to live by: The faster the industry clockspeed, the shorter the half-life of competitive advantage. A drumbeat of unexpected, unlikely events in recent decades has put companies of every stripe, and every clockspeed, at risk; for example,

- *Shocks to the business environment.* How many mink farmers went bankrupt when the animal rights movement targeted fur coats? How many billions have been spent on pollution control and restoration for waste disposal practices that used to be an accepted part of doing business?

- *Economic shocks.* When oil prices skyrocketed in 1973, the market value of the auto industry was decimated. When interest rates soared to 20 percent later in the decade, thousands of fortunes were lost.

- *Technological shocks.* The innovation of jet aircraft sent propeller manufacturers into a tailspin. Personal computers destroyed the value of word-processing companies such as Wang and minicomputer companies such as Prime.

- *Shocks from competitors' breakthrough products and services.* Federal Express ran many a traditional package delivery company out of business. Disposable diapers changed the changing habits of generations of parents and pushed many a diaper delivery service over the edge.

- *The shock of a new and newly dominant business model.* Superstores such as Wal-Mart chased out mom-and-pop stores and downtown department stores across the United States. Amazon.com helped send many small bookstores packing.

To be sure, business leaders have always had to contend with change, but in times past, the shocks tended to be fewer and farther between. Most industries crawled along at turtlelike clockspeeds. Companies carried on for generations, far longer than the career of any given manager. When a worker started a career with a company, he or she "knew" the structure of the company and industry would last a lifetime. Today, whether you work for a powerhouse such as Boeing or Microsoft, or an Internet startup such as Marimba, Inc. (a company that develops technology for transferring graphics and software on the Internet), you have little ground for such confidence.

As a result, companies and individuals must learn to focus directly on two distinct sets of priorities: exploiting their current capabilities and competitive advantages while also consciously and purposefully building new capabilities for the inevitable moment when the old ones no longer provide an advantage. As a result, the strategic planning process should consist of trying to think through the company's series of temporary advantages.

Of course, this approach flies in the face of most of the accepted wisdom in the field of strategic management. That wisdom emphasizes the necessity for a company to develop *sustainable* competitive advantage by *locking in* its advantages with unique capabilities, thereby *locking out* the competition.[2] There is, however, a fly in this ointment: These solutions were conceived in an era of slower clockspeeds. In fact, I think of sustainable advantage as a slow-clockspeed concept. In contrast, temporary advantage is a fast-clockspeed concept.[3]

In sectors where the clockspeeds are relatively slow, achieving a position where one's advantages or architectures[4] are locked in and competitors are locked out can provide significant and durable streams of profit. Just look at the IBM of the 1970s or General Motors in the 1950s and 1960s. Even in the fast-clockspeed information technology arena, a company can lock in an advantage or lock out a competitor for a time. That said, no one really expects people such as Bill Gates to rest for long on their laurels: Gates knows that his Windows franchise does not have the half-life of a 747, so he's hard at work on his next act. And in the truly fast domains—for instance, the information and communication industries—even such slowpokes as AT&T are trying to, well, sprint.

We can see some of these issues and the transience of advantage played out in the recent, turbulent history of the photolithography industry, which produces equipment essential for the manufacture of semiconductors.[5] A state-of-the-art photolithographic stepper costs upwards of $5 million, and a semiconductor factory may need a dozen or two of these complex, high-tech behemoths.

Photolithography is the process whereby light is projected through the gaps in a template called a mask and onto a silicon wafer, printing integrated circuits on the wafer's surface. Early photolithography machine tools, called aligners, were simple: The equipment put the mask directly on top of the wafer. But there was always the danger that this so-called contact alignment would damage the mask or contaminate the wafer.

In 1973, Canon challenged the industry leader, Kasper, by introducing a new technology intended to eliminate that threat. Called a proximity aligner, it used a sophisticated mechanism to separate the mask from the wafer and to control the gap between them.

Kasper responded by producing a copycat version of the proximity aligner, but the company treated the advance as nothing more than a minor modification in a single component of the system. Kasper was so committed to its old capabilities that it failed to see the new technology for what it was—an architectural shift, a rethinking of the relationship between the gap-setting mechanism and all the other components of the machine. In the marketplace the copycat version of Canon's mechanism had no claws.

For a while Canon was the king of aligners, but not for long. In 1974, Perkin-Elmer entered the market with an aligner that used optical scanners to project the image of the mask onto the wafer. Its advantages were manifest: increased speed and accuracy. Yet within a few years, even Perkin-Elmer was displaced by another company, GCA, whose new aligner projected the image of the mask through a refractive lens and "stepped" the image across the wafer. And in the early 1990s, Nikon toppled GCA by introducing a second-generation stepper machine with larger lenses.

This roster of winners-that-became-losers is all the more remarkable because, in all cases, the demands of the new photolithography products seemed within easy reach of the reigning companies. Yet from one generation to the next, the inability of the leading company to evolve, even incrementally, prevented it from adapting successfully to technological advances. Although apparently within the grasp of the incumbent, advantage in each generation proved ephemeral.

Adjusting to the Age of Temporary Advantage: The Case of Kodak

Consider one of the most venerable names in American business: Eastman Kodak Company.[6] When Kodak invented photographic film, it controlled a long and highly integrated value chain, including the camera, the film, the paper, the chemicals, and the chemical processing. Kodak marketed preloaded cameras that the photographer would return to the company for processing. An 1888 marketing slogan summarized Kodak's approach to the market: "You press the button. We do the rest."

The business world that founder George Eastman lived in was a highly vertical one. In his hometown of Rochester, New York, one could buy foods, clothing, even automobiles that were locally produced.[7] The challenge of running a vertical organization appealed to Eastman. In 1915, he wrote to a friend: "Between you and me, this is the most varied and interesting business in the world. It embraces, at one time or another, almost every problem that comes up in science, art and industry."[8] One can imagine that the company was flexible and innovative as it approached the challenges that it faced. But it did so in a very insular way, creating integral solutions to the problems it faced.

George Eastman was successful not only in defining a new industry, but in maintaining near-monopolistic control over it. While this control enabled Kodak to enjoy high profit margins, the lack of competitors and external suppliers locked the company into a vertical structure. As a result, the organization became hierarchical and bureaucratic. In such lopsided industry structures, innovation often slows since few pressures force the monopolist to keep ahead of the competition. Each product generation—for example, the Brownie, 126, 110, the Instamatic, the instant, and the disc cameras—was highly integral: Kodak provided the camera, the film, the chemicals and paper, and even the processing.

This trend was broken in the course of the 35mm camera boom. In the 1980s, many companies began providing cameras that were compatible with Kodak's 35mm film. During this period, Kodak was developing another completely integral photographic system, the disc camera and its high-grain, low-resolution film. When it became clear that the consumer preferred 35mm photography to the high- grain, Kodak was caught off guard. Nevertheless, Kodak still controlled the part of the value chain where most of the value lay: the film. Thus, rather than being a wake-up call, the 35mm boom was seen as a great source for growing revenue. Having won the photography battle, Kodak turned its attention elsewhere, investing for a time in pharmaceuticals, chemicals, and household products such as Lysol and D-Con.

In process technology, Kodak took a vertical/integral approach as well. The lack of suppliers of photographic chemicals and components with highly reliable quality led the company to invest in chemicals, plastics, metals, and optics. What started as a "no one else can, so we have to" justification turned into a "we can, so we will" mentality. Even today, it is common to hear Kodak veterans use phrases such as "We start with earth, wind, and fire" and "From soup to nuts." In the typical 35mm film manufacturing process, every part—including the tape that attaches the film to the spool—is manufactured in-house.[9]

While Kodak may have started as a relatively fast clockspeed company, its pace of change slowed as two things happened. First, the technology matured. Although new products are continually developed, the basic silver halide technology pioneered in Kodak's early days still drives the vast majority of Kodak's profits in film. Second, as Kodak enjoyed a near-monopolistic position in its field, the competitive pressure to operate at a fast clockspeed simply did not exist. No matter what the people at Kodak did, it seemed that they always made enormous profits.

But the winds have shifted. The competitive environment looks much different for Kodak in the age of digital everything. Digital image processing technology will likely be governed by Moore's law rather than incremental advances in a comparatively mature area of chemistry. Foreign competitors, notably Fuji, have meanwhile eroded

Kodak's historically high profit margins and market share. In October, 1993, George Fisher became the first person outside Kodak to become CEO of the company.

In response to Kodak's years of stagnancy, Fisher put into motion a major restructuring of the organization, selling the sideline businesses and cutting 15,000 jobs. Within four years, he had almost doubled the stock price to $94 a share. Then, suddenly, the bloom was again off the rose. Sales and profits began to tumble. Five months later, the stock had fallen to $68 a share.[10]

What went wrong? In a word: Fuji. The Japanese giant had declared war: Fuji cut its prices on film by as much as 50 percent and vastly increased its low-cost photo-finishing capacity. It built a $1 billion plant in South Carolina to produce film and paper. It spent record sums promoting its products in the U.S. market. Its state-of-the-art film has even been grabbing market share among finicky professional photographers.[11]

Kodak finally recognized that its glory days alone atop the consumer photo market are gone. Its 35mm monopoly has been undercut by Fuji and will never come back. In response, the company has diligently sought new worlds to conquer—substitute sources of revenue, that is—by investing heavily in digital imaging. In this technology, Kodak has come to a major crossroad: whether to develop this technology by itself end-to-end as it did with photography or to assume that the technology will end up modular as it has done in the PC industry. If the latter case proves true, Kodak would then face the challenge of choosing which components to play in, hoping to hold the keys to the scarce links in the chain, as it did in film and as Intel has done in PCs.

With all due respect to Aesop and his fables, it is worth observing that the tortoise seldom wins the race. In a business environment where all advantage is temporary, organizations must either evolve faster than their competitors or fall behind. The fruit flies of business teach us that the key to victory today is to avoid holding on too long to waning capabilities and advantages and to go for the best new—albeit temporary—advantage again and again and again.

Herein lies the even more difficult challenge Kodak faces. Not only must Kodak learn and develop a strategy for a dramatically different technology supply chain in digital imaging, but it must now learn to play in a game with not one direct competitor, as it did in the 35mm battles with Fuji, but with many competitors such as Intel, Hewlett-Packard, Canon, Xerox, Sharp, Matsushita, Sony, and myriad others in the electronics industry.

In tumultuous, fast-clockspeed markets, you cannot hide behind a lock-in strategy. You must continuously develop new capabilities in preparation for the inevitable new opportunities and battles just around the corner. And you must maintain an organization that is flexible enough to jump when jumping is called for. No company can be assured a lock forever, and the end often comes just when it is least expected.

Microsoft and the Tumultuous Road Ahead

By the mid-1990s, Microsoft appeared to have an absolute lock-in. The vast majority of the personal computer industry was totally dependent upon the company's proprietary technological standard in PC operating systems. Yet, as we have seen in chapter 2, the company was blindsided by the emergence of Internet browsers and the upstart Netscape, which threatened the future of traditional operating systems.

Microsoft has responded powerfully, of course, but just as it seemed to have the browser war under control, it came under heavy attack from state and federal governmental authorities for alleged antitrust violations over its use of its market power in PC operating systems. These developments have raised questions that might earlier have seemed presumptuous or even absurd: Is Microsoft in for some serious trouble? In all my research, I have been unable to find a single instance in war, politics, sports, or business that contradicts the theme of this chapter—namely, that all competitive advantage is temporary. Why should Microsoft be different?

Despite its market penetration, Windows is not the most admired of operating systems. Many PC owners criticize the company's software as "bloatware" and less than user-friendly.[12] It has attracted nothing like the devotion accorded the Macintosh operating system. Will the public stay loyal to Windows if a viable hardware-software alternative comes along?

By the same token, Microsoft has few friends in the industry other than Intel. Most of its allies are partners under duress. But this is an industry that is highly dependent on technological complementarity: No company is an island. Will these partners stay loyal to Microsoft if they have a viable alternative?

In the computer industry, the low end always seems to eat the high end: Personal computers displaced mini-computers, just as mini-computers had bumped mainframes a decade earlier. At this point, Microsoft is the high-end standard. Will it be able to hold off challenges to its hegemony from low-end threats such as personal digital assistants and multifunctional cell phones? No one accuses 3-Com's Palm Pilot of exhibiting bloatware.

On the other hand, there are reasons to believe Microsoft may prove the exception to the business genetics rule—at least for a while. Bill Gates is an astute businessman and a relentless competitor. Moreover, he is continually surveying the broad landscape, watching for changes in industrial structures, identifying opportunities and pitfalls. In effect, he practices business genetics.

In addition, Microsoft has a huge pool of available capital, much of it invested in creating opportunities for further growth. When the dominant industrial giants of yesteryear—AT&T, IBM, General Motors, RCA, Xerox—generated megaprofits in their epochs of dominance, they each invested generously in R&D organizations—Bell Labs, Watson Labs, GM Research Lab, Sarnoff Lab, and Xerox PARC—intended to develop technologies to extend their dominance into the future. In most cases, these laboratories delivered marvelous inventions such as the transistor, the hard disk drive, low-cost anti-lock brakes, color TV, windows and mouse-based computing, the laser printer. The corporate downfalls, when they occurred, were caused by strategic and operating errors in these companies, often in spite of huge technological leads. In similar fashion, Microsoft has invested heavily in creating Microsoft Labs[13]—a research and development organization formed to push the technological frontiers in its industry. One expects that the technological fruits of this investment will come. The critical ingredient will then be management decision making and execution.

The most compelling argument for the company's continued survival and dominance lies in the fact that its systems have become the technological standard of a critical system (the personal computer) in a vast information industry. The significance of that fact is best illustrated by observing the history of the keyboard layout to be found in virtually every computer in the English-speaking world.[14]

The QWERTY keyboard, so called after the letters of the top left row of letter keys, was designed in the nineteenth century to prevent typists from pecking away too fast and jamming the keys. Even after typewriter keys became virtually unjammable and then disappeared altogether, typists continued to be trained on QWERTY keyboards, which have remained the standard in English-speaking (and many other) countries. Another design, known as the DVORAK Simplified Keyboard, was developed, with the most-used keys all on the keyboard's "home row." All other things being equal, DVORAK-trained typists are much faster than their QWERTY counterparts. In fact, a study by the U.S. Navy concluded in the 1940s that the payback time for a typist's switch to DVORAK was no more than ten days.[15]

Nevertheless, much of the industrialized world seems stuck with QWERTY—not exactly the outcome you might have predicted from a hypercompetitive capitalist economy.

In discussing the economics of the QWERTY keyboard, Paul Krugman, an economist at the Massachusetts Institute of Technology, notes that

> the story of the QWERTY keyboard is not just a cute piece of trivia. Like the description of the pin factory with which Adam Smith began *The Wealth of Nations,* it is a parable that opens our eyes to a whole different way of thinking about economics. That different way of thinking rejects the idea that markets invariably lead the economy to a unique best solution; instead, it asserts that the outcome of market competition often depends on historical accident.[16]

Consider the story about the standardizing of U.S. rails to 4 feet 8.5 inches. This story was posted on the Internet by Professor Thomas O'Hare, Department of Germanic Languages at the University of Texas at Austin. The account has been disputed by some,[17] but it is so germane to this discussion of standards and economics that I think it is possible to read it as another parable about the persistence of technological standards with far-reaching impact. It appears that some standards might have begun as mere accidents:

> *How Mil Specs (Military Specifications) Live Forever*
>
> The U.S. Standard railroad gauge (distance between the rails) is 4 feet, 8.5 inches. That's an exceedingly odd number. Why was that gauge used? Because that's the way they built them in England, and the U.S. railroads were built by English expatriates. Why did the English people build them like that? Because the first rail lines were built by the same people who built the pre-railroad tramways, and that's the gauge they used. Why did "they" use that gauge then? Because the people who built

the tramways used the same jigs and tools that they used for building wagons, which used that wheel spacing. Okay! Why did the wagons use that odd wheel spacing? Well, if they tried to use any other spacing, the wagons would break on some of the old, long distance roads, because that's the spacing of the old wheel ruts. So who built these old rutted roads? The first long distance roads in Europe were built by Imperial Rome for the benefit of their legions. The roads have been used ever since. And the ruts? The initial ruts, which everyone else had to match for fear of destroying their wagons, were first made by Roman war chariots. Since the chariots were made for or by Imperial Rome, they were all alike in the matter of wheel spacing. Thus, we have the answer to the original questions. The United States standard railroad gauge of 4 feet, 8.5 inches derives from the original specification (Military Spec) for an Imperial Roman army war chariot.[18]

Standards are a wildcard in the fast-clockspeed games that most industries play. We have an arcane keyboard standard that has survived many generations of typewriters and workstations over many decades and arcane military standards that have survived generations of military vehicles over many centuries. Industry evolution marches on, however, both because of and despite the standards, but the dynamics of standards evolution follow a different metronome than those of other industrial products or industries.

We have a personal computer industry wedded to two technical standards—QWERTY for the keyboard and Windows for the operating system. Perhaps the most striking difference between the economics of the Windows standard and the QWERTY standard is that every time someone buys a QWERTY keyboard, no royalties are paid for the right to use that standard. However, with Windows, Bill Gates shares with his fellow Microsoft stockholders as much as $50 in gross margin for each of the tens of millions of PCs sold each year. Gates and Microsoft charge a "tax" on an economic standard that is now as ubiquitous as the QWERTY keyboard. No wonder Microsoft seems able to mint money.

The standards factor is the wildcard in forecasting the decline of Microsoft's franchise despite the fast clockspeed industry the company is in. Can Windows hold on as long as QWERTY—or perhaps even as long as the military specifications for Rome's chariots? Both time-spans seem unlikely, given the complexity of the information-entertainment industry and the attractive returns to rivals who might find ways to unseat Windows.

The bottom line of this chapter: All advantage is temporary. Accept it. Live with it. Plan your life and strategy around it. Don't throw away a period of lock-in if you do happen to gain control of an important standard, but don't rest on your laurels in such situations either. Railways are being paved over with asphalt every day.

4 THE SECRET OF LIFE

Harnessing the Power of the Double Helix

In 1953, two scientists discovered the secret of life—
the double helix, the molecular structure of DNA.
Now, it seems, business has a double helix, too.

In 1962, James D. Watson and Francis Crick received the Nobel Prize in medicine for their discovery of the molecular structure of DNA and the mechanism of genetic replication. They found that the nucleus of each living cell contains two long, parallel strands of alternating phosphate and deoxyribose units twisted into the shape of a double helix. In his firsthand account of their work, *The Double Helix,* Watson said that he and Crick had discovered "the secret of life."[1]

By examining the "molecular" structure of companies—their capability chains—business genetics helps us to understand their mutation, evolution, and eventual survival or demise. Business genetics features the industrial equivalent of the double helix—a model based on an infinite double loop that cycles between vertically integrated industries inhabited by corporate behemoths and horizontally disintegrated industries populated by myriad innovators, each seeking a niche in the wide open space left by the earlier demise of the giants.

The business double helix illuminates how these vertical and horizontal epochs determine the fate of companies, industries, and sometimes the economic fortunes of nations. Internal and external forces—niche competitors, the strain of maintaining technological parity across many products, and the organizational arteriosclerosis that so often afflicts market leaders—drive vertically integrated companies toward disintegration and a horizontal industry structure. On the other hand, when an industry has a horizontal structure, the forces exerted by powerful component suppliers and by individual firms' incentives to promote their own proprietary technologies create strong pressures toward reintegration.[2]

To observe these dynamics in vivid motion, let us turn, once again, back to the fruit flies, and to the remarkable history of the computer industry.

In the 1970s and the early 1980s the computer industry's structure was decidedly vertical (see figure 4.1). The three largest companies, IBM, Digital Equipment Corporation (DEC), and Hewlett-Packard, were highly integrated, as were the second tier of computer makers, including Burroughs, Univac, NCR, Control Data, and Honeywell, commonly referred to as "the BUNCH." Companies tended to provide most of the key elements of their own computer systems, from the

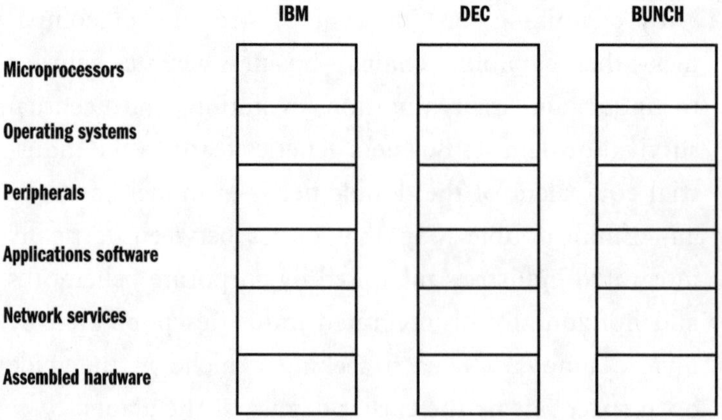

Figure 4.1. Vertical Industry Structure and Integral Product Architecture in the Computer Industry, 1975–1985[3]

operating system and applications software to the peripherals and electronic hardware, rather than sourcing bundles of subsystem modules acquired from third parties.

In this era, products and systems exhibited *integral architectures*. That is, there was little or no interchangeability across different companies' systems. DEC peripherals and software, for example, did not work in IBM machines, and vice versa—so each company maintained technological competencies across many elements in the chain.

IBM had significant market power during that time and was very profitable. By holding to its closed, integral product architecture, the company kept existing customers hostage—any competing machine they bought would be incompatible with their IBMs.[4] At the same time, Big Blue emphasized the value of its overall systems-and-service package, determined to stave off competitors who might offer better performance on one or another piece of the package. But storm clouds were gathering. The task of maintaining its competencies over such a broad array of technologies and capabilities was daunting, and the pace of innovation in the industry was accelerating.

In the late 1970s, IBM faced a challenge from a new quarter. Upstart Apple Computer had cobbled together a so-called personal computer, tiny by IBM's standards, which had captured the imaginations of growing numbers of sophisticated buyers in the electronics and computer markets. In response, IBM chose to launch a new business division and a new personal computer of its own.

For the new PC, as we saw in chapter 1, IBM's newly created PC division turned its back on vertical integration and integral product architectures. Instead, it opted for a modular product architecture, outsourcing the microprocessor to Intel and the operating system to Microsoft. IBM's mutation catalyzed a dramatic change throughout the industry, which quickly moved from a vertical to a horizontal structure. The dominant product was no longer the IBM computer, but the IBM-*compatible* computer. The modular architecture encouraged companies large and small to enter the fray and supply subsystems for the industry: semiconductors, circuit boards, applications software, peripherals, network services, and PC design and assembly.

A single product/supply chain decision (by a dominant producer) set the stage for a momentous structural shift—one that provides instruction for many other industrial species—from a vertical/integral industry structure (figure 4.1) to a horizontal/modular one (figure 4.2). The universal availability of the Intel and Microsoft subsystems led dozens of entrepreneurs to enter the personal computer business with IBM-compatibles. The modular (mix-and-match) architecture created significant competition within each "row" of the horizontally structured industry depicted in figure 4.2, rather than across the vertically integrated "columns" of the structure shown in figure 4.1.

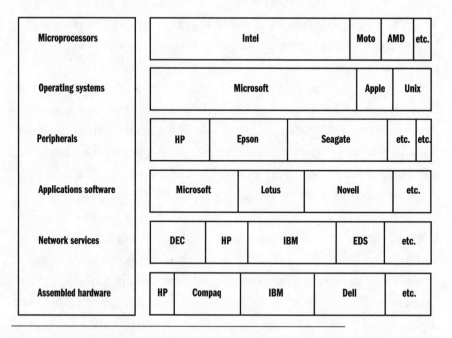

Figure 4.2. Horizontal Industry Structure and Modular Product Architecture in the Computer Industry, 1985–1995[5]

One leader of the new era was Compaq, the first of many producers of PC "clone makers" who led the way in modularizing the industry in the image of the product's modular architecture. Compaq was nimbler and more focused than IBM. Its managers sensed what was required to go head-to-head with one of the world's most admired and feared competitors. By working closely with IBM's suppliers, Compaq beat IBM to the market in 1985 with Intel's new 80386 chip and then again with the first version of Microsoft's Windows. By focusing its energies and resources on product development—and leaving technology development in the hands of its suppliers—Compaq was running rings around Big Blue.

In this industry, so recently organized along monolithic, vertical lines, there now appeared a spate of separate subindustries—not only for microprocessors and operating systems, but for peripherals, software, network services, and so on. Within each of the categories, new businesses emerged, making it easier and easier for a computer maker to shop around for just the right combination of subsystems.

On balance, this spread of competition has been a healthy development for the industry and for computer buyers, but certainly not for IBM shareholders, who saw their company lose about $100 billion in market value between 1986 and 1992.[6] Some observers have speculated that this model of horizontal competition, which also evolved in telecommunications in the 1990s, might be the new industrial model for many industries.[7] However, further examination suggests that the horizontal/modular structure may also prove to be quite unstable—as unstable as the vertical/integral structures that give birth to it.

Why might the horizontal/modular structure be short-lived? Let's look again at the fruit flies in the PC industry.

Horizontal structures tend to create fierce, commodity-like competition within individual niches. Such competition keeps the players highly focused on their survival. However, over time, a shakeout typically occurs, and stronger players—those that manage to develop an edge in costs, quality, technology, or service, for example—drive out weaker ones. Once a firm is large enough to exert some market power in its row, it sees the opportunity to expand vertically as well. Microsoft and Intel, both of which came to dominate their respective rows, have exhibited this behavior. Intel expanded from microprocessors to design and assembly of motherboard modules, making significant inroads into an arena typically controlled by the systems assemblers such as Compaq, Dell, and IBM. In addition, with each new microprocessor generation, Intel added more functions on the chip (functions that applications software suppliers traditionally offered), thereby making incursions into that row as well.[8]

In the case of Microsoft, dominance in PC operating systems has led to the company's entry into applications software, network services, Web browsers, server operating systems, and multimedia content development and delivery. In short, Microsoft looks a little bit more each day like the old IBM—attempting to dominate increasingly large slices of the overall industry and earning monopoly-like profits in the process. Exploiting market power in this way is as old as shipbuilding—when the nations that built the best ships also controlled the most lucrative trading routes. Microsoft's ability to integrate across the rows is particularly vivid (to both competitors and regulators) because its market share is so large and information technology is so flexible.

The Forces behind the Double Helix

Figure 4.3 illustrates the entire dynamic cycle with the double helix. When the industry structure is vertical and the product architecture is integral, the forces of disintegration push toward a horizontal and modular configuration. These forces include

1. The relentless entry of niche competitors hoping to pick off discrete industry segments;

2. The challenge of keeping ahead of the competition across the many

dimensions of technology and markets required by an integral system; and

3. The bureaucratic and organizational rigidities that often settle upon large, established companies.[9]

These forces typically weaken the vertical giant and create pressure toward disintegration to a more horizontal, modular structure. IBM, it might be argued, had all these forces lined up against it: Constant pressure from niche entrants, particularly in software and peripherals; competitors who took the lead in some technological segments (Intel's invention of the microprocessor, for example); and the many layers of bureaucracy that grew up as IBM expanded its head count to almost half a million employees at its peak in the 1980s.

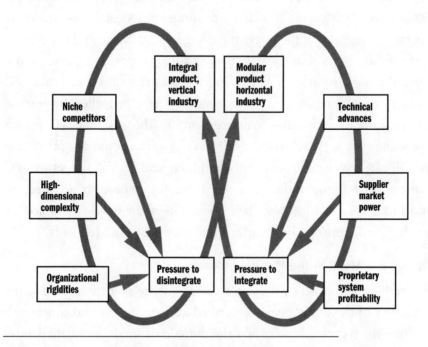

Figure 4.3. The Double Helix, Illustrating How Industry/Product Structure Evolve from Vertical/Integral to Horizontal/Modular, and Back[10]

On the other hand, when an industry has a horizontal structure, another set of forces push toward more vertical integration and integral product architectures. These forces include

1. Technical advances in one subsystem can make that the scarce commodity in the chain, giving market power to its owner.
2. Market power in one subsystem encourages bundling with other subsystems to increase control and add more value.
3. Market power in one subsystem encourages engineering integration with other subsystems to develop proprietary integral solutions.

To apply the power of the double helix, consider the plight of Apple Computer in light of the history of the personal computer described so far. In the mid- to late 1980s, Apple's Macintosh computer was clearly the technically superior product in the PC industry. However, Apple failed to realize that the principal advantage of its computer was in its operating system, not the integral package of hardware and software it was offering. As a result, Apple tied its superior operating system in a vertical bundle to inferior hardware, whereas the IBM-compatible PC industry raced ahead, subsystem by subsystem, propelled by intense competition in each subsystem segment. In the end, the Macintosh operating system, shackled to a hardware anchor, could not match the overall rate of improvement in the modular and highly competitive PC market. Had Apple understood the dynamics of product architecture and industry structure described above, it might have uncoupled its product and controlled the catbird seat now held by Microsoft.

The Double Helix in the Bicycle Industry

The bicycle industry provides a clear vantage point for viewing the dynamics of the double helix described above.[11] In the mid-nineteenth century, the bicycle industry was the domain of small, innovative, integrated firms in England, France, Germany, and the United States—most of which controlled the complete engineering and manufacturing of their bicycles. This industry structure changed, however, once everyone settled on the dominant design of the "safety bicycle" in the late nineteenth century and demand exploded along with general economic growth in the United States in the 1890s.

The Schwinn Bicycle Company provides a vivid illustration.[12] Arnold, Schwinn & Company was founded in 1895 with financing from Adolph Arnold, a meatpacker, and engineering and business talent from Ignaz Schwinn, an immigrant who had learned the bicycle trade in Germany. Schwinn came to Chicago just in time for the great economic and bicycle boom of the 1890s. Ignaz Schwinn, his company, and Chicago were to bicycles and economic development in the 1890s what Henry Ford, the Ford Motor Company, and Detroit were to automobiles and economic development in the 1920s. Bicycles transformed urban life in the 1890s, a decade that saw the national horse population decline by 7 million as the bicycle population soared to over 10 million.[13]

By 1899, when the boom peaked, the industry had completed the first turn along the double helix—that is, from vertical/integral to horizontal/modular. More than 300 bicycle companies existed in the United States, but they were mostly assemblers (à la Compaq Computer) that bought components from larger metal machining companies and sold their products in highly competitive markets through outlets such as Sears, Roebuck & Company and Montgomery Ward.

By 1905, two years after the first Ford automobile was sold in Chicago, only 12 bicycle companies remained. Total annual industry production had dropped from more than a million to only about 250,000.[14] For the next 30 years, bikes were viewed as products for children only, whereas adults aspired to cruise in motorized vehicles. In the early twentieth century, Schwinn and the other surviving companies all turned out nearly identical products constrained both by the department stores, which insisted they could sell bikes only at rock-bottom prices, and by component makers (including the dominant supplier of tires, U.S. Rubber), who refused to invest in any quality-improving innovations because they believed that the public would not pay more for "children's toys."

In 1925, F. W. Schwinn, the son of the company's founder, wrote:

> Cycle manufacturers were completely at the mercy of these large volume buyers, aided and abetted by the principal parts makers, who were quick to see which side their bread was buttered. [Other bicycle manufacturers] had supinely accepted the standardization of parts so profitable to the parts maker, hadn't even chirped when the parts maker sold more than half of his bicycle to the customer direct, depriving him of any profit thereon, and besides, the good little fellow was always too grateful for the bone that was left him.[15]

What happened next provides significant evidence for the maxim "Necessity is the mother of invention." When the Great Depression hit, business became even worse for the bike companies. Stymied by the refusal of U.S. suppliers to make higher quality components for him to support development of higher quality bikes, Schwinn went on a "cycle research" visit to Europe and came back threatening the U.S. supply base that he would import European components of higher quality if suppliers at home would not respond to his requests. Although the rest of the industry laughed at Schwinn's ideas of selling premium bikes in an economic depression, the U.S. suppliers blinked and responded to his demands, triggering a decade of growth that led to unchallenged dominance for the Schwinn Bicycle Company.

Granted over 40 patents during the 1930s, Schwinn turned out innovations and market hits such as the "Super Balloon Tire Bicycle," the "Aero Cycle" (with a lifetime guarantee), the built-in "Cycle Lock," the "full-floating" saddle, the "knee-action" spring fork, and many others.[16] Moreover, he pulled the entire bicycle industry (which had copied his innovations as quickly as it could) out of the depression to a sales level by 1940 of 1.3 million, exceeding the industry's previous peak set in 1899.[17]

Performing their own engineering and cost estimating, the people at the Schwinn Company used their volumes to play suppliers off against each other and to achieve the power to keep them in line.[18] If the suppliers would not respond as desired, Schwinn was more than willing to resort to vertical integration and make the part internally. At the same time, Schwinn turned his fire to the other end of the value chain as well: the distributors and retailers. "Schwinn-built" developed a cachet like "Cadillac" in its day, and Schwinn used this leverage to award franchises to dealers who promised to focus their sales efforts on Schwinn bikes.

The Schwinn dominance lasted through the 1970s. In the previous decade, the company's super hit "Sting Ray" sported high handle bars, a banana seat, and a "sissy bar" in back. In the 1970s adults thought twice about bikes being for kids only and turned to the 10-speed "Varsity" and "Continental" as a way of dealing with skyrocketing oil prices. Hitting a peak of 15.2 million bicycles sold in 1973, the bicycle industry had turned from horizontal back to vertical. Schwinn was as powerful in its industry as IBM or General Motors were in their respective heydays.

Schwinn's dominance was so great that the industry was ripe for its next turn on the helix back toward disintegration. In their striking history of the Schwinn Bicycle Company, Judith Crown and Glenn Coleman relate the story of this transition:

> Two distinct odors wafted across the rugged hills of California's Marin County in the early 1970s: Marijuana . . . and burning grease.
>
> Both tainted the air when gonzo cyclists raced down Mount Tamalpais on clunky old two-wheelers at speeds topping 40

miles per hour. High from the thrill, and often the dope, they'd worked their brakes so hard the grease would turn to vapor, smoke spewing from the battered bikes long after ride's end. . . .

Not for the timid, nor for any old bike. As riders thrashed their clunkers one day and overhauled them the next, they scoured junkyards and bike shops for stronger frames, wheels, and components. The models that seemed to last the longest were those big and heavy ballooners from the 1930s.[19]

Gary Fisher—the California entrepreneur, innovator, and bike racer, who at the age of 24 launched the mountain bike industry—built his bikes on the frame of a classic: the 1937 Schwinn Excelsior.

Fisher's innovation sparked a local cottage industry that drew the attention of executives at Schwinn Bicycle Company of Chicago. A team of engineers was dispatched to Marin County in the late 1970s and visited Fisher's new MountainBikes Company. But the callers from Schwinn snickered when they saw his contraption: This wasn't a bicycle, it was a mongrel. "This guy in his fifties was looking down at me like I was some kind of jerk kid who didn't know anything," Fisher recalls. "The Schwinn engineers were going, 'We know bikes. You guys are all amateurs. We know better than anybody.'"[20]

The once-proud Schwinn Bicycle Company petitioned for Chapter 11 bankruptcy protection on August 26, 1992.[21] The vertical era of the bike industry, triggered by Schwinn innovations during the depression, had completed the turn on the helix back to a horizontal structure. But Schwinn failed to make the turn with it. Since that time, the name and assets of the company were bought by a turnaround firm, Zell-Chilmark, and unsecured creditors received about 35 cents on the dollar. The Chicago factory is long gone, and the company with completely new management has moved to Colorado. About all that's left of the original company is the brand name Schwinn, which still has a distinct ring, enough to sell about 500,000 bikes a year.[22]

But that's only a part of the story.

The Bicycle Industry (Redux)

Mountain bicycles have an almost instant appeal.[23] With a more upright, stable ride, shock absorbing tires, and wide range gearing, these bicycles remind you that riding is supposed to be fun. They have heavy-duty frames and rims to withstand potholes and even curb hopping. By the mid-1990s, approximately 80 percent of bicycles sold in specialty dealers' shops were mountain bikes, and the bicycle industry in the United States had become segmented into two markets, a low-end and a high-end one, based on price, quality, and features.

At first glance, domestic companies appear to dominate the bicycle industry in the United States. In 1995, 9 of the 11 top-selling brands were U.S. companies. Only 2 brand names—Diamondback, owned by China Bicycle Company, and Giant, a Taiwanese company—appear to be significant foreign players in the U.S. market. Further analysis, however, reveals a quite different picture of the strength of some of these U.S. companies. These brand-name companies are often merely the end sellers; they make neither their own component parts nor even their own frames for bicycles in the $200–$400 price range.

Of the domestic companies, only Cannondale, Raleigh, Ross, and Trek make their own frames at the lower price point. And of these four, only Cannondale distinguishes itself by making aluminum frames instead of the steel ones that the rest of the industry uses at the lower price points. Most of the frames sold in the United States are manufactured by either Giant or the China Bicycle Company (CBC). For example, Schwinn purchases frames from CBC for its bicycles retailing under $350 and from Merida, another Taiwanese company, for its high-end bicycles.[24]

Many of the U.S. bicycle companies do not even perform their own assembly. (Similarly, many computer companies outsource circuit board assembly to the likes of SCI Systems and Solectron.) Because frames are made in either Taiwan or China, and because the majority of components are produced in Asia, it is cheaper to have the bicycle assembled by the frame manufacturers. Although "CBC Inside" had significant market share, its brand name was invisible to the consumer, a missed opportunity for sure. A component manufacturer named Shimano tried a different marketing strategy.

Horizontal Again and Ripe for "Intel Inside"?

The bicycle companies such as Trek and Schwinn buy everything that attaches to the frame from outside vendors—and Schwinn buys the frame as well. The Schwinn Company supplies only the name. Purchased components include drive-train parts (derailleurs, shifters, crank sets, chains, and gear clusters), brakes, and other items. Because of the bicycle's inherently modular design, a large number of suppliers, ranging from small mom-and-pop shops to large highly technical organizations, provide component parts. As a result, the components industry is a highly competitive business in which bicycle companies always try to reduce their costs and reach certain price points for their products by combining various components from different vendors on their bicycles.

As of 1995, Shimano, a Japanese components manufacturer, had gained control of the market for major components to bicycle assemblers in the United States. With worldwide 1995 sales of over $100 million, Shimano spent as much as $5 million to advertise its products in the United States. In *Bicycling* magazine's Super Specs database of over a thousand 1993 models, 86 percent of the bicycles came with Shimano components. Of the 536 mountain bikes in the database, 509 (95 percent) had Shimano components. And of the 157 mountain bikes selling in the under $500 range, the most popular category, 154 or 98 percent came with Shimano parts,[25] which even the company's detractors concede are high-quality products. As one observer noted:

> Shimano has captured an estimated 85 percent–95 percent of the component business for derailleur-equipped bikes by offering equipment that has made cycling easier, simpler, and more fun. Only the grouchiest purists would return to the days before innovations such as index shifting, combined brake/shift levers for road bikes, more effective brakes, clipless mountain bike pedals and maintenance-free bottom brackets, all of which Shimano either pioneered or perfected for the mass market.[26]

As another indication of its dominance, industry observers compared Shimano to Intel, the premier component manufacturer in the computer industry. As former CEO Andrew Grove of Intel put it, "Somebody got me a clipping from a bicycle magazine about Shimano gears, and there's a quote in there that Shimano is the Intel of the bike industry. [We've made it] when biking magazines use us as the thing to compare to."[27]

Shimano built market control by bundling its components (for example, a brake set with derailleurs and shifters, cranksets, chains) into groups at different price points and degrees of quality. A bicycle assembler could save money by buying the bundled group, taking advantage of Shimano's discounts of approximately 10 percent for bundled products and volume sales. The bundled components cost much less than they would if sold separately, and the logistics of the transaction were both simpler and less expensive.

Shimano also built market share by integrating traditionally modular components, particularly the drive train. Shimano introduced indexed shifting in 1985, which then required components such as shift levers, rear cogs, derailleurs, and chains to be designed to work integrally. The company expanded this integration by combining the rear hub and cog set in such a fashion that other brands of cogs and hubs were incompatible. Then, Shimano integrated its shift levers into the braking system, requiring bicycle assemblers to purchase Shimano brake and shift levers as a single unit. (This strategy, by the way, parallels Intel's integrating its microprocessor into a module with expanded functions. Similarly, Microsoft bundled its Windows operating system with Internet Explorer—and claimed that the package was inextricably integral.)

Facing a vertical/integral Goliath that had wrested significant industry control from the assemblers, how could other component suppliers compete with the Intel of the bicycle industry? The successes and stresses of one company that developed a new device for gear shifting prove instructive. Founded in 1987, SRAM developed Grip Shift, a mechanism that allows bicyclists to shift gears by rotating a dial on their handle bars rather than pushing two levers up or down as they do with Shimano's RapidFire system, which has nearly 100 pieces. In contrast, the Grip Shift has 20 pieces, only 2 of which move. As added features, the shift weighs a bit less, and the moving parts don't wear out as easily. Grip Shift also allows riders to shift gears without releasing their grip on the handlebars, eliminating the insecurity some bicyclists feel when they have to release their grip while shifting.

After initial attempts to introduce the product for road bikes, SRAM successfully convinced Trek to put the shifter on its hybrid bikes—an insignificant segment of an industry dominated first by mountain bikes and then by road bikes. The shifters were a hit, although the hybrid bicycle market never grew; as a result, SRAM increasingly concentrated on the mountain bicycle market.

Although somewhat slow to be accepted, Grip Shift eventually helped make SRAM a major player in the industry. At least 65 of the 1994 models included Grip Shift, whereas the previous year only three models did, a clear indication of the product's rapid rise and success. As of the end of 1995, SRAM's Grip Shift had gained approximately 60 percent of the shifter market, and SRAM had manufacturing plants in Chicago, Ireland, the Netherlands, Taiwan, and China. This increase resulted in part from SRAM's 1989 lawsuit against Shimano for unfair bundling practices. While never admitting fault, Shimano settled the case out of court with an award somewhere between $2 million and $4 million. What is more, Shimano discontinued its heavy discounting for bundling component group purchases.

Adding further injury to Shimano was the fact that Grip Shift's shifters did not accommodate Shimano's integrated brake design. Assemblers, therefore, had an excuse to collect competitive bids for those components as well. In addition, SRAM developed its own integrated strategy, which it used against Shimano. By designing brake systems that were integral to the Grip Shift system, SRAM began capitalizing on the demand for its own shifters.

Success with one product does not guarantee the long-term success of SRAM as a bicycle components manufacturer, however. Shimano retained a strong presence in most of the drivetrain components. Additionally, Taiwanese-based SunRace and the European heavyweight Sachs quickly copied (and perhaps improved upon) SRAM's Grip Shift idea.

SunRace, for example, aggressively offered drivetrain components at discounts of up to 50 percent off of Shimano's wholesale prices. SunRace, in turn, went after market share at the lower end, offering product compatibility with Shimano rather than technological innovation. And Shimano wasn't the only company SunRace was willing to copy. It also came out with its own version of Grip Shift called Turbo-Grip. Not far behind SunRace came a number of other Taiwanese companies, most of which concentrated on offering discounted prices on up-to-the-minute copies of Shimano freehubs, gear clusters, crank sets, and brakes. For bicycle assemblers, these companies offer substantial savings, particularly attractive in less visible components on the bicycle.

The threat of competition also looms from the bicycle assemblers themselves. Trek and Specialized—to name but two of the assemblers—have long placed their names on such parts as seats that are in fact manufactured by low-cost suppliers. In addition, Cannondale began to design its own components, including cranks, which could then be outsourced at the lower price points. Although Cannondale chose to make its more expensive Coda line of crank sets, it outsourced its lower-end crank sets to such companies as Sugino, an established low-cost Japanese components company.

As this brief survey suggests, the bicycle industry went from vertical in the late 1800s to horizontal around the turn of the century to vertical (around Schwinn) in the mid-1900s to horizontal in the early 1980s and briefly back to vertical (around Shimano) in the early 1990s. In the some 125 years of its history, the bicycle industry has thus taken two trips around the double helix. Without having seen the helix among the fruit fly industries—where computers, for example, traversed the whole cycle in less than two decades—one might not have thought to look for such patterns elsewhere. But, once you have the model in mind, it opens up new ways of viewing opportunities and threats in any industry. This point is well illustrated by the automobile industry.

The Double Helix in the Auto Industry

In the United States at the turn of the century, approximately a hundred "coach makers" grew up in the Detroit area, each involved in some aspect of offerings by the "horseless vehicles" industry. By mid-century, from that beginning as a horizontal, fractured industry, Henry Ford and Alfred Sloan had overseen the consolidation of the industry around a few massive, vertically integrated corporations such as Ford and General Motors. Recently, the industry has started to move back around the double helix and take on a much more distinctly horizontal/ modular structure—similar to the one we saw in the PC industry, albeit with a much slower clockspeed. In the computer industry, Compaq was the first assembler to drive the shift around the double helix. In the automobile industry, that distinction goes to Chrysler.

Compaq bought components from IBM's suppliers, bundled them into an IBM-compatible personal computer, and dramatically undercut and outmaneuvered IBM. Chrysler began doing much the same to Ford and General Motors in the early 1990s.

Chrysler's strategists launched one of the most dramatic back-from-the-brink stories in business. In the 1980s, Chrysler was so cash-poor that to generate operating capital for survival, it had to sell its new, billion-dollar engineering center to a finance company and then lease it back. At that time, Chrysler was also in a difficult spot with its suppliers. As the smallest of the Big Three automakers, Chrysler typically stood third in line with suppliers, who were continuously at the beck and call of the much stronger and larger Ford and General Motors. In that vertically structured era, U.S. car manufacturers tended to keep in-house the intellectual and product-development work for components and subsystems, typically outsourcing only the low-level production of individual parts according to detailed specifications. The automakers also worked to keep component prices down by demanding bidding competitions for each job.

At one of its darkest hours, Chrysler met with suppliers and, partly out of desperation, proposed a radical change in the way the company would do business. Instead of dictating to suppliers and trying to pit them against each other, Chrysler promised to commit to long-term relationships for developing entire subsystems and to share the benefits of any cost-saving ideas with suppliers. Long the norm in many Japanese companies, this mode of operation represented for Detroit a major departure from business as usual.

At the same time, Chrysler dramatically reduced its component development and technology development activities and, as a result, the corporate overhead associated with them. It designs, assembles, and markets vehicles to which it contributes little of its own innovative component technology. Instead, the company relies on mutually beneficial partnerships in which suppliers grace Chrysler's autos with the latest advances.

Chrysler's strategic shift must be judged an outstanding success. From near bankruptcy, the company achieved the lowest cost structure of the Big Three and the highest average profit per vehicle. Corporate sales and profits skyrocketed. Furthermore, from having a stock price well down in the single digits, Chrysler was judged to be worth over $60 per share by Daimler-Benz when it made its historic takeover offer in 1998.

In an effort to compete with the new Chrysler, Ford and GM have also scrambled to separate their components operations from their automotive operations. Rumors that Ford or GM will sell its component operations continually resurface, a sure indicator that Chrysler has played the role of the Compaq of the auto industry. Just as Compaq helped to drive the entire computer industry to a horizontal/ modular structure, Chrysler's strategy allows suppliers—even Ford's and GM's internal suppliers—to strengthen their capability to develop whole automotive subsystems, thereby pushing the entire structure of the industry from vertical toward horizontal.

The double helix helps us observe two phenomena: First, the assembler portion of the industry is moving from a vertical structure to a state where it is facing significant pressure to disintegrate. Second, the supplier sector is moving from a horizontal structure to a state in which there are significant incentives to integrate. Let us look at these dynamics from the perspective of each position in the chain.

Helix Strategies for Automakers

So what do you do if you are a player in the automotive industry? If you are an automaker, the risks are clear: To remain vertically integrated in the face of industry disintegration is to risk the fate of IBM in the 1980s—a slow behemoth beset by agile niche competitors. Interestingly, General Motors, the auto industry heavyweight that has lost billions of dollars and millions of car sales worth of market share in the 1980s and 1990s, has an asset it might be able to exploit: Delphi Automotive, GM's $32-billion-a-year auto parts powerhouse. If, as the fruit flies have taught us, the automotive industry is headed for an era where suppliers may take control, it is certainly vital to note that by far the biggest and strongest automotive supplier on the planet is wholly owned by General Motors. The trick for GM will be balancing the health of the child with that of the parent. IBM lost control of its industry partly because the entrenched mainframe division could not stand the thought of subjugating itself to the upstart PC division. Will GM's car folks stand in the way of Delphi's rise to power? Managing that balancing act will be key to GM's future.

In the case of Toyota, there is no asset such as Delphi to help hedge against the danger of "Denso Inside" overtaking what we might call "Toyota Outside." What Toyota has, however, is the world's premier lean machine of the automotive world. The company has a tremendous lead in the combination of cost, quality, and development speed. Its knowledge base of automotive development and technologies is very deep. And, its ability—and willingness—to explore new technological frontiers (such as hybrid gasoline-electric engines) is impressive. These assets probably assure Toyota safe passage unless an extremely powerful player in components or retailing emerges.

A recent *New York Times* article reported on a joint venture between a Toyota subsidiary and Texas Instruments to build a $1.5 billion semiconductor factory that would make memory chips and automotive electronic components. The article also noted Toyota's earlier moves into telecommunications and software, and it twice used the word "puzzling" in reference to Toyota's strategy behind this venture.[28]

To a student of business genetics, however, these moves are anything but puzzling. They indicate clearly that Toyota managers have intuited the lessons of the double helix, concluded that auto industry clockspeed will approach that of the electronics industry, and that some car companies may fall victim to the automotive equivalent of "Intel Inside" computers. Thus, they are continually adjusting their supply chain design to position themselves for the coming changes.

If you are Chrysler, you play the Compaq/Dell strategy to the hilt. Chrysler leads in that strategy by a large margin. If you are Daimler-Benz, you either follow the Macintosh strategy—higher quality to a small, discerning niche—or you buy a Chrysler and try to be a premier, full-line player such as Toyota. That's a tough row to hoe, but it may be more promising than playing Apple among increasingly powerful suppliers and large, powerful rivals.

On balance, the world's major automotive manufacturers are adjusting their strategies for a tougher, faster-clockspeed world, but they are not acting as if they believe a turn in the helix is inevitable in the short term. Because the automobile as a manufactured product may never be as modular as the Windows-plus-Intel PC, this could be the best course. In the automotive supplier sector, however, the preparations for a horizontal/modular world are in full swing.

Helix Strategies for Auto Suppliers

The players that produce automobile seating systems illustrate well an aggressive stance toward the turn to horizontal/modular. For most automakers, seats are the biggest single externally purchased item for their vehicles—more than $1,000 per set in some cases. Through the 1980s, most Big Three carmakers, consistent with the vertical structure of the industry, designed and assembled seating systems, but purchased the seat parts—the metal frames, fabric, and electronic controls. By the mid-1990s, however, the seat industry was dominated by giants such as Lear and Johnson Controls, each of which saw its annual sales skyrocketing from under $1 billion to more than $7 billion. In this new environment, when an automaker begins to plan the seats for a new vehicle, there is a limited set of possible suppliers, each of which has significant clout in the industry.

Furthermore, these seat companies have begun to acquire related businesses—suppliers of interior panels and carpets, for example. Thus, if Ford, for example, wants to specify Lear seats for a new car, it may be told, in effect, "We're not a seat company anymore. We are now an interiors company. If you want our seats, you have to buy the whole integral automobile interior: our carpets, our headliners, and our dashboards as well." Because Ford has a limited choice of seat suppliers and because each seat supplier seems to be pursuing a similar vertical integration strategy, a pattern begins to emerge: Once niche players have built significant market power in the now horizontally structured industry, they often move vertically to exploit their newfound market power. This activity is little different from Intel's bundling of graphics chips with its microprocessors or Microsoft's bundling of its Web browser with Windows.

Despite the depth and market power of suppliers such as Delphi, Bosch, Denso, Johnson Controls, Lear, and others, no one in the auto industry has a monopoly grip that even approaches that of Intel or Microsoft in the computer industry. And, although suppliers are consolidating across subsystems—a sort of hedging strategy like the one we saw in the MICE industry in chapter 2—automakers can still play suppliers against each other. That game, however, is much trickier than it once was because of the dramatic increase in industry concentration in many segments. A supplier that becomes too ambitious too fast can find itself shut out of many car programs. Yet a supplier that is too timid can find that its competitors are winning contracts by flexing their muscles in exactly the way that Intel did when it launched its "Intel Inside" campaign—by going directly to the final consumer.[29] In the computer industry case, a typical consumer in effect tells the sales channel: "I don't care who made the box, just give me 'Intel Inside.'"

If this type of campaign can work with a computer chip, which customers can neither see nor touch, then surely it has a chance to work in the automotive industry, where visual and tactile appeal count a great deal in a customer's evaluation of the vehicle. Certainly, customers can be made much more aware of the value they place in the seats or electronic controls in a car. However, even for lesser systems, direct advertisement to the customer might prove fruitful. Consider the following example: In 1996, UT-Automotive, a broad-based supplier of components and subsystems to the automotive industry, ran an advertisement in a number of business magazines touting its electronic security systems. The print ad featured a photo of a high-tech car thief, who used a device to capture electronically the code to a car's security system as the owner "beeped" it into the alarm mode with a remote key-chain device. UT-Automotive's ad boasted a security system feature that could scramble the code and reset it with each use, so that the code picked up by the thief would not be the right code for the next deactivation of the alarm. The ad noted that the system was available on some GM, Honda, and Nissan vehicles, in effect saying: "You shouldn't focus on who made the box; just ask for 'UT-Automotive Inside.'"

The suppliers in the automotive world have far more to gain from a shift to horizontal/modular than do the assemblers, except perhaps for Chrysler since it has already aligned itself with such a model. The suppliers, in addition, have girded themselves for war should one arise. I believe the automakers should be wary. The PC industry teaches us that once the horizontal/modular trigger has been tripped, neither market share nor technological depth, neither financial strength (in the case of IBM) nor superior product technology (in the case of the Apple Macintosh) can withstand a tidal wave of exuberant entrants into the breach.

Because even a Toyota could probably not retain its standing if all other firms evolved into horizontal/modular structures, the critical

concern of automakers is how to prepare for and
major industrial shift. Individual capabilities that are criti.
era may become commodities in the next. As a result, more importan.
than any individual capability—in technology or manufacturing, for
example—is the ability to foresee the coming changes and choose
which capabilities will be of greatest value. This is the theme of the
next part of the book: supply chain design. Design of the organization's entire value chain network (that is, supply chain)—especially
determining which capabilities to invest in and which to outsource—
is the most important competency in a company's arsenal.

SUPPLY CHAIN DESIGN:

THE *ULTIMATE* CORE CAPABILITY

5 THE PRIMACY CHAINS

Capability Chains Make a Business

A company is its chain of continually evolving capabilities—that is, its own capabilities plus the capabilities of everyone it does business with.

NO CAPABILITY IS FOREVER. That is one of the key messages of the fruit flies and of Part I of this book.

No capability exists by itself, isolated from all others. That is the first key message of Part II. The old maxim that a chain is only as strong as its weakest link is as true in business as it is in mechanical systems. In the physical world, mechanical system designers know this law well and design their chains accordingly. In business, strategy designers must respect this law as well.

To build a company or a capability without regard for the chain in which it is embedded is a recipe for disaster. I argue in this chapter and those that follow that there is no competency more critical than that of superior design of one's capability chain—from the final consumer all the way upstream to the sources of raw materials and new technological concepts.

To begin, let's look at the role of chain design through the handiwork of one of the most inspired supply chain designers on the planet: Michael Dell. As of May 1998, the stock price of Dell Computer had increased 26,900 percent in the decade of the 1990s—higher than that for

Intel, Microsoft, Coca-Cola, Disney, or Cisco Systems.[1] Dell Computer has no proprietary technology propelling it to such stratospheric growth and profitability. In fact, the company's position in the supply chain has it squeezed between Intel and Microsoft upstream, two of the computer industry's most powerful players, and a downstream market populated by millions of well-informed consumers who can choose from dozens of computer companies that assemble almost indistinguishable personal computers. In terms of direct rivals, Dell must contend with powerhouses IBM, Hewlett-Packard, Compaq, plus myriad low-cost Asian and American players who have taken advantage of the low costs of entry into the PC industry. By any Porter-style analysis,[2] Dell's industry position looks anything but attractive.

Yet Dell not only thrives, its sales and profit growth can take your breath away. The company's primary advantage is its preeminent supply chain design, augmented with precise supply chain *management*. Although difficult to believe, throughout the 1990s Dell's supply chain management has been driven by "vintage software" for materials requirements planning (MRP).[3] The story of Dell's success is fascinating and important, in part because it illustrates a brilliant supply chain design in a fast-clockspeed industry.

Using parts ordered from catalogs, Michael Dell began assembling and selling computers from his dormitory room at the University of Texas. When his roommate kicked him out because of the electronic clutter, Dell just moved to bigger quarters and has continued to expand ever since. Fortunately, Texas is a big state and has afforded him plenty of space to grow.

Dell Computer takes orders for customized PCs and workstations over the telephone and on its Internet site, begins building the machines almost immediately after the orders are complete, and ships the completed products as soon as they are built, often within 24 hours.

The company carries no finished goods inventories, nor does it employ any distributors or retailers who carry inventory. It ships all products directly from its factory to the final customer. Furthermore, Dell carries almost no materials inventories: Every part the company buys goes immediately into a machine that is then built and sold.

How does Dell know what it will sell? To understand the answer, it helps to frame the question the other way around: Dell sells whatever it has purchased. The only variable is price.[4]

Dell's sales organization is responsible for forecasts and decisions on what components to purchase. Because commissions are based on Dell's profit margins, salespeople must sell whatever they order, including components for which buyers misjudged customer demand. If demand falls or customers no longer want a component, the sales organization must lower the price so that the product sells no matter what.

How does the company avoid getting burned? First, it gets good prices from suppliers because it buys in volume. Second—and this is the real key—if in doubt about likely customer preferences, buyers always opt for ordering components of latest technology because those have the longest shelf life. Because the company carries no inventories and has no resellers, it can be the lowest-cost producer. In addition, because high-end users usually purchase the latest components, Dell services this select group and keeps its profit margins healthy (see figure 5.1).

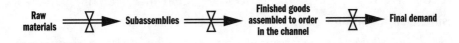

Figure 5.1. Dell's Supply Chain

And here's the real kicker: The faster the clockspeed of the computer industry, the greater the advantage Dell wields over its competitors. How does this work? Every other major PC maker builds to stock and sells through resellers who carry inventory. In this industry, inventory does not age gracefully.[5] In fact, aged inventory in the computer market is downright ugly. What could be worse than holding a large inventory of PCs with built-in 28K modems when the new 56K modems hit the market? Who would have wanted to have on hand several thousand Pentium processors when Intel introduced the Pentium II and prices of the old Pentiums dropped through the floor?

In the lightning-speed PC industry such obsolescence is practically an everyday occurrence. The more inventory in the chain, the higher the obsolescence costs. And the faster the clockspeed, the higher the obsolescence costs. So whoever has the leanest chain wins—and the faster the clockspeed, the larger the margin of victory. No wonder Michael Dell is printing money.

Why can't Compaq, IBM, HP, and the others just copy Dell's model, given that there are no secrets or proprietary patents? Actually, those companies are trying to do exactly that, as fast as they can. The problem is that they are all dependent on their current channel resellers for sales (see figure 5.2). Any attempt to eliminate those resellers is likely to cause sales to plummet until the new model is fully worked out. Meanwhile those lost sales will go to Dell Computer Corporation or another competitor and may not come back. Thus, the resellers/channel-dependent producers are forced to adopt a gradual conversion rather than go cold turkey, so to speak. But a gradual conversion in a fast-clockspeed industry can seem like a lifetime. As a result, Dell Computer remains in the driver's seat—for now.

Dell Computer Corporation illustrates a richer way of thinking about supply chain design—not as a static collection of contractors, but as a company's most important competency. Most of the literature on business strategy has focused on the individual corporation as the

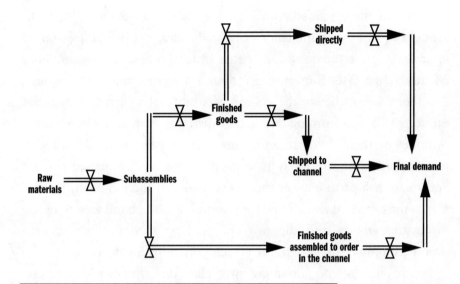

Figure 5.2. Standard PC-industry Supply Chain[6]

appropriate unit of analysis. In this line of thinking, the supply chain is taken as given, and the challenge is characterized primarily as managing the chain: stewardship of the relevant network of organizations and assets to provide value to final customers.

This static, passive view of supply chain design, however, is inadequate to describe what is actually happening in the personal computer industry, where companies are continually reassessing their supply chain designs in search of temporary advantage. Considering the industry's fast clockspeed, firms must pay attention to designing the *extended* organization, defined here as the corporation per se as well as its supply network, its distribution network, and its alliance network.

Just as the manufacturing management community discovered in the 1980s the enormous power of the product *design* activity for leveraging improvements in product *manufacturing* performance, a well-designed supply chain offers enormous payoffs in managing the

the extended company. Supply chain design ought to be thought of as assembling chains of *capabilities*, not just *collaborating organizations*, in the quest for a series of temporary advantages. Since no advantage lasts forever, these design activities must be ongoing, and therefore constitute the "core" capability of a firm in a dynamic economy. Top-performing companies distinguish themselves from the ordinary by their ability to anticipate better where in the chain lucrative opportunities are likely to arise and to invest in the capabilities and relationships to exploit them. Especially in the long run, fortune favors the prepared firm. Therefore, superior market and technological forecasting ability and superior competency portfolio management (that is, supply chain design) are critical functions for the organization.

Jazz musicians who jam in the same place day after day learn to create great art by inviting other musicians to join them, people who might be passing by and interested in a short gig. There's a core of players, but the real creation is not theirs alone. That opportunity arises when outsiders, some of whom may be very talented musicians, join the creative process. Once everyone feels the rhythm and intuits the direction of the musical line, the creation is spontaneous but not entirely subject to accident or fortune. A lead musician still directs the burst of inspiration and innovation.

Similarly, a company's *real* core capability—the inner core, if you will—lies in the ability to design and manage the supply chain in order to gain maximum advantage, albeit temporary, in a market where competitive forces may change at lightning speed. To see a corporation piecemeal, element by element, affords but a limited and usually distorted sense of the entire enterprise. One might just as well study a heart or a liver in hopes of determining what sort of person the owner is. Looking at a company in the context of its supply chain and stakeholders renders a much fuller view, a holistic image of activities, a seamless chain of capabilities or know-how, both its own and that of the organizations with which it is allied. Like the world around them, these capabilities and the relationships among them are constantly changing and evolving. Therefore, a company must monitor and manage them all.

[In a fast-clockspeed world especially, companies must focus strategic thinking on their entire value chain, not merely on individual capabilities. Individual capabilities can lose value overnight, hastened by new or rapidly evolving technologies or by the new tactics of competitors. These observations are borne out by three cases from vastly different industries: Silicon Graphics in computer workstations, Toshiba in computer chips, and Merck in pharmaceuticals.]

Silicon Graphics, Inc.

If ever there was a golden-haired child of high-tech fortune, it was Silicon Graphics, Inc. (SGI). Its powerful computer workstations and three-dimensional graphics dazzled its Silicon Valley neighbors and Wall Street analysts alike. In 1995, its sales soared past $2 billion a year; its profits grew at an annual rate of over 50 percent, and its stock had reached an all-time high of almost $45 a share.[7] A pioneer in interactive TV, Silicon Graphics had even staked out a place for itself on the ground floor of the Internet, with its servers operating some of the day's hottest Web sites. The sky was the limit, or so it seemed.

Within two years, however, the company's fortunes had plummeted. Its stock price plunged below $13 a share, and for the first half of 1997, those spiraling profits reversed course in a maelstrom of losses. Old customers complained about product quality and delivery, while new customers were harder and harder to find. Interactive TV turned sour, and Sun Microsystems' Java software stole the Internet applications market. Above all, Hewlett-Packard and Sun were now selling workstations whose 3-D graphics were closing in on SGI's high-performance levels—and selling them at a much lower price.

What went wrong? Critics compiled a virtually endless list.[8] But the real culprit was a kind of corporate hubris—an assumption that the company's technical wizardry could guarantee SGI's continued success. With its strategy tightly focused on these technology elements of its capabilities chain, SGI lost control of the chain as a whole, and the results were dire.

To supply advanced graphics chips for its new workstation line, the company chose Toshiba, which had no experience making the chips. Major delays in delivery put production of the new stations behind schedule. At the same time, delays elsewhere along the supply chain led to a last-minute crunch in manufacturing and assembly, with predictable effects on the quality and quantity of the product.

Even after the workstations were completed, supply chain failures dogged the company. A defect in the microprocessor, built by NEC, meant that SGI engineers had to chase down every machine and replace the chip. Meanwhile the expected demand for the new machine among commercial customers, a new market for SGI, turned out to be far smaller than predicted as customers purchased older, proven versions instead. That reversal led to a costly oversupply of the new machines and a shortage of the old ones. In short, a capabilities chain in disarray and the invasion of competitors' new, lower-priced machines taught management at SGI a hard lesson in fast-clockspeed capability chains.

The rapid reversal at Silicon Graphics serves as a pointed reminder of the vulnerability of even the most time-honored, secure capability a company possesses, if it does not also manage the portfolio of capabilities that support that key asset. Especially in high-speed, unpredictable business environments, companies must understand and manage the whole of their capability chains.

Of course, there are certain constants, even in the most volatile environments. The actual function of an industry capability chain, for example, is likely to remain intact over a long period of time. That is true even of the most rapid-clockspeed industry, infotainment, whose function is to produce and deliver information content to consumers ravenous for information. Thus, if a company's executives begin from the premise that they want to supply one or more elements of that chain, then they are on solid intellectual ground to begin a strategic assessment of their capacity to do so. On the other hand, if a company's strategy derives simply from its hope to exploit an existing capability by inserting itself into the chain, the strategy rests on shaky intellectual grounds and can easily lead to a rapid, costly exit from the industry.

Toshiba Corporation

With the next case study, on the chain of supply for dynamic random access memory chips (DRAMs), we can move directly to consider one of the most powerful themes of supply chain design—the capability chain analysis. In particular, we need to answer these questions: Where, exactly, in the chain are the greatest opportunities? Which resources in the chain will be in the shortest supply? Where in the chain will the lion's share of the money be made in the months and years ahead?

DRAMs are an essential player in the economy of the Information Age. Aside from the microprocessor, they are the critical semiconductor component of personal computers and many other electronics products. DRAMs have historically been manufactured by an all-star cast that included IBM, Motorola, Texas Instruments, Toshiba, NEC, Hitachi, Matsushita, Samsung, as well as a number of new entrants from Singapore, Taiwan, and China, among others. The DRAM supply chain starts with process technology companies such as Applied Materials (AMAT) and Nikon, which make the machines that make the chips—process tools such as the photolithographic steppers described in chapter 3. Once the chips are made by Samsung, Toshiba, and others, they are shipped to firms like Compaq, Dell, and HP to be placed in workstations and personal computers, which are then sold to resellers or directly to end users (see figure 5.3).

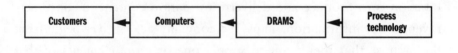

Figure 5.3: The DRAM (Dynamic Random Access Memory) Supply Chain

Now, consider the position of Toshiba Corporation in this chain. Toshiba has been a major player in both the computer segment of this chain and the DRAM segment. In addition, Toshiba has supported great internal technical depth in some process technologies, most notably photolithography, where the company has often developed its own experimental tools that were one to two generations ahead of what was available from suppliers like Nikon.[9] Such advanced process technology permits earlier product development of the latest technology chips. Interestingly, however, Toshiba has not typically offered its deep capability in lithography for sale to other companies.

When we examine profit opportunities in this chain, the computer market is not likely to be the most attractive link. The market is crowded, fiercely competitive, and margins are constantly under pressure. The same is true of the DRAM production link, which seems to get more crowded daily. So technologically deep Toshiba labors mightily in two of the most hotly contested segments in this chain.

Given the competition in its chosen segments, Toshiba must be vigilant to cut costs steadfastly. One possible target is the army of researchers focused on lithography. Other DRAM makers have a leaner cost structure because they rely on suppliers for lithography knowledge. So Toshiba might feel pressure to save money and disband its advanced process technology research group.

But a capability chain analysis suggests another possibility. Perhaps a greater opportunity lies in process technology, where the competitors are relatively few, the entry barriers are high, and the profit margins are relatively fat (although the volatility of demand is high).

Photolithographic tools, for instance, are produced by a select few firms such as Nikon and Canon, sell for as much as $5 million apiece, and are found by the dozen in all the major semiconductor factories around the world.

Instead of cutting its lithography group, Toshiba might consider making and selling its own photolithographic steppers. Such a strategy is not without risk. As Toshiba's loyal stepper supplier, Nikon would surely not be amused. Nonetheless, we see that in more and more industries the greatest threats and opportunities sometimes lie in the battles of vertical competition—battles along the chain—as opposed to horizontal battles with traditional rivals. This is why supply chain design is so challenging and so critical.

Merck & Co., Inc. and the Bio-Pharmaceutical Industry

Finally, let us turn to a sector, pharmaceuticals, where new technology —genomics and biotechnology—has unleashed an explosion of vertical competition to complement the already white-hot horizontal competition.

If you weren't invested in the information industry in the 1980s when fortunes were made by buying stocks in the likes of Intel, Microsoft, Compaq, and Cisco, you could console yourself a bit had you guessed that the major pharmaceutical companies would continue to enjoy their explosive growth. From 1982 through 1992, industry sales grew at an average rate of 18 percent a year, and profit margins were typically over 70 percent in the United States, rivaling even the margins at Intel.[10] In fact, the entire period from the 1950s to 1990, called the "golden age for the pharmaceutical industry"[11] by Harvard's Gary Pisano, was a slow-clockspeed, high-prosperity era for all the major players such as Merck & Co., Inc., Eli Lilly and Company, Bristol-Myers Squibb Company, and Pfizer, Inc. Successful drug development projects typically took well over a decade to complete, had exclusive patent protection once approved, and enjoyed very high barriers to entry. Only one new entrant, Syntex Chemicals, Inc., the developer of the oral contraceptive, successfully entered the industry after World War II.[12] Like the aircraft industry in the same era, this was a high-technology, but slow-clockspeed, industry.

The fantastic financial results at the major pharmaceutical companies were both a beneficiary of and a contributor to what many perceived as runaway costs in the U.S. health care system. After four decades of red-hot results, however, the drug industry got a very cold shower beginning in the early 1990s. From both upstream and downstream—in what had been seen as a dormant supply chain—the pharmaceutical companies experienced attacks on two flanks. Downstream, the U.S. federal government talked of controlling runaway health costs that threatened to dominate the budget and explode the federal deficit. At the same time, American corporations, having made their factories and operations as lean as possible, targeted the high price of health care as a way of further reducing costs and thereby increasing their competitiveness against aggressive rivals at home and abroad.

Upstream, meanwhile, the news was no less disconcerting. Biotechnology was absolutely decimating the exclusivity of the small club of drug-creation factories. During the "golden age," large pharmaceutical companies had achieved a high degree of vertical integration in their research and development. In fact, they viewed their R&D function as the lifeblood of the industry: Here lay the opportunities for finding, synthesizing, and testing chemicals for their efficacy against human ailments. But, by the early 1990s, this search-and-synthesize approach to drug discovery and development was well past its point of diminishing returns—yielding fewer and more costly "blockbuster drugs"—just as the revolution in genetics and biotechnology was exploding.[13]

The biotechnology industry is an outgrowth of major advances in the field of molecular biology. Prior to the advent of biotechnology, most pharmaceutical compounds were made using synthetic chemistry. This approach to drug design required an R&D facility to have a large number of chemists in order to synthesize a vast array of distinct, small-molecule chemicals used in the drug screening process. The key benefit of molecular biology is the capacity of this technology to make complex protein molecules and DNA available as therapeutic agents, or as therapeutic targets for more traditional approaches to drug development. This advance has allowed biotechnology companies effectively to address a wide range of human diseases. By 1994, there were more than 220 biotechnology products under development, and sales of these compounds on the market exceeded $60 billion.[14] Biotechnology provides not only innovative new drugs with unique characteristics but also a scope of potential applications that dwarfs those available using synthetic chemistry.

In addition to increasing the number of diseases that can be addressed by pharmaceuticals, biotechnology has led to a shortening of the product development cycle for pharmaceuticals. What used to take anywhere from seven to eleven years to develop now requires between four and eight years.[15] Because biotechnology requires skill sets that synthetic chemistry scientists usually do not possess, biotechnology can be viewed as a competence-destroying technological discontinuity in the pharmaceutical industry.[16] However, biotechnology-based compounds face the same regulatory and distribution constraints as traditional pharmaceutical compounds, allowing pharmaceutical industry leaders to maintain their edge in the downstream parts of the supply chain against the competence-destroying biotechnology firms.

The explosion of knowledge in biology, combined with similar increases of capability in information technology, has created an environment in which four powerful but distinct technology platforms create value.[17]

Perhaps the foremost of these technology platforms is genomics, the study of the human genome (DNA sequence) and its comparison with the genomes of other organisms, such as the mouse and the fruit fly. Although there is a worldwide International Human Genome Project, slated to have the entire human genome and its three billion components mapped by 2003, there were already in 1997 eight private firms trying to race ahead of the government-funded project in search of salable advantage. Obviously this is no longer a sleepy-clockspeed industry.

The genomics technology platform is complemented by a screening (bioassay) platform for determining gene function and assessing drug libraries and a combinatorial chemistry platform for increasing the rate (a hundredfold!) at which compounds can be generated and tested. This new model, dubbed the "drug development triad,"[18] is supported further by bio-informatics, which enables computer-simulation of drug effects to replace work previously done with compounds and organisms in the laboratory, plus robotics and micro-fabrication for the molecular-level manufacture of new drugs.

This splintering of the value chain has led to one of the most complex industry structures in business today. Around the world, well over a thousand biotechnology companies plus a large number of pharmaceutical service companies offer any bit from the drug development triad one could ask for. Virtually any part of the value chain can be outsourced.[19] This splintering has dramatically lowered the cost of entry in practically every link in the pharmaceutical value chain.

In response, most of the large pharmaceutical companies have launched a new supply chain design strategy: Outsource or acquire biotechnology capability rather than develop it in-house. The tremendous increase in the technology clockspeed for pharmaceuticals has left the large firms little choice but to begin competing aggressively for technology acquisition outside their historical supply chain structure. It has also created a huge incentive for creative biotechnologists to launch companies and sell out to the highest bidder.

These new pressures are the main impetus behind several horizontal mergers: In 1996, Ciba Geigy AG and Sandoz AG formed Novartis AG in a \$36.3 billion merger; the following year, Glaxo Holdings and Burroughs Wellcome merged in a \$14.7 billion deal.[20] But such mergers do not create new drugs—the ultimate driver of value. Mergers usually just thin out the competitive field.

Producing innovative drugs requires pharmaceutical companies either to adopt new research strategies or to acquire late-stage drugs from companies with innovative research platforms. The most common response in terms of supply chain design to this new playing field is the creation of alliances along the drug development triad. Consider that the number of strategic alliances focused on therapeutic development between biotechnology companies and the top 20 pharmaceutical companies increased from 85 in 1988 to over 200 in 1996.[21]

According to George Post, president of research and development at SmithKline Beecham,

> The escalating cost and complexity of technical specialization has rendered self-sufficiency unattainable. Companies must establish increasingly diverse networks of technical alliances to ensure access to the full range of resources and skills needed for competitive survival. The evolution of the extended enterprise, and building the managerial skills required to sustain a fluctuating network of alliances, will be increasingly influential in corporate success.[22]

Many pharmaceutical and biotechnology companies are now looking at ways to exercise greater control over the supply chain and thereby gain better access to technologies that comprise the drug discovery triad. A near exponential growth has occurred in the last several years in the number of pharmaceutical alliances with genomics companies, which has risen from 1 in 1992 to 18 in 1996.[23] Most of the top 20 pharmaceutical companies, in fact, have followed an alliance strategy that strings together genomics, bioassay, and combinatorial chemistry companies into a "virtual network" devoted to their drug discovery needs.

These alliance networks utilize a number of different kinds of financial relationships, including equity investments, licenses obtained by the pharmaceutical companies to use a biotech company's technology, milestone payments upon completion of targets toward reaching a drug's final approval, and royalties on the sales of certain drugs.[24] Some European pharmaceutical companies have been especially aggressive in developing alliances in the drug discovery triad because they have traditionally focused on innovation-driven research, whereas their American counterparts tend to be more market-driven companies.[25] By 1997, for example, SmithKline Beecham had formed alliances with Human Genome Sciences in genomics; Cadus, Gliatech, Arris (now AXYS Pharmaceuticals, Inc.), and EvoTech, Inc. in bioassay technology; and Orchid Biocomputer, Inc. and Oxford Glycosciences Plc in combinatorial chemistry. Similarly, Roche had alliances with Human Genome Sciences, Inc., Incyte Pharmaceuticals, Inc., and Millennium Pharmaceuticals, Inc. in genomics; with Affymetrix, Inc., Aurora Biosciences Corporation, and Caliper Technologies Corp. in bioassay technology; and with Alanex Corporation, ArQule, Inc., and Combi-Chem, Inc. in combinatorial chemistry. Roche also held a major interest in Genentech, Inc., the third largest biotechnology company.

In stark contrast to the horizontal/modular supply chain design strategies that SmithKline Beecham, Roche, and many others have crafted, Merck & Co., Inc., the bluest of the blue-chip pharmaceutical companies, has opted to retain a strong vertical/integral structure, mostly eschewing alliances with supply chain members.

Merck is arguably the first among equals leading the pharmaceutical industry. In August 1996, Lehman Brothers analyzed a sample of 70 biotech companies that collectively had 284 drugs in development and a market capitalization of $50 billion. They compared this sample with Merck, which had only 26 drugs in development, but a market capitalization of $80 billion at the time.[26] Either market investors assign much lower probabilities or returns to the drugs from the small biotech firms, or they simply trust Merck to continue to deliver as the company has historically done.

Or could it be Merck's supply chain design? Unlike most of its fellow travelers in the pharmaceutical industry, Merck shows great confidence in its ability to go it alone and remain a vertically integrated powerhouse.[27] Merck's supply chain design reflects the company's strategy to cope both with increasing pressures from customers and payees over the costs for health care and with the accelerated technology clockspeed in research and development. The company's multi-billion-dollar acquisition in 1993 of Medco, the largest pharmaceutical benefits management firm in the United States, goes a long way toward assuring that Merck's pharmaceutical solutions to any human ailment get a fair hearing, at least as a medical option for the 50 million Americans under Medco's guard.

Thanks to its high degree of vertical integration, Merck spends only about 5 percent of its research and development externally, as opposed to its competitors, which spend up to 80 percent.[28] Merck has essentially chosen to internalize the entire drug development triad, whereas the rest of the industry outsources it. Persuaded that the quality of its research and drugs are unparalleled, Merck also seems to believe that it will get higher quality solutions from within its own walls than it could receive if it merely cobbled together the interests and technologies of various suppliers and alliances as many of its competitors have set out to do.

So far, Merck continues to deliver. The company reported record sales and profits in 1997 and can boast of a stream of successful mega-drug launches.[29] Whether Merck can buck the trend as the industry turns along the industrial double helix—from vertical to horizontal— remains to be seen. In the absence of an Intel/Microsoft effect in this industry, Merck's strategy seems viable if not superior to that of its

:s. Although its costs are perhaps higher because of the internaᵤᵤ.ᵤ.ition of processes, it expects the corresponding revenues to be higher as a result of higher quality.[30]

Furthermore, technological interfaces along the pharmaceutical value chain may prove to be much less modular than in the personal computer industry, raising transaction costs for those companies reliant on myriad alliances. However, if one of the genomic companies, such as Human Genome Sciences, manages to get a proprietary, Wintel-like[31] lock on a large portion of genetic knowledge, non-partnering companies are likely to suffer severely.

So how is supply chain design the *ultimate* core competency? In the case of Dell, it provides a cost advantage whose magnitude continues to increase as the industry clockspeed accelerates. In the case of Silicon Graphics, inattention to supply chain design led to a nasty fall. In that of Toshiba, it offers potential directions for greater profitability. And in the case of Merck, supply chain design involves betting the company on the winning structure of the industry. What could be more deserving of the most thoughtful attention of a company's strategic leaders?

These examples point out some of the complexities of supply chain design and management for companies in the relatively fast-clockspeed computer industry and the somewhat slower (although still rapid) pharmaceutical industry. Although Merck has chosen a different path than many other members of its industry and has elected to expand its internal processes to respond to market pressures and the demand for new drug technologies, the company recognizes that it is only as strong as the chain of its continually evolving capabilities.

In chapter 6, we look more closely at occurrences in the extended enterprise to see what inferences we can draw about "laws" of supply chain dynamics. Thereafter, the discussion turns in chapter 7 to ways of mapping the extended enterprise: Where will breakdowns most likely occur? How is it possible to avoid them?

6

LAWS OF NATURE

The Dynamics of the Extended Enterprise

Sometimes clockspeeds and volatility ripple through the chain; sometimes they roar. Knowing what to expect pays big dividends.

MOST BOOKS ON SUPPLY CHAIN *MANAGEMENT* focus their attention on the important issues that arise in managing the logistics of materials and inventories across the supply chain. This book, however, focuses primarily on supply chain *design*, which precedes and must anticipate the challenges of logistics and materials management. I do not intend to cover here those logistics issues that are thoroughly discussed in other places.[1] Because strategic supply chain design decisions, however, have such a large impact on the available options for supply chain management, addressing some of the areas of overlap is critical. This chapter, then, takes up several supply chain design issues that can have a significant impact on those challenges, and it presents options for structuring and improving supply chain management.

[Specifically, I begin with what I call the first and second "laws" of supply chain dynamics. The first is the law of *volatility amplification*, better known to the supply chain management community as the "bull-whip effect" or the "beer game effect,"[2] a phenomenon whereby the volatility of demand and inventories in the supply chain tend to be amplified as one looks farther "upstream"—that is, away from the end user.]The focus here is on some of the strategic supply chain design issues that arise from this phenomenon.

[The second law is new and introduced here for the first time. I call it *clockspeed amplification*, whereby clockspeeds tend to be amplified as one looks farther "downstream"—that is, toward the final customer.[3]]

After describing the dynamics specified by these two laws, I discuss how they influence tiering of the supply chain, the increase of which is an important trend in supply chain design and management. "Tiering" is the phenomenon whereby a designer or assembler of a complex manufactured item (a computer, an automobile, or an airplane, for instance) outsources complex systems to "first-tier" suppliers, who, in turn, outsource subsystems to "second-tier" suppliers, who in turn outsource sub-subsystems to the "third tier," and so on. In contrast to this approach, many major U.S. manufacturers in the 1980s and earlier outsourced only very simple individual components to a single tier of suppliers and integrated the majority of systems and subsystems themselves.[4]

Volatility Amplification

At an MIT supply chain conference in 1995, Richard Kegg, then vice president of Cincinnati Milacron, one of America's few remaining large machine tool companies, began his talk by showing a slide of a graveyard. Each tombstone carried the name of an American machine tool company that had gone out of business. The message was clear: Within the supply chain, machine tool companies are an endangered species. To understand this phenomenon better, consider the data in figure 6.1.

From 1961 to 1991, while the gross domestic product (GDP) in the United States swung in the range of plus or minus 2 percent to 3 percent and automotive production swung in the range of plus or minus 20 percent, orders in the machine tool industry fluctuated in the range

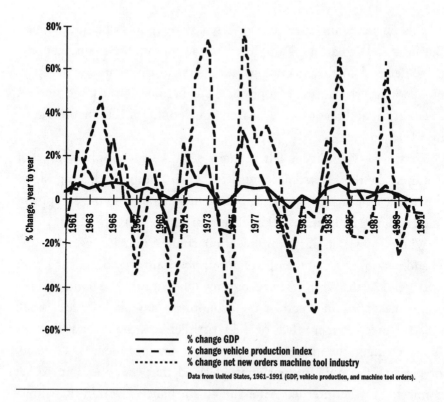

Figure 6.1. Supply Chain Volatility Amplification: Machine Tools at the Tip of the Bullwhip[5]

of plus or minus 60 percent to 80 percent. And the graveyard population soared with every cyclical free fall. Figure 6.2 shows this phenomenon incontrovertibly: A ripple at one end of the supply chain can trigger a tidal wave at the other.

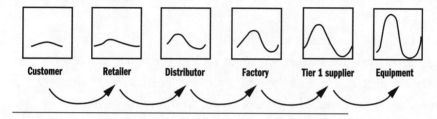

Figure 6.2. The Bullwhip Effect: Supply Chain Volatility Increases Upstream

This phenomenon gives us the first law of supply chain dynamics: Business cycle volatility is amplified as one goes up the chain, from the customer end to the technology suppliers. In my opinion, this phenomenon has the stature of a physical law because of the large amount of empirical and theoretical research (much of it at MIT) that has gone into verifying it.[6]

That same volatility is felt in many sectors of a supply chain. For example, in the electronics industry, when computer buying slows down, the chip makers see a steep drop in demand, and the equipment makers, large and small, feel as if they are careening off a cliff.

Where does volatility amplification come from? To visualize the phenomenon, think of the upstream supply chain members as the knot at the end of the whip of the economy. One month, the handle of the whip, the "consumer end of the economy," may experience a small "disturbance," a mere flick of the wrist: Perhaps the Federal Reserve Board changed the interest rate; perhaps a new president was elected, or perhaps ten million consumers decided that they just had to get connected to the Internet. After the "disturbance," within the supply chain, one observes some information lags (it takes time to realize and respond to demand changes), delivery lags (it takes time to adjust the inventories and flow levels in the supply lines), some misperceptions or miscalculations of the magnitude of the triggering event, over- and under-ordering (adjusting to new levels of demand can generate over-shooting or undershooting), and some lumpiness in orders or layoffs. These effects accumulate, resulting in amplification as they ripple up the chain.

The upstream members of the supply chain will feel the same cyclical characteristics as the consumer end of the economy, but because they are at the "end" of the whip, the distance traveled is greater, the speed is higher, and the effects more pronounced. What was just a flick of the wrist at one end cracks with a sharp snap at the other.

Historically, the machine tool companies have attempted to damp demand volatility by shifting sales to export markets when domestic markets ratcheted down. Of course, if there are simultaneous recessions at home and abroad in key machine tool markets, then the cyclicality cannot be exported. This strategy of shifting to export markets during downturns at home is also hampered by the intensity of competition in world markets. American, Japanese, German, Swiss, and Italian companies are among those that seek to strengthen their export sales during domestic downturns while competing intensely in their own home markets.

Toshiba has developed an interesting strategy to deal with volatility in the demand for capital equipment. The company maintains a central division that supplies manufacturing equipment to its various product-manufacturing divisions. When demand from one product division slows, personnel are reassigned to work on equipment for other divisions. No doubt employees who normally work on semiconductor equipment are less effective when assigned to design and build metal-cutting machines, but there are some skills such as controls programming which transfer relatively easily. This practice also encourages insights and expertise from one area to be applied to another.

Many American machine tool builders traditionally resorted to the strategy of collecting a large stock of backlogged orders to tide the company over during downturns. Backlogs meant that when orders dried up, tool builders did not get caught with excess manufacturing capacity of their own. When the U.S. machine tool industry had little foreign competition, this strategy worked fine for the tool builders, although customers did not particularly like it. In the 1970s and 1980s, however, foreign competitors challenged American machine tool companies in the U.S. market not only with new technology and competitive prices, but also with rapid delivery. By 1986, the American industry was reeling.

The volatility problem is one reason that the machine tool industry can never be complacent. Believing that the industry is a strategic asset to any nation, business leaders, consultants, academics, and government leaders all seem to worry constantly over the fate of the industry.[7] Similarly, corporations sometimes have strategic suppliers that they must seek to protect from the ravages of volatility amplification.

Cincinnati Milacron and Market Volatility

Consider the example of Cincinnati Milacron, one of the major survivors of America's machine tool industry cataclysm of the past three decades. At any time, the next quarter can bring a 100 percent upswing in orders, completely swamping the company's ability to respond. Just as unpredictably, the company can experience a 75 percent drop in orders, driving it to seek and hoard cash as well as lay off some highly skilled, difficult-to-replace human assets to assure short-term liquidity and survival.

Supply chain collaboration is one source of salvation. In Milacron's case, the company has a very good customer in Boeing, not necessarily because Boeing buys more machine tools than anybody else, but because Boeing, in a cyclical industry itself, appreciates the vulnerabilities inherent in cyclical industries. It understands the huge lag times required to rebuild a world-class, skilled workforce once a company such as Milacron has suffered significant layoffs. If, during a slump, Boeing's machine tool orders are down, or if the machine tool industry experiences a downturn, Boeing may offer Milacron a special project in research and development: "Why don't you see if you can develop a tool to automate this production process?" company managers might ask.[8] Even such small efforts, if timed at the bottom of the cycle, can have a significant effect at ameliorating the most severe damage.[9]

What happens otherwise is that companies go out of business or they strip away important technological capabilities. If you are not sure whether your company can even survive through the next quarter, then the people who are conducting research and development for the next product generation are "expendable." Historically, industries that experience high-magnitude volatility cannot easily develop and sustain internal technological capabilities. When the downturn comes, they end up having to cut a fair amount of their R&D capability. So it's nice if, like Milacron, you have a customer willing to help you out during a downturn.

Volatility and Its Implications for Supply Chain Design

In Japan, the vast majority of the machine tool industry exists inside large manufacturing companies. Toyota, Nissan, Honda, Mitsubishi, Toshiba, Hitachi—all have their own machine tool companies. In such vertical corporate structures, the customer often commits to taking care of the more volatile upstream domains; thus, company managers do not have to lay off their technologically skilled people or slow down their new product development activities just because of a temporary (albeit possibly severe) downturn. In the United States, however, the vast majority of the machine tool companies are independent. They reside in market-mediated environments where they suffer the full brunt of the volatility.

What are the implications for supply chain design and management? The farther you look upstream in your technology supply chain, the more volatility you see. Customers are foolish if they don't spend any time (or resources) thinking about the health, survival, and possible independence of their core technology suppliers.

Consider the U.S. auto industry and its relationship with the machine tool industry when the automakers in Detroit took the attitude that "it's not our job to worry about the health of the machine tool industry. Those guys are independent business people. If they merit the business, they should guard their own." They couldn't, of course, take care of themselves without help. And the United States, which once led the world in machine tools, fell behind Japan and

Germany in yet another high-technology, high-value-added sector during the 1980s.

In 1994, I gave a talk on some of these ideas to a group of executives at Toyota's manufacturing headquarters in Toyota City, outside of Nagoya. The day before my Toyota presentation, I visited Okuma, Japan's second-largest independent machine tool company. Okuma managers traced for me the proud 100-year heritage of their company, but bemoaned the recent past when, for the first time in the company's history, they had been forced into involuntary layoffs—approximately 30 percent of the workforce. After I recounted for the Toyota executives the woes of Okuma and the context of the first law of supply chain dynamics, those executives replied, "It's not our problem. They are an independent company. If they overbuilt capacity in the 1980s because of a large surge of orders, then they will have to figure out how to resolve it themselves."

My reply: "That was the attitude of the U.S. auto industry for many years, and look at the machine tool infrastructure it ended up with! If Toyota, Japan's largest and strongest manufacturer, does not worry about Japan's industrial manufacturing infrastructure, who will?"

What are the lessons of the first law? No corporation is an island. Every company is dependent on others in large supply chains and distribution chains. As a result, limiting strategy to within the corporate enterprise is as meaningless as the purported boundaries of such entities.

Individual capabilities are the building blocks, the genetic material, of business strategies today. If a critical capability happens to reside inside your machine tool supplier, you must consider it as precious as the critical capability that sits in the office next to you. Competitive advantage comes from the DNA of business—the strands or chains of capabilities which flow into, through, and around corporate legal boundaries. In short, corporate strategy is insufficient; capability chain strategy must augment it.

Clockspeed Amplification

Practitioners and theoreticians alike have spent many years trying to understand supply chain volatility amplification. In contrast, we are only in the dawn of understanding the second "law" of supply chain dynamics: *As you move closer to the end customer in the supply chain, the clockspeed increases, sometimes dramatically.*

Illustrating this law, figure 6.3 presents a simplified version of the technology supply chain for fiber-optic telecommunication applications. At the upper end of the chain, we have fiber optic cable, which Corning and AT&T developed over a period of more than 20 years. It can be characterized as a stable product technology with an nominal incremental rate of improvement in process technology for its manufacture.[10] Fiber-optic cable is the high-bandwidth communications conduit for the information superhighway in the foreseeable future. No fruit flies on the horizon here.

Figure 6.3. Clockspeed Amplification in Information Technology

Moving down the supply chain from the fiber-optic cable are the communications networks. Cables and connections are planted under roads, buildings, and oceans with the expectation that they will stay put and in service for years or even decades. Although the switching technologies are evolving, the basic architecture of these systems is not changing rapidly. The local versions of these systems—local area networks or LANs—have very similar structures. The clockspeed is faster here, but not overwhelming. AT&T, MCI, Sprint, and myriad other companies are in this business, and their immediate survival does not seem to hinge on differences in network technology.

At the next level in the chain, system applications and Internet applications software, we see much faster clockspeeds. Software to create new Internet-accessible products and services is under constant development. Think of Fidelity mutual funds as a developer of applications (tools to be used over the World Wide Web) to sell financial services to their customers over the Internet. Finally, as the last link in the chain, consider an individual investor who continually fine-tunes her portfolio strategy and uses Fidelity's Web tool to implement her resulting investment changes. The clockspeed here is very high: Such mutual fund strategies seem to change almost as frequently as the *Wall Street Journal* is published.

As a second illustration, consider part of another chain in the electronic world—the chain for development of content sites on the World Wide Web, represented in figure 6.4. At the far downstream (left) end, the typical Web page content has a far shorter life cycle than even the skittish fruit fly—often changing on a daily or weekly basis. Upstream from the Web developers are the suppliers of personal computers (such as Dell and Compaq), where four to six months is the average amount of time a product will be on the market before it is revamped

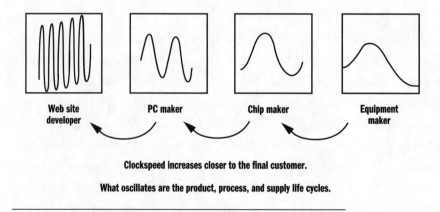

Clockspeed increases closer to the final customer.

What oscillates are the product, process, and supply life cycles.

Figure 6.4. Clockspeed Amplification in Information Technology

or upgraded. The PC makers use microprocessors (primarily from Intel) where the typical life cycle has been two to four years between generations. Finally, the chip makers buy semiconductor manufacturing equipment from equipment suppliers such as Nikon and Applied Materials, whose equipment turns on a cycle of perhaps three to six years.

Wherever we look, we see dramatic increases in clockspeed as we move from the technology source to the customer application. High returns attributable to differentiation of products and services to the final consumer constantly churn up product offerings. At the technology end, large investments in technological infrastructure preclude the frequent scrapping of those investments and the frequent invention and commercialization of wholly new technologies. Certainly capital obsolescence occurs, and in the semiconductor industry, for example, at relatively fast clockspeeds. As fast as semiconductor factories tend toward obsolescence, however, the downstream computer and consumer products that use the chips make that trip even faster.

Tiering and Competitive Interdependence

How does one use these laws of supply chain dynamics? To investigate this question, one must first consider recent developments in supply chain evolution, where two trends stand out: tiering and competitive interdependence. Let's consider tiering first.

Until the 1990s, the Ford Motor Company had several thousand suppliers—individual companies with their own problems and demands to be met. Ford managers were responsible for dealing with each of them and keeping the whole system going. In the 1980s and 1990s, Ford, like Xerox and many other companies, moved to cut drastically the number of its suppliers and to change the supply base according to a multi-tiered design. Ford managers continue to deal with first-tier suppliers, who provide major automotive systems such as interiors or brake systems. But now the first-tier suppliers are expected to have unprecedented skills in developing products and managing projects. For instance, they must manage a group of second-tier suppliers, who in turn manage a group of third-tier suppliers, and so on back up the line.

This trend has sent shock waves through the supply chain. Suppliers are scrambling to learn a whole new set of managerial skills and carry this substantial extra burden. This need stretches them in the short run, but new opportunities always stimulate the growth of new management abilities, allowing the successful companies to expand more easily in the future. Ford and other companies have eliminated a set of expensive, difficult tasks, although in doing so, they have ceded some of the knowledge and control that the previous structure had supported.

The second major important trend in supply chain management is the growing recognition of the interdependence among competitors. Historically mortal enemies in the microprocessor market, Intel, Motorola, and Texas Instruments still had tightly aligned interests when it came to the capabilities of companies such as Applied Materials, the world's largest supplier of semiconductor manufacturing equipment. Far ahead of many other industries, the semiconductor industry organized Sematech to cope with this competitive interdependence.

Sematech began as a response to an American fear of "Japan, Inc." in semiconductors.[11] In the mid-1980s, the U.S. semiconductor industry was losing market share to the Japanese at the rate of several percent a year. The semiconductor equipment suppliers were losing share at about twice that rate. American chip makers, who compete aggressively with each other, realized that in order to exist and compete, they had to find a way to cooperate on areas of perceived common interest. At the time, they focused on maintaining a technologically and economically strong American supply base. Today Sematech (the chip makers' association) and Semi-Sematech (the suppliers' association) thrive as private associations. They seek to develop consensus technology road maps to guide development in this fast-clockspeed industry. By sharing information about the most fruitful technological directions, these associations strive to reduce the investment risk of all the members.

Applying the Laws of Chain Dynamics

Given the trends of tiering and competitive interdependence, we can apply the first and second laws of chain dynamics to forecast some of the challenges companies will face in the coming years. And the message is not what those companies want to hear:

- Each tier adds amplification.

- More tiers mean more amplification—in both volatility and clockspeed.

These two corollaries predict that the need to cope with the challenges of amplification of volatility and clockspeed will only increase.

So, how can you use these laws to advantage in supply chain design? We have already seen one example in Dell Computer Corporation. Michael Dell's supply chain design reflects the understanding that more tiers and more time in the chain mean more volatility and a rougher ride. Dell's design minimizes the tiering and the time to its great advantage.

Amazon.com and Its Supply Chain Design

Another organization that has used the laws of supply chain design to upset the equilibrium in its industry is Amazon.com. Amazon launched its Internet book selling service in competition with the likes of Borders Books, Barnes & Noble, and your long-time neighborhood bookstore, changing forever the process of book buying and selling as well as most people's idea of how to build Internet commerce.[12]

Booksellers in the United States seem to be pursuing most vigorously two kinds of customers, both upscale: those who like to sample books over a caffè latte and those who want to buy their books quickly and efficiently from their homes or offices. This distinction is not unlike the one faced by Dell vis-à-vis competitors Compaq, HP, IBM, and others. Dell offers the quick-buying experience over the Internet for customers who can decide what they want without trying it out. In the competing channel, computers are sold through resellers, and retail stores hold inventory that customers can see and touch before buying.

Although it was still reporting negative earnings in early 1998, Amazon.com had a market value of $2 billion based on three assets. First, Amazon's opportunity in supply chain costs is similar to Dell's. That is, absence of retail stores means fewer links in the physical chain and result in lower chain inventories. Second, Amazon has inundated the Web with its presence, with over 30,000 Web sites as partners, compared to only 5,000 that its closest competitor, Barnes & Noble, has—a very aggressive alliance-based strategy.[13] Third, Amazon.com not only sells books, but it attracts what the Internet marketing community calls "eyeballs"—that is, viewers who may be subjected to advertising by other marketing messages. Whereas it took Amazon.com 27 months to acquire its first million customers, the second million took less than six months.[14]

To date, Amazon.com has not taken full advantage of its structural supply chain advantage because it has relied heavily on middlemen such as U.S. book wholesaler Ingram Book Group, which exploits extensive economies of scale for managing logistics and the necessary inventories in the chain.[15] As its volumes increase, however, Amazon.com can justify handling an increasing fraction of the high-volume books through its own warehouse system, thereby pumping up its profit margins considerably. These high-volume books are like the high-value components that Dell stocks: They have fast turnover and, as a result, low holding costs.

Amazon.com's model provides another built-in advantage over storebound competitors. The tradition in the book publishing industry is for retail stores not only to place big orders for books to stock their shelves but also to have the right to return all unsold copies to the publishers. This policy is extremely expensive for the publishers because they end up shredding millions of books that the retailers ordered but did not sell. Since Amazon.com does not need stacks of physical inventory to sell its wares on the Internet, another set of players in the chain—the publishers—are likely hoping that the site prospers. Accordingly, they might be inclined to help Amazon.com along.

Of course, its rivals such as Borders Books and Barnes & Noble are not standing still. Each has launched an extensive Web site to sell books as well. Although Barnes & Noble lost $134 million on Internet sales of $9 million in the first quarter of 1998, one analyst characterized the competition as follows: "Barnes & Noble has declared war on Amazon.com. They're going to spend $25 [million] to $30 million this year on advertising with, hopefully, generating revenues of about $100 million."[16] As Compaq has discovered in selling computers, however, the more successful BarnesandNoble.com is, the more resentful its retailers are likely to become—perhaps providing some built-in limits on how aggressive Barnes & Noble can be in its electronic commerce.

Overall, Amazon.com's chain is shorter and therefore experiences less inventory volatility. Amazon can hold a book in storefront virtual "inventory" indefinitely at essentially no cost, thereby extending a book's retail lifetime (and clockspeed), slowing its relegation to the shredder. Amazon is also able to pool its inventory for all demand, thereby needing less of it than the geographically dispersed storefronts of Borders Books and Barnes & Noble.

Regardless of how this competition turns out, what we see from this example is that the battlefront in today's competitive wars is the design of the supply chain. No longer can it be relegated to the company's tacticians; rather, it must be part and parcel of the organization's key strategic thinking. To inform this thinking, however, you need to have a clear image of what your supply chain design looks like, who is doing what for whom, and where the "clockspeed bottle-necks" are occurring. The next chapter provides the necessary tools for mapping and assessing your current and ideal supply chains to help form a more accurate picture of opportunities and threats in the chain.

7 DNA MAPPING

Strategic Assessment of the Chain

The practice of clockspeed analysis begins with mapping an existing chain of capabilities to identify its weak spots—and its opportunities.

ANALOGOUS TO MAPPING DNA ON THE human genome, understanding and redesigning a company's capabilities chain also begins with a map, one which identifies the organizations involved in that company's activities, the subsystems they provide, the capabilities they bring to the value proposition, and the technological contribution each makes to the company's final product. Sometimes that understanding arrives from the most unexpected source imaginable.

Chrysler and Kitty Litter

Consider Chrysler Corporation. During the 1990s, Chrysler became a corporate pacesetter in making supply chain design a core competence of the corporation. The leader of this endeavor was Thomas Stallkamp, who designed and executed this process as executive vice president of procurement and supply. In 1997, against all traditions in the industry, Chrysler's board of directors named Stallkamp as the company's new president. Then in 1998, when Daimler-Benz launched its merger with Chrysler, the newly announced organizational structure featured two CEOs, one each from Chrysler and Daimler-Benz, but only one worldwide president: Stallkamp. As the clockspeed of the automotive industry accelerated in the 1990s, Chrysler and Stallkamp led the field in applying fast-clockspeed principles to supply chain design.

Chrysler estimates that approximately five million people and 100,000 organizations are involved in the company's Extended Enterprise. And each person and organization in this network can affect in some way the customer's perception of quality as she drives her new car or used truck off the dealer's lot and onto the road. Appropriately, Chrysler finds it humbling to contemplate the complexity of coordinating a massive meta-organization of this scale. Consequently, in the early 1990s, the staff of Chrysler's Procurement and Supply organization decided to begin mapping this enormous system.

The staff began with the Jeep Grand Cherokee—one of Chrysler's most important products at the time.[1] Going one step up the chain, they examined the source of Jeep's V-8 engines—obviously an important subsystem in the vehicle—which are manufactured in one of Chrysler's own plants.

At the next level of the chain, the team traced the source of a roller-lifter valve—a small but critical component in the engine. This component was supplied by Eaton Corporation, a large global automotive supplier that manufactured the lifters in large quantities.

At the chain's next level, the team visited the source of the raw metal castings that the Eaton Corporation precision-machined for the roller-lifter valves. These castings were sourced by Eaton from a small shop near the Eaton factory. After visiting this casting shop, the Chrysler team chose to go back even further to visit the company that supplied the clay for the foundry where the castings were made.

Upon visiting the clay supplier, the team made a remarkable discovery: This supplier, which provided clay of a unique chemistry needed by the casting company, had for some time lost money in its business. Without informing any other members in the chain, the company owner had decided to get out of the unprofitable casting clay business and reorient his business to processing the same raw materials into kitty litter! Imagine how the Chrysler executives must have looked at each other in horror as they quickly realized that this strategic move into kitty litter could soon shut down manufacturing of one of the most profitable product lines in the entire Chrysler Corporation.

The Power of Mapping the Chains

I once worked with a semiconductor company that experienced high maintenance costs on a bottleneck process for several of its capital-intensive chip plants. Upon exploring the supply chain for one of the key high-consumption spare parts required for the maintenance operation, company managers found a "gem" at a fourth-tier metal plating supplier: Employees at a key plant were dumping the highly toxic chemical plating wastes into their backyard. This was triply horrifying to the semiconductor company because of the environmental destruction, the potential liability to all members in the chain for that destruction, and the potential loss of output from shutting down the plater if a replacement could not be found quickly.

As a business manager, you can trace the production sources of every item used in creating, distributing, and marketing your products. The power of this mapping lies in the sometimes shocking discoveries you will make, discoveries that can help you avoid potential crises down the road if you take the necessary steps now to correct the problems. But to take full advantage of this prediction of present or future stress points, you will need to master the cartographer's skills.

In a typical atlas, one map color-codes the average rainfall or temperature in all the cities of the region. Another illustrates population density or income distribution. A third shows the gradations in elevation. To begin to understand the region thoroughly, you have to examine all the maps. Similarly, to understand a capabilities chain thoroughly, you have to view it—map it—in multiple dimensions: organizations, technology, and capabilities.

This chapter presents four case studies to illustrate the variety and richness of the chain maps that may be plotted and the clockspeed analyses that can be extracted from them. First I continue the Chrysler case study above to show the three levels on which chains may be mapped: the organization chain, the technology supply chain, and the capability chain. Next I present a case from AlliedSignal in chemical production, which illustrates that within these chains one can observe and respond to management challenges due to acceleration in product clockspeeds, process clockspeeds, and organization clockspeeds. Finally, I present a dynamic clockspeed analysis methodology, which is then illustrated for cases in the defense aerospace and information-entertainment industries.

Three Chain Maps at Chrysler

Consider the three chain maps illustrated in figure 7.1, which elaborate upon the Chrysler story above. The diagram indicates three levels of supply chain mapping that can be used to identify various pitfalls and opportunities in the chain. The first level—*mapping the organizational supply chain*—is straightforward conceptually, but can be difficult logistically, because of the large number of entities in the chains of many organizations. The data required for this effort, however, will typically be maintained by the organization in its customer and supplier databases. The second and third levels—*mapping the technology supply chain* and the *business capability chain*—are both conceptually and logistically more challenging to develop. Most of the data required to develop them is not in any organizational database, but needs to be constructed by people intimately involved in the technological and business processes of the organization.

Chain mapping affords valuable tools for revealing risks and opportunities in the value chain. Managers will be most familiar with the

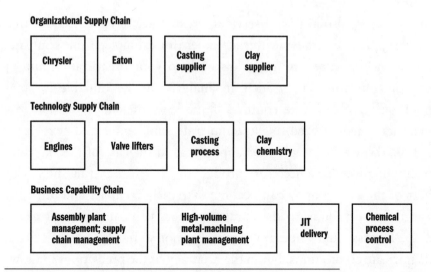

Figure 7.1. Organizational Supply Chain, Technology Supply Chain, and Business Capability Chain

organizational supply chain map, which arrays the entire set of organizations—all the way from the uppermost supply tiers—that add value in the chain to the final customer. Although easy to conceptualize in the abstract, this task can be enormously complex in actuality—as evidenced by Chrysler's estimate of the 100,000 organizations in its extended enterprise.

Because mapping such an entity in its entirety is clearly a monumental task, you must be judicious in choosing which strands to illuminate and explore in greatest detail. The most important to explore carefully are those with clear strategic importance and those with fast clockspeeds since fast clockspeed domains are the most likely to create dramatic industrial restructurings.

Drawing such a map is not unlike creating a family tree. Taking either a product or a process view of your organization, you begin by enumerating each of your suppliers who provide raw materials or components (be sure to state what these are) that your company uses to provide its products and services. Next, trace any connections that these suppliers may have with each other (for example, is one company providing the same raw materials both to your organization and to one of your suppliers?). Such an analysis can be valuable for pinpointing possible future conflicts if suddenly the supply of that raw material is jeopardized. Next, enumerate suppliers in the next tier—that is, those who supply the suppliers, as in the case of the clay supplier who provided a necessary product to Chrysler's casting shop. This part of the cartography can become extremely complex and intricate, and there is no limit to the number of tiers you can represent in the map. The essential value of the map lies not so much in the details of its intricate connections, but in the accuracy of the predictions it allows you to make about the future of your company or industry.

The next challenge is to attack the mapping of the technology supply chain. Even if a firm's technology is relatively simple and straightforward, as in the case of an Internet server and e-mail, it is important to trace the lines of dependency from your organization upstream and downstream to the suppliers and customers who provide and use the technologies that lie out of your immediate sight. These dependencies can turn out to be pivotal.

Product and process engineers must sit down with procurement and supply experts to sort through the product bills of materials and the process plans for fabrication and assembly. Drawing a map of the key technologies deployed in the company's value chain helps you not only visualize the connections between the technologies and your company's capabilities, but also plan for alternatives if technologies fail or become unavailable. Like the organizational supply chain, the complete chain map typically will be vast. Therefore, much judicious thought must go into identifying the high-leverage, high-risk, high-clockspeed, and high-opportunity elements in the chain—then mapping them into a usable tool.

The map outlined in figure 7.1 highlights a few of the key technologies in the Chrysler chain—engines, valve lifters, the casting process, and clay chemistry. Other examples include the genomics-related technologies critical to Merck, the bicycle components purchased by Schwinn, and the photolithography technology used by Toshiba. In each case, there is not one, but an entire chain of technologies to be elucidated and examined.

Perhaps the most conceptually challenging is the business capability chain. To map it requires a team comprising experts in your organization's key business processes—product development, research, production, purchasing, logistics, human resources, and so forth. This team should be tasked with identifying and mapping the key business process capabilities along its value chain.

Again, the map in figure 7.1 shows several key capabilities in the Chrysler chain: assembly plant management, supply chain management, high-volume metal-machining plant management, JIT delivery, and chemical process control. Other examples include Web site development at amazon.com, continuous product upgrading and logistics management at Dell Computer Corporation, and management of science-based research and development at Merck.

The value of chain mapping continues to impress me. Some years ago a group of executives from one of the "Baby Bell" companies called me for advice about a nascent telecommunications joint venture. At first they had trouble defining exactly who were members of their chain. Then they debated whether particular links were important or not, whether they were first- or second-tier. They had no clear sense of each organization's specific contributions to the chain. As we continued our discussions, it became evident that they had little understanding of the relationships among members of the chain.

I urged those executives to map their chain as a means of answering questions about the relative importance of chain members. This exercise was a revelation for them: They learned, for example, that their chain was conceptually organized in tiers, but that arrangement was often ignored. The company paid first-tier suppliers to deal with second-tier members, but then devoted significant time and effort to working directly with the second-tier suppliers as well.

What's more, the executives discovered that certain parts of the existing chain simply made no sense. Some links really added little value. The presence of this or that supplier was determined as a nod to old relationships that no longer had any economic rationale.

The company's executives also began to look more closely at their own role in the chain and posed hard questions: Why are we still insourcing this part of the value chain? Is there really any comparative advantage now? Was there ever? Time and again, the managers discovered that the practices stemmed from aged decisions that no longer made sense. The mapping exercise drove the executives to begin asking these crucial questions, which led eventually to the redesign efforts on their entire chain.

Product, Process, and Organization Clockspeeds at AlliedSignal

AlliedSignal Polymers (ASP) is a vertically integrated and process-oriented business within AlliedSignal Inc., a Fortune 100 manufacturing company with diverse business units.[2] ASP's internal value chain consists of two chemical plants, two fiber plants (one in Chesterfield, Virginia, another in Columbia, South Carolina), a film plant, and a plastics plant (mapped in figure 7.2). Although the products and processes have remained relatively stable for over 40 years, competition has been steadily increasing over the past few years, nudging up the industry clockspeeds. Global competitors have aggressively entered the domestic market. Upstream suppliers are expanding into activities that historically have followed their primary function (forward integration), whereas downstream customers are going the other way, as more and more of them take on functions usually furnished by their suppliers (backward integration). These conditions have increased the demands for higher quality and customized products

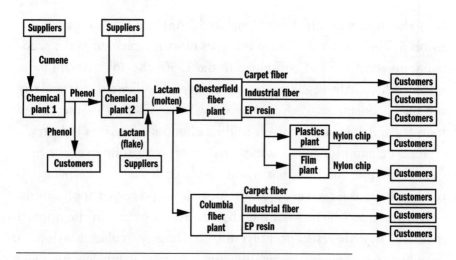

Figure 7.2. AlliedSignal Polymers: Nylon Value Chain Inside ASP

while depressing profit margins. Faced with increasing clockspeed, ASP has accelerated its pursuit of new concepts to remain competitive. Figure 7.2 depicts the production flow of value from suppliers to customers.

Nylon, a versatile polymer first patented by Dr. Wallace Carothers at the DuPont Company in 1937, represents approximately 4 percent of the total 1990 world polymer consumption. Although many different varieties of nylon are produced, the two most important commercial nylons are nylon-6 and nylon-6,6, which together comprise over 98 percent of the total nylon production.

These two nylons have almost identical chemical and physical properties. However, nylon-6,6 has a higher melting point and a faster polymerization processing time (2 hours versus 12 hours), but is slightly more expensive since it is produced from two raw materials instead of one.

Raw material production and fiber/polymer manufacturing exhibit significant economies of scale; both are dominated by large, vertically integrated chemical firms. DuPont and Monsanto are market leaders for nylon-6,6, whereas AlliedSignal and BASF are market leaders for nylon-6. The nylon value chain becomes more fragmented as the product approaches the end consumer. In the 1990s the downstream parts of the value chain began to become more consolidated, particularly through acquisitions such as those by Shaw Carpets in the carpet industry and Johnson Controls in the automotive interiors industry.

Total demand for nylon is expected to grow steadily over the next decade, despite the fact that nylon has been losing market share to other polymers in certain applications. In low-end carpet applications, polypropylene, which is cheaper, has displaced nylon. In the apparel industry, wrinkle-resistant polyester has largely replaced nylon in broadwovens. And in the manufacture of tires, nylon has also lost market share to polyester, which delivers superior performance.

Apart from these fiber applications, nylon resins and films have seen steady growth. Because of their light weight, nylon resins, for instance, have found increasing uses in automotive components.[3] Nylon films are also finding many more uses in medical applications and food packaging.

Faced with increasing clockspeeds due to global competition, ASP has begun to pursue many of the manufacturing policies used in fruit fly industries. To understand this strategy, it is helpful to see how ASP has responded to three varying clockspeeds: one for its products, another for the process of recycling, and a third for organizational structure.

As a diversified business, ASP has to deal with various clockspeeds across its product lines. Products for very mature industries such as commodity chemicals (phenol, acetone, and other compounds) can have life cycles well over thirty years. In contrast, the clockspeed for moderately mature industries, such as textiles and carpets, is typically five years. That is, new product launches occur about every five years. In some faster-moving markets such as industrial fibers, engineering plastics, and films, product clockspeed may be as fast as two to three years. In these markets, low switching costs and technology improvements reduce barriers to entry and allow competitors to imitate successful new products. Thus, the half-lives of any first-mover advantages for ASP are short.

As if it were not enough to deal with varying clockspeeds for its products, ASP also has to attend to an increase in the clockspeed of its nylon production process. While the process for producing the raw materials—phenol and caprolactam—has remained relatively constant for over 40 years, pressure has mounted from citizens' groups and the government to recycle nylon-based products. To meet this demand, AlliedSignal has patented a process to recycle used carpets by depolymerizing the nylon back to caprolactam for reuse. To be sure, this recycling effort may provide, at least initially, a public marketing advantage for AlliedSignal. But this advantage, too, may be short-lived because competitors are pursuing their own recycling efforts.

Similarly, the production process is changing. To produce the nylon fibers, ASP has to engage in a labor-intensive process, quite distinct from the processes it uses to produce chemicals. Foreign competitors, who often operate with much lower labor costs, have forced ASP to adopt the strategy of replacing its old process, which had many steps, with a new single-step process called ZIP ("zero interruption process"). Even the distribution processes are affected by cost-minded customers. In an attempt to reduce their labor costs, many customers now want to buy what is known as "bulk continuous filament." This packaging delivers carpet fibers on large spools, which are easier to handle, rather than in bales. And finally, ASP is changing its product mix to satisfy major customers who want to buy the lower-cost nylon resins as opposed to fibers.

Like many other companies, ASP has undergone some version of reengineering. Ten years ago, the company was organized functionally to focus on manufacturing, but recently it has adopted a more customer-focused structure designed to ensure that customers have the highest quality products that they need. To reduce overhead and promote knowledge transfer within manufacturing, ASP has formed "virtual plants." By tradition, manufacturing leadership positions were filled by "lifers," who might spend 20 years or more in the same position. Now, however, a single leadership team manages two or more plants with similar product lines or functions, such as the two chemical plants. Further, all manufacturing leaders rotate positions, geographically and functionally, every two or three years. These steps have helped reduce organizational clockspeed to about six months and prevent the formation of "silos" or proprietary internal functions.

Thus, we can see that ASP has responded to increases in clockspeeds across its products, processes, and organization structures. Building on these insights, I next present a systematic methodology for dynamic clockspeed analysis of the chains and illustrate it with examples from defense aerospace and information-entertainment.

Bringing the Maps to Life with Clockspeed Analysis

Analyzing the static maps of the organizational supply chain, the technology supply chain, and the capability chain can help you discover hitherto hidden facts about the supply chain and provide insights that can deeply affect the setting of corporate strategy. Still more valuable insights come from examining the chain maps and their constituent parts in conjunction with dynamic clockspeed analysis.

The beauty of clockspeed analysis is that it is simple, but powerful. Beginning with the three basic maps described, then, for each element of the chain, we ask a series of what I call the clockspeed analysis questions:

1. What is the clockspeed of this chain element and the industry in which it is embedded?

2. What factors (for example, increased competition from new entrants, new technological innovations in the industry, new regulations, and the like) are driving the clockspeed of this element?

3. What are the prospects for a change in clockspeed in this chain element as a result of expected changes in competitive intensity or in rates of innovation?

4. Where is its industry located on the double helix? That is, is the industry primarily in a stage of horizontal structure with modular parts or primarily vertical with highly integrated parts?

5. What are the current power dynamics for this element in the chain?

The following examples illustrate how the clockspeed analysis questions can help illuminate the usefulness of the capabilities chain and assist managers in predicting future events.

Lockheed Martin Defense Aircraft Clockspeed Analysis

Consider the challenges of developing a state-of-the-art jet fighter.[4] The end of the 1990s features a contest between the two largest aerospace companies in the world, Boeing and Lockheed Martin, competing to win the prime contractor role for the "Joint Strike Fighter" (JSF) jet that is expected to be the mainstay of U.S. airborne military capability for the first half of the twenty-first century. The total lifetime value of the contract has been estimated at over a third of a trillion dollars.[5] The "fly-off" competition is expected to occur in the first decade of the second millennium, and volume production is expected to begin in 2008.

The development challenges for this project are staggering. Among them is the need to reconcile the high clockspeed of the electronic capabilities of military warfare with the much slower clockspeed of airframe evolution and the long time scale of the project.

Figure 7.3 provides a simple diagram of two components of the technology supply chain for this project: the airframe and the electronic controls. To be concrete in illustrating the analytic approach, I will make some assumptions about the facts of the case where precise numbers are classified or not available.

The first of the clockspeed analysis questions—namely, what is the

Figure 7.3. Two Components of the Joint Strike Fighter (JSF) Technology Supply Chain

clockspeed of this chain element and the industry in which it is embedded?—suggests estimating clockspeeds for the products and processes involved. Let's suppose that major technological improvements are expected to occur roughly every three years in the controls domain and every ten years in the airframe domain. (Three years is far longer than the interval of consecutive Intel microprocessors, for example, but more in line with slower-evolving complex software systems, such as Microsoft Windows.) Further, let's suppose that the processes for electronics and airframe manufacture undergo major technological improvements every five years and ten years, respectively. Given the faster clockspeeds in the electronics arena, designing the jets in order to equip them so that they have the latest electronic control systems is a major challenge and critical to the aircraft's performance. One need study military history no further back in time than the Gulf War with Iraq in the early 1990s to appreciate the value of superior electronics.

The second question of the analysis asks what factors are driving those clockspeeds. For the electronic controls, the clockspeeds are, in part, driven by hardware innovations from the electronics industry that are completely outside the control of the aircraft industry. On the other hand, software development in electronics controls to exploit the latest hardware is driven by the tradeoffs in the costs of developing and writing new software and the expected benefits. Those benefits depend on the state of the competition's capabilities and technologies, which may be influenced, say, by the state of the arms race at a given moment in history. The clockspeeds of airframe products and processes, in contrast, are much more directly influenced by investment rates within the aircraft industry itself.

The third question—what are the prospects for a change in clock-speed in this chain element as a result of expected changes in competitive intensity or in rates of innovation?—requires some crystal-ball gazing and reliance on what technology companies say about future developments in their industry. In the electronics domain, for instance, Intel has claimed that it can keep up the pace in developing micro-processors and semiconductors well into the second decade of the twenty-first century.[6] In software development, estimates are likely to show greater variance, depending in part on the pace of software development tools. In the case of airframes, one possible factor in development might be aggressive investment in composite materials development by the automotive industry. This scenario seems unlikely since the aircraft industry has typically led the automotive industry in advanced material usage, although a new set of policies to radically reduce automotive emissions and fuel consumption is possible during the lifetime of the JSF project.

Fourth, we ask where on the double helix is the industry located. Is it primarily horizontal and modular or vertical and integral? In electronics hardware, for instance, the industry and supply chain are currently horizontal and modular, with little momentum toward a more vertical structure. In fighter jet controls software, the structure is much more vertical and integral, and there are very few players in the world who can supply the required technology and knowledge base. In airframe products and processes, the available supply chains include the major aircraft makers in the world, most of which have modularized their supply chains to some degree so that they can outsource significant amounts of component fabrication. However, given the consolidation in the U.S. aircraft industry in the 1990s, we might expect that little additional integration will occur and that any movement along the double helix is likely to be in the horizontal/modular direction, although probably at a slow pace consistent with historical clockspeeds in the industry.

With respect to dependency dynamics in the chain (the fifth clockspeed analysis question), the jet makers will likely continue in their dependence on electronics supply chains for hardware, but given the absence of high concentration in that industry, this dependency will likely pose few strategic problems. In controls software, the major firms are dependent on some suppliers for subsystem controls, but tend to keep "in house" the system's design and integration because of the direct dependency of overall system performance on this function. In the case of airframes, the jet makers tend to do the design and assembly internally, but outsource the fabrication. Depending on the part of the airframe, some of the fabrication components are sourced in markets where few suppliers could provide the capabilities.

For the sake of space and exposition, this analysis has taken a very simplified view of an enormously complex project. Nevertheless, assessing the answers to these five clockspeed analysis questions does yield useful insights. First, the rapid clockspeed of the electronics sector and the structure of the supply chain for electronics suggest several policies for the jet manufacturers. For example, the aircraft product design, the controls software, and the development and manufacturing process must allow for some modularity in electronics so that new hardware developments from suppliers can be integrated into the product. Furthermore, given the confidence of firms such as Intel in their ability to continue to push hardware performance, some of those projections probably ought to be designed into the systems. Vertical integration into the hardware would be expensive and might not provide competitive hardware advances.

Second, although airframe design and assembly have traditionally been considered as absolutely core to aircraft suppliers, the relatively slow clockspeed of the technology, the availability of a number of airframe makers around the world, and the fact that any relevant innovations in airframe materials are likely to come from existing or new suppliers, all suggest that some amount of airframe outsourcing would be strategically safe. Keeping airframes solely inside might be optimal given the integrality of the airframe with other subsystems (such as weapons or cockpit), but within the example examined here, some outsourcing, given the right supplier opportunity, seems reasonable.

Of course, all these arguments apply readily to a peacetime situation, but would certainly be tested vigorously in the event of war. In that case, which is arguably the only one that really matters, assemblers presumably want on-shore supply capability. As discussed earlier, Boeing's commercial business does not have this (and may not need it). However, in defense aircraft, supplier location and nationality is surely an important consideration.[7]

Information-Entertainment Clockspeed Analysis

To show the contrast to the slow-clockspeed aircraft industry, let's consider a light-speed example, this one from the entertainment production and distribution industry, where the likes of Disney, Paramount, and Universal compete at a pace that rivals the life cycle dynamics of the fruit fly. For the sake of illustration, a simplified relationship between production and distribution is presented in figure 7.4.

For the first two clockspeed analysis questions (clockspeed measurement and drivers), the improvements in digital image manipula-

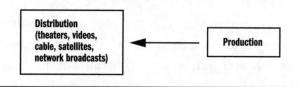

Figure 7.4. Two Components of the Entertainment Technology Supply Chain

tion that allowed hits such as *Jurassic Park, Titanic,* and *Toy Story* to be created have hastened the clockspeed of movie production technology. Although this evolution is continuous rather than discrete, we can conservatively peg the turnover rate at once every two or three years. In distribution, enhanced Internet and telecommunications technologies, as well as a proliferation of new distribution channels, suggest a rate where one might expect a new, important technology to appear almost on an annual basis, if not more quickly.

In both production and distribution, the clockspeed is driven primarily by the electronics industry. Faster microprocessors and faster, larger storage devices allow companies such as Silicon Graphics to develop faster graphics-intensive computers whose increased capabilities permit new and different production possibilities. Distribution clockspeed is also driven by the intense competition for viewers that new channels hope to win.

With respect to changes in clockspeed (the third clockspeed analysis question), although difficult to fathom, far more signs point to a speeding up rather than a slowing down. Widespread availability of powerful computers and universal access to the Internet may encourage entry into both production and distribution. Just as the Internet and computing technology have powered an explosion of entry into print media, there is every reason to believe that an analogous explosion in video may follow as the costs come down and the number and variety of channels increase. As much as the media moguls try to control the distribution channels to wring maximum value from their franchises, new technologies and a huge potential viewer market should keep up the innovation, entry, and clockspeeds.

With respect to the position of the industry on the double helix (the fourth clockspeed analysis question), as discussed in chapter 2, the industry seems to be integrating,[8] in part because of the desire to hedge uncertainty in the relative future values of the contributions to the different supply chain components. Also, this vertical consolidation by some players has encouraged even more consolidation (by other players) as each production studio moves to assure itself of distribution channels that are not captive to a direct competitor. Perhaps surprisingly, this integrated supply chain structure is accompanied by a highly modular product structure. Virtually every movie production can be delivered on any of the available delivery platforms (for example, network broadcasts, cable, satellite, or movie theaters). This mismatch serves only to amplify the volatility that the industry is likely to see. Little synergy in delivering value to the customer is achieved by the existing vertical media supply chain structures.

In terms of dependency dynamics (the fifth clockspeed analysis question), I think that the field is still wide open. As discussed in chapter 2, any of several possible links in the chain could become the scarce resource. Despite this uncertainty, let me suggest another tack by asking what windows of opportunity exist in this industry.

Consider the fraction of movies viewed that involve a trip to the video rental store. To watch a video, the consumer drives to the rental store, chooses a movie, and drives home with it. After watching the movie, this customer has to drive back to the rental store to return the cassette, and then drive home again. The final score: Four one-way automobile trips, one video consumed. (No wonder the oil and automobile industries have been bigger than the movie industry in Hollywood!)

Here, however, we find an open window of opportunity: Who will first find a way to make driving to the video store obsolete? Whoever creates a convenient, efficient, easy-to-use means of accessing the world's video libraries from the home will fill a giant gap in the industry's structure and make a fortune at it. A huge opportunity awaits the right entrepreneurial idea and technology. A clockspeed analysis suggests pointedly, however, that this window of opportunity, great as it appears, may not be open for long.

We see, then, that a mapping of the supply chain can be followed fruitfully by a clockspeed analysis of its elements. I would emphasize that the analyses presented in this section—namely, that of the Joint Strike Fighter (JSF) technology and the infotainment industry's production and distribution segments—are intentionally short. The purpose is simply to offer a glimpse into the possibilities of the clockspeed-based capability chain analysis. In the next chapter, we examine actions that you should take in response to a clockspeed analysis, actions that involve the simultaneous design of products, processes, and the supply chain in order to take the fullest advantage of those three elements in setting a workable strategy for your company. Although advantage is only temporary, there is much to be gained from bringing all elements of your company in line with those of your entire chain in order to avoid costly delays and setbacks. I call this action *three-dimensional concurrent engineering,* or 3-DCE for short. As we will then see in chapter 9, clockspeed analysis can also help address a question that has plagued managers ever since people began building pyramids or trading for spices, namely whether it is better to make an item oneself or to buy it already made from someone else.

EXECUTING STRATEGY IN THE AGE OF TEMPORARY ADVANTAGE:

THREE-DIMENSIONAL CONCURRENT ENGINEERING

CHAPTER

8   CLONING IN THREE DIMENSIONS

Simultaneous Design: Product, Process, Supply Chain

In a fast-clockspeed world, advantage arises from the concurrent design of products, processes, and capabilities.[1]

IN THE SPRING OF 1989, two researchers at the University of Utah announced that they had discovered the principle behind "cold" fusion, a remarkable process that would shake up the scientific community (this "discovery" later proved untenable). In the swirl of shock and debate that followed this announcement, a cartoon appeared in various newspapers showing the Earth from a vantage point far out in space. In the cartoon, one of the researchers in Utah exclaims, "I believe we have demonstrated cold fusion!"—to which his colleague responds, "Yes, I think we have finally replicated cold fusion." On the other side of the globe appear two other dialogue bubbles: One announces, rather matter-of-factly, "The cold-fusion-powered Toyotas will be shipped today," while the other states, "The cold-fusion-powered Hondas will go on sale next week."

Regardless of the ultimate fate of cold fusion and the Utah researchers who "discovered" it, the underlying message of the cartoon strikes home: In the 1980s (as well as in other decades), while Americans were focused primarily on research and development breakthroughs in the laboratory, the Japanese rapidly adopted these discoveries and built them into their product and process development systems.

In the 1970s and 1980s, the transition to Japanese market leadership—in many industries once dominated by Americans—was attributed to all sorts of factors ranging from deep-seated cultural differences to sheer arrogance on the part of American corporate leaders who thought themselves invincible. Throughout these decades, American companies and research facilities served as fountainheads for new ideas and technologies, but they were less well prepared than the Japanese to manufacture reliable products in high volumes and at low costs for consumer markets. Japanese firms ran circles around the Americans in many cases.

One infamous example of this dysfunction in process and product development was RCA, the company whose name was synonymous with television technology and markets in the mid-twentieth century. By the early 1970s, RCA had developed a viable technology for home video players, which would enable customers—for the first time ever—to rent or buy prerecorded video entertainment and play those recordings on their televisions wherever and whenever they chose. Although people had long talked about such technology, it still seemed the stuff of science fiction. Many entrepreneurs could envision the demand for such a product, but perhaps only the most clairvoyant of them could imagine just how widespread that demand would become.

RCA developed a viable product technology, but failed to solve the manufacturing problems to deliver the players reliably in high volume at low cost. In the words of Michael Cusumano and Richard Rosenbloom, technology management scholars at MIT and Harvard who closely followed the industry's technology, "RCA and [its key supplier] Bell and Howell never could bridge the gap between design and manufacture."[2] Sony and Matsushita (JVC), however, had mastered the techniques of manufacturability or concurrent engineering (CE). Although these Japanese powerhouses started out behind RCA in the race to market, their technology management, particularly their focus on the integration of design and manufacturing, put them in a decidedly better position to win.[3]

Throwing It over the Wall

RCA's approach to design and manufacturing was anything but an aberration in the United States. Prior to the 1980s, in most Western manufacturing companies, the work of marketing, designing, developing, and delivering products proceeded according to a fixed sequence of events, all directed by a bureaucracy of managers, research directors, and technicians. In industries such as consumer electronics and automobiles, where innovation is the watchword, product designers sat in their labs at the top of the hierarchy, developing marvels of technology. They left it to the drudges in manufacturing to figure out how to churn out their inventions in high volumes at costs that would make the manufacturing venture feasible. In its turn, the purchasing department served the needs of manufacturing: The purchasers sought compliant, low-cost suppliers to deliver components or materials to the factories where these new products could be mass-produced.

The operating policy these companies adopted has been called "Throwing it over the wall." That is, a typical company, much like a medieval castle, constructed protective walls around certain groups, functions, or departments, in effect keeping out people who did not belong. The research laboratory, for instance, was certain to have the highest walls, and only the initiated might enter its sacred chambers. Having invented a new product, these architects of the imagination would toss their designs over the walls of the lab and down to the people in manufacturing, who might well have to guess what the design was for—and then how to make it.

Often oblivious to the realities of the supply chain, these fabricators, in turn, would throw their requirements down to the purchasers, who would scurry around in search of the right commodities and the least expensive suppliers. When discussions did occur between any of these groups, they were haphazard at best; and at worst, relations were deeply acrimonious. The inventors never liked to hear that they had designed products that could hardly be manufactured without costing a fortune. Meanwhile, those who actually built the item would point fingers at the purchasers for not securing the right materials on time. Product manufacturing often fell hopelessly behind schedule.

Further complicating the manufacturability problem, many companies adopted the age-old functional organization structure for their product development. In a typical U.S. or European automobile company, for example, the head of a product development project for a new vehicle would have to "borrow" engineers—some of whom might be assigned to multiple projects—from functional departments such as body development, fuel systems, or electronics. These engineers, however, identified primarily with their home departments, not with the project group to which they were temporarily assigned. After all, their rewards and career opportunities came from the heads of those functional departments, not from the ad hoc project managers who wielded little clout in the great organization scheme.[4]

The disasters in industrial performance such as those of RCA and General Motors have been thoroughly documented. Clark and Fujimoto, for example, have surveyed the severe disadvantages suffered by U.S. and European automotive firms in contrast to the relative success enjoyed by Japanese automakers.[5] Such woes are further catalogued in numerous other industries in the best-selling *Made in*

America,[6] based on industrial performance research conducted over several years at MIT.

The Power of Concurrent Engineering

The general malaise in U.S. manufacturing competitiveness in the 1970s and 1980s caused many companies to seek a revitalization by benchmarking successful Japanese companies. Analysis of their innovations in supply chain management, manufacturing, inventory control, and other areas brought to light such concepts as "lean production"[7] and "concurrent engineering."[8] Sometimes referred to as "design for manufacturability" (DFM), concurrent engineering (CE) seeks to improve manufacturing performance not only by making changes, substantive or incremental, at the factory (for instance, installing appropriate automation, streamlining the assembly line), but by coordinating the design of products with the actual production system in the factory. This is, in essence, the principle behind designing a product for manufacturability. Those designers, used to working in isolation behind the walls of their laboratories, would need to have a crash course to learn how better to collaborate with their colleagues in procurement and manufacturing if the company hoped to meet the success of foreign companies that had already mastered the techniques of CE.

Following is a list of what I consider to be the key procedures of concurrent engineering.[9]

Key Steps in Concurrent Engineering

1. Analyze first the architectural design of both processes and production in order to identify fundamental problems. Then scrutinize the details of the actual design of products and the processes in place to produce them.

2. Break down the product and process systems into their component parts, or subsystems, and identify the interactions within and across them.

3. Align the requirements for the actual design of the product with those for the process design and organizational structure.

4. Explore alternatives for the primary product design process and manufacturing processes.

5. Estimate early the costs of adopting various process options.

6. Estimate early the time requirements—in person-hours, but especially in the critical path time effects—of executing different design options.

7. Identify and alleviate any bottlenecks in the CE process.

8. Manage the design process with multifunctional teams, working concurrently.

9. Align incentives for design such that trade-offs associated with selecting alternative design options will be made from a global, product life cycle perspective.

Concurrent engineering is a model technique for a fast-clockspeed world. When companies have little competitive pressure and slowly evolving technologies, the burden of time weighs relatively lightly. In the absence of time pressure, the penalties for working slowly and sequentially rather than concurrently—and for iteration and reworking—are mild. As the clockspeed of industry after industry has begun to heat up from the driver of global competition, the necessity of concurrency has struck home.

Although concurrent engineering of product and process led to great improvement in performance in the 1980s and early 1990s, those tools no longer provide significant *differential* advantage in many industries.[10] A significant number of the most competitive companies have already adopted standard CE methodology. The best of them are now seeking to master the next leap in process capability—namely, three-dimensional concurrent engineering (3-DCE).

Concurrent Engineering in Three Dimensions

If the traditional two dimensions of CE are insufficient to ensure competitive advantage, what must be added to bring the theoretical model in line with current and future market realities? The answer to this question lies in the design and development of the supply chain. Of course, many companies already make significant efforts in designing their supply chains. Often they do so, however, without full corporate consciousness of the strategic issues at stake or of the opportunities that would be available to them if they were to focus on designing the supply chains strategically and concurrently with their products and production processes. In short, supply chain issues are hardly newcomers to manufacturing and design processes, but in the traditional way of considering concurrent engineering, many companies have treated development of the supply chain as an afterthought.

As is evident in the examples of Intel, Toyota, Chrysler and Boeing, discussed later in this chapter, the supply chain forms the third axis of concurrent engineering. Taken with process and product design, it invites us to look at CE in three dimensions rather than the traditional two, and it thereby offers even very successful companies a significant opportunity to establish and enhance their competitive advantage.

When firms do not explicitly acknowledge and manage supply chain design and engineering as a concurrent activity to product and process design and engineering, they often encounter problems late in product development, or with manufacturing launch, logistical support, quality control, and production costs. In addition, they run the risk of losing control of their business destiny.

Supply chain design has particular importance when the effects of the chain relationship are long-lasting. This occurs especially when the competitive impact of supply chain design and development decisions extend over several generations. Even the most innocuous decision affecting supply chain designs can have enormous ramifications extending all the way to the continued survival of a company or an entire industry. In the personal computer industry, for instance, IBM's supply chain design practically handed over the reins of the industry to Microsoft and Intel. Although IBM has regained some of the ground it lost, it occupies only a spit of land that it might have controlled if the company had taken a three-dimensional view of concurrent engineering. Its failure to do so represents a decision that changed the course of the world's computer industry.

Architectures in 3-D: Product, Process, and Supply Chain

In chapter 4 we saw the double helix partly through the lens of product architectures. As these evolved from integral to modular and back to integral again, we saw synchronization with the evolution of the industry and supply chain structures, which themselves modulated from vertical to horizontal and back to vertical again. To approach three-dimensional concurrent engineering, we can again stand at the level of architecture, but this time we examine it in three dimensions represented by products, processes, and supply chains.

Analyzing product and process design problems at the architecture level provides a strategic, high-level perspective on how supply chain design can be integrated into concurrent engineering. In a seminal paper, Karl Ulrich describes product architecture as the scheme by which the function of a product is allocated to its constituent components.[11] He distinguishes between integral and modular product architectures, a distinction that is fundamental to three-dimensional concurrent engineering.

To understand these concepts, think of integral architectures as exhibiting close coupling among the elements of the product. An integral product architecture might feature, for example,

- components that perform many functions
- components that are in close proximity or close spatial relationship

- components that are tightly synchronized.

In contrast, a modular architecture features separation among a system's constituent parts, whereby

- components are interchangeable.
- components are individually upgradable.
- component interfaces are standardized.
- system failures can be localized.

Applying these distinctions, we would expect to see integral architecture products with principal components having multiple functions. Engineers call this "function sharing."[12] For example, consider the very simple product of a carpenter's hammer. The claw head of this everyday tool typically exhibits an integral architecture. The steel head, a single component, performs two distinct functions: The head end drives nails, whereas the "claw" removes them.

A more complex example is the wing structure of a typical commercial jet airplane such as the Boeing 777. The wing must be designed and constructed to perform (at least) two functions: It must provide lift to the aircraft, and it must serve as a hollow tank for storing jet fuel.

An equally intricate example is the frame of a modern motorcycle, such as a model built by Honda.[13] In contrast to an automobile— which has separate body, engine, and gasoline tank components— motorcycles have a complex frame structure that integrates structural body functions with engine and gas tank components.

Products also exhibit characteristics of an integral architecture if some of their functional requirements must be delivered by various subsystems and cannot be reduced to a single component or subsystem. For example, automobiles and airplanes have stringent requirements for total weight, a functional requirement that spans virtually all of their subsystems (such as chassis, fuel consumption, exhaust, braking, to name a few). Similarly, mainframe computers require that the enormous amount of heat generated by key components be eliminated; otherwise, the system runs the risk of becoming damaged.[14]

Modular architecture products, in contrast, exhibit interchangeable components, each of which has a single or only a few functions. One common example is a home stereo system, for which customers mix and match receivers, speakers, compact disk players, and other components, often from different manufacturers. This mix-and-match convenience is now possible because the interfaces across those components have been standardized throughout the industry. Desktop personal computers, with their motherboards, disk drives, DRAM chips, modems, monitors, and keyboards are also highly modular.

In contrast to motorcycles, for instance, most modern bicycles (as discussed in chapter 4) are also highly modular. Manufacturers now build frames that can accommodate a wide variety of interchangeable components such as seats, brakes, chains, freewheels, and gear shifters from a multitude of suppliers.

In many cases, there is considerable tension between choosing integral or modular designs. As the Teledesic case study in chapter 11 illustrates, arguments for the integral design are often largely technical or performance-based, whereas arguments for the modular tend to be based on business concerns such as cost and time to market.[15]

Supply Chain Architecture

Building on the product architecture concept enables development of the construct of supply chain architecture, a richer concept than that of traditional make/buy or vertical integration, which focuses primarily on the ownership of assets in the supply chain.[16] The supply chain architecture concept is one of the keys to a deeper analysis of the make/buy challenge, which will be examined in chapter 9. This concept also is essential in extending the integral-modular distinction from products to supply chains. An integral supply chain architecture features close *proximity* among its elements. Proximity is measured along four dimensions: geographic, organizational, cultural, and electronic.[17]

Geographic proximity can most simply be measured by physical distance. Although electronic communication technologies have reduced in many cases the importance of geography, for many other product and process engineering projects, geography significantly affects the project outcome. Especially for highly integral product designs, continuous iteration among design parameters for key interrelated subsystems is most efficiently handled by co-located (essentially integrated) engineering teams.

Measuring *organizational* proximity is a bit more complex, but can be approximated by constructs of ownership, managerial control, and interpersonal and interteam dependencies. Thus, a customer and supplier who are owned within the same corporate structure have interlocking corporate ownership, report to the same general manager or CEO, and have tightly interconnected work processes among functions or teams. They can usefully be described as having close organizational proximity.

Cultural proximity captures commonality of language, business mores, ethical standards, and laws, among other things. Matsushita Electric Industrial, Co., Ltd. exemplifies a global company with a well-established value system and philosophy, which was enunciated by the company's founder, the late Konosuke Matsushita. Even today, those values continue to motivate and direct Matsushita employees and company policies.

Finally, *electronic* proximity, or what today might be termed a "virtual vicinity," can be captured through e-mail, electronic data exchange (EDI), intranets, video conferencing, and other technologies among members of the supply chain. Both Ford Motor Company[18] and Toyota,[19] as examples, have invested significantly in computer-aided design software that can be used across the supply chain for 3-D concurrent engineering, fostering electronic proximity within the supply chain.

A supply chain with a high degree of integrality, therefore, is one in which a manufacturer and its principal suppliers are concentrated in

one city or geographic region, have common or interlocking ownership, share a common business and social culture, and are linked electronically. Excluding the last of these dimensions, the well-known
"lean production system"[20] was developed within a highly integral
supply chain. This highly respected and widely imitated system was
conceived and nurtured by Toyota Motor Corporation in the
Nagoya/Toyota City industrial region within a highly uniform culture
and with significant ownership and managerial participation by
Toyota and its suppliers.

Interestingly, Toyota's early efforts at integrating North American
suppliers into a global product development extension of its Toyota
City model met numerous difficulties.[21] That is, even the widely
respected Toyota struggled when it tried to implement *global* three-
dimensional concurrent engineering from a highly integral supply base.
Toyota's solution to these problems featured a dramatic improvement
in electronic proximity with sophisticated CAD (computer-aided
design) tools shared across a network between engineers in Toyota-
Japan and its North American suppliers.

In contrast to the integral system, a modular supply chain exhibits
low proximity along most or all of the dimensions listed above. That
is, modular supply chains are those that may well exist over a huge
expanse of geographical territory and have autonomous managerial
and ownership structures, diverse cultures, with low levels of electronic connectivity. Of course, extremely low levels of proximity in all
these dimensions would render a supply chain unmanageable in a fast-
or even moderate-clockspeed industry, so some degree of close proximity along one or more of these dimensions is necessary for survival
in most cases. If you do not have high geographic, organizational, or
cultural proximity, then you probably need significant electronic proximity to coordinate a globally distributed chain like that of the merged
Daimler-Chrysler organization combined with its acquired Nissan
Truck operation, for example.

We can still observe significant differences, however, in the extent of proximity across successful supply chains today. Modular supply chains tend to feature multiple, interchangeable suppliers for key components. As one example, consider the personal computer industry. The supply chains for these devices are widely dispersed across myriad companies, primarily in North America and Asia. Those companies— including semiconductor fabricators, circuit board assemblers, modem manufacturers, disk drive makers, and software houses—are located in the United States, Japan, Taiwan, Singapore, Malaysia, Thailand, China, India, and many other countries. They share neither geographic, nor organizational, nor cultural proximity. Only the advent of technologies for electronic proximity has allowed these highly modular supply chains to thrive.

In contrast to that of Toyota City, the supply network resulting from the "global sourcing" policies of General Motors has retained significant component development, manufacturing, and integration capabilities internal to the corporate entity. These internal capabilities enable GM to treat many of its suppliers as interchangeable to some degree and to outsource components in a competitive bidding mode while the company does the integration work itself. This policy has resulted in a collection of suppliers that are widely dispersed geographically, organizationally, and culturally, even for a fairly integral product such as an automobile.

A complex of a different sort is offered by the garment manufacturing industry in Italy.[22] This industry comprises hundreds of small firms, many of which specialize in just one step of the garment-producing supply chain. That is, a firm might concentrate on designing, spinning, weaving, dyeing, cutting, or sewing, rather than on trying to perform all of these steps. Members of this supply chain, although they often share geographical and cultural proximity, still exhibit modular characteristics of interchangeability.

Finally, consider the example of telecommunications services.

Although the U.S. system was developed by a highly integrated "Ma Bell" in the middle of the twentieth century, by the 1990s, partly as a result of the historic spin-off of the local service providers ("Baby Bells") in 1984, the industry structure evolved. Consumers now build their own supply chains, choosing separately the interchangeable suppliers of telephone handsets and hardware, local service, long distance service, cellular service, repair service, Internet access, and the like. This evolution shows another instance of movement along the double helix and reinforces that we ought to expect to see significant variety in the supply chain architectures of different industries.

Concurrent Design of Product and Supply Chain Architectures

Before integrating the complexities of process architecture into this discussion, let us consider the relationship between product architecture and supply chain architecture as discussed above. To a significant degree, product and supply chain architectures tend to be aligned along the integrality-modularity spectrum. That is, integral products tend to be developed and built by integral supply chains, whereas modular products tend to be designed and built by modular supply chains.

In essence, product and supply chain architectures tend to be mutually reinforcing. As we saw in chapter 4, the Chrysler Corporation helped ensure its survival by taking the extraordinary step (extraordinary for Detroit automakers) of modularizing its product design and its supply chain to offer suppliers greater autonomy and the potential for increased revenues. The Schwinn Bicycle Company, on the other hand, was forced into bankruptcy when it failed to make the turn from integral products and supply chains back to modularity along the double helix of the industry's development in the latter part of the twentieth century.

In the case of the personal computer industry, modularity in product architecture enables manufacturers to use modular supply chains.

By extension, the existence of a strong modular supply chain encourages the further development and use of modular products, as evidenced by Compaq, Dell, and other makers of personal computers. Similarly, the more complex the development process for integral products, the higher degree of integration we can expect in integral supply chains. This effect results from the intensive, iterative communication required for development, as exemplified by the companies that produce aircraft for defense purposes. Fighter jets comprise highly integrated subsystems that are extremely difficult (if not impossible) to decompose into independent modules for outsourcing to highly independent suppliers.[23]

These relationships are illustrated in figure 8.1.

Figure 8.1 illustrates the cases of our discussion so far. Toyota automobiles in Toyota City and telephone systems in the mid-twentieth century zenith of "Ma Bell" were both examples of integral products provided by integral supply chains. At the other end of the spectrum, modularity in product design enables the modular supply chains of apparel design and manufacture, General Motors' global sourcing, personal computers, and telephone service in the 1990s.

Now, consider an off-diagonal example. BMW products are among the highest performing luxury sedans in the world. In its product development process, BMW sacrifices much in cost and development time in order to create a vehicle that will thrill customers—many of whom are sophisticated automobile enthusiasts—and deliver the best possible acceleration, braking, handling, and the like. To achieve this high level of product performance, BMW has historically crafted a highly integral vehicle design, relying on an integral supply chain centered in the Munich area, around the company's corporate headquarters. This high level of integrality assures tight control of all vehicle specifications and process interactions among all key subsystems.

In the early 1990s when BMW decided to build a factory in the United States, the company also chose (reputedly under some pressure

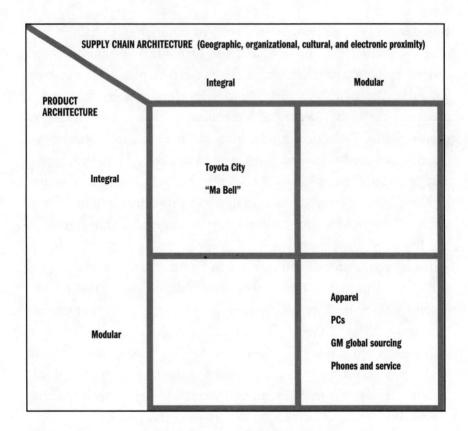

Figure 8.1. The Interaction Effects between Product and Supply Chain Architectures

from local governments) to use a number of American suppliers instead of bringing all of its German suppliers to the North American site. To the company's chagrin, BMW engineers discovered that some of their American suppliers, although highly skilled in working with their traditional American customers, were ill-equipped for the highly integral and iterative product development and launch processes that were second nature to the skilled craftsmen in the German supply base. As a result, BMW's first U.S. manufacturing process experienced delays and a costly launch, when the company and its suppliers scrambled to reengineer the modular supply base to meet the demands of BMW's integral vehicle designs.[24]

Process Architecture

Like the architectures for the product and supply chain, it can also be useful to locate your process architecture along the line extending from the extremes of vertical-integral and horizontal-modular. Whereas we used four dimensions (geographic, organizational, cultural, and electronic) to characterize the degree of integrality and modularity in the supply chain architecture, for process architecture we use only two dimensions: time and space. That is, process architectures can be integrated in both time and space (highly integral), integrated in either space or time, or dispersed in both space and time (highly modular). For example, a significant portion of the developed world's just-in-time production efforts of the past two decades has been devoted to reducing or eliminating time dispersion in production systems. Nevertheless, one can still observe differences along this dimension, although the variance is far smaller than that of twenty years ago.

To illustrate the concept, consider the following examples in figure 8.2. As we saw in chapter 5, Dell Computer Corporation's computer assembly process is tightly integrated in time. An entire computer is built in a few hours to be rushed off to its future owner. Dell's assembly process is tightly integrated in space as well: All assembly operations take place in a single work cell in a single factory operated by a very small team.

Contrast this process with newspaper production such as we might find at the *Wall Street Journal*. Journalists adhere to a tight schedule, usually a 24-hour deadline for product completion, but the reporters contributing to the product are highly dispersed geographically as are the printing presses on which the product is run. Another example in this category is software development. A software company can implement full assembly and testing of a product prototype once every 24 hours if it wishes, even though the software engineers may work in dispersed facilities on several continents.

In the opposite quadrant of the space and time dimensions, premium-brand wine making serves as an example of a process that

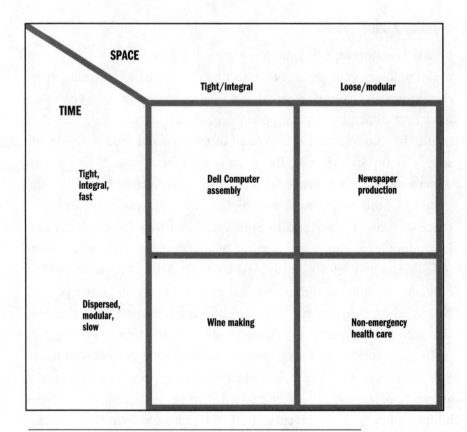

Figure 8.2. Different Process Architectures along the Dimensions of Time and Space

requires an extended time component. The fermentation process often extends many years, whereas most of the work—growing, picking, processing, fermenting, and aging—occurs in a single location, the winery.

Finally, services such as nonemergency health care tend to be spread out geographically—for example, in a large hospital complex or across multiple facilities within a large city. These services often span months or years, depending on the ailment being treated. (Emergency care, on the other hand, tends to be very tight both in time and in space.)

Some apparel making, in addition, is widely dispersed in both time and space. For example, the ski-wear maker Sport Obermeyer has a production system that spans the Pacific Ocean and requires several months for product completion.[25]

The Imperative of Concurrency

Figure 8.3 illustrates several interactions across product, process, and supply chain development activities. Where the three ovals overlap we locate those activities that need to be undertaken concurrently, either bilaterally or collectively, among the three functions. This diagram further illustrates that not all of the activities undertaken within any of the three functions need to be performed in conjunction with members of the other groups. That is, not all work must take place in "integrated product teams" (IPTs). Rather, IPTs would concern themselves only with tasks where activities of two or all three functions overlap.

Figure 8.3 attempts to capture visually many of the ideas in Part III of this book. One can consider how architecture decisions are made through discussions within and across the product, process, and supply chain organizations. In addition, many of the tools—for make/buy decisions and product development, as examples,—discussed in the following two chapters can be placed within the framework of this diagram.

A further refinement of the overlapping areas of concurrency across product, process, and supply chain development appears in figure 8.4, which also highlights the imperative of concurrency. This figure divides each of the three developmental areas—product, process, and supply chain—into two subactivities:

- *Product development* is subdivided into activities of architectural choices (for example, integrality versus modularity decisions) and detailed design choices (for example, performance and functional specifications for the detailed product design).

- *Process development* is divided into the development of unit processes (that is, the process technologies and equipment to be used) and manufacturing systems development—decisions about

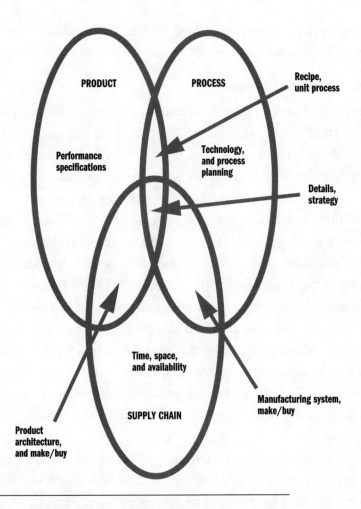

Figure 8.3. Overlapping Responsibilities across Product, Process, and Supply Chain Development Activities

plant and operations systems design and layout (for instance, process/job shop focus versus product/cellular focus).

- *Supply chain development* is divided into the supply chain architecture decisions and logistics/coordination system decisions. Supply chain architecture decisions include decisions on whether to make or buy a component, sourcing decisions (for example, choosing which companies to include in the supply chain), and contracting decisions (such as structuring the relationships among the supply chain members). Logistics and coordination decisions include the inventory, delivery, and information systems to support ongoing operation of the supply chain.

For purposes of this chapter, the most important aspect of figure 8.4 is the series of overlapping arrows at the bottom of the chart. These arrows highlight the linkages across the three activities, emphasizing where concurrent development takes on paramount importance. Three of these bilateral links are emphasized. We call them, respectively, Focus, Architecture, and Technology (FAT).

The Architecture link is discussed above in reference to figure 8.2— aligning product and supply chain architectures. The Technology link encompasses the coordination of detailed product designs with process capabilities, which is the domain of traditional (two-dimensional) concurrent engineering.

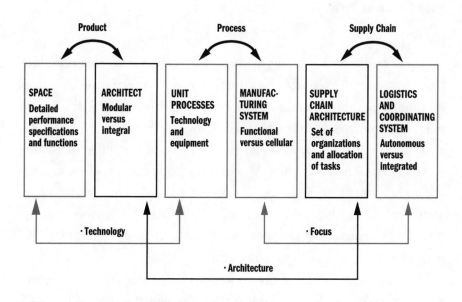

Figure 8.4. The "FAT 3-DCE Decision Model"

Focus decisions link choices about the manufacturing system design with those in logistics and materials system design. Since the supply chain logistics management system is typically an extension of the in-house manufacturing system design, these process and supply chain design areas are often tightly linked. An important set of decisions in the domain of process design is the extent to which the manufacturing system is "process focused" or "product focused."[26] Traditional job shops and semiconductor fabrication plants tend to be process focused, grouping together all like sets of equipment and unit processes. Concurrently, as the supply chain logistics and materials system is designed, managers must make decisions about the chain management system. For instance, should it be tightly integrated as Dell's is, or should it remain a loose-knit group of autonomous system suppliers as we find in the manufacture of defense aircraft?

The next four cases—Intel, Chrysler, Toyota, and Boeing—further illustrate these ideas.

Four Cases in Point

Intel

In an era and industry of unprecedented clockspeed acceleration, Intel Corporation has risen about as quickly as any corporation in history as a major manufacturer. Most of Intel's growth to a $25 billion corporation occurred over less than a decade, a period during which the company built highly capital-intensive factories and introduced new products at a blistering pace. Much of the company's success in keeping competitors at bay during the period of explosive growth can be attributed to its ability to execute new product and process development with many new suppliers at breakneck speed. In short, Intel proved to be a master of fast-clockspeed 3-DCE.

Given the complexity of the underlying technologies, we can gain a valuable understanding of how Intel simplified the daunting 3-DCE challenges it faced. Its approach offers lessons for any company contemplating a shift to three-dimensional concurrent engineering. Intel's microprocessor product families—popularly known as the 286, 386, 486, and Pentium processors—were the result of a massive product development process, involving hundreds of engineers and scientists working over multiple sites and multiple years.[27]

Historically in the semiconductor industry, where DRAM products absorbed the lion's share of new investment, each new generation of product—64Kb RAM, 256Kb RAM, 1Mb RAM, and so forth—each product launch occurred on an all-new generation of manufacturing process (typically denoted by the smallest line-width on the integrated circuits). Thus, for a DRAM manufacturer, launching a new product meant simultaneously launching a new process—always a complex affair. Through most of the 1980s, the Japanese semiconductor companies concentrated on DRAM design and production, exploiting their skills in precision clean manufacturing. The Japanese tended to be the process technology leaders into each new smaller line-width process generation.

By the early 1990s, however, Intel found itself in the position of needing new processes (for example, more metallization layers) in advance of the DRAM industry's needs or its willingness to invest in such processes. As a result, the DRAM makers no longer unequivocally drove process development. Having emerged as the 800-pound gorilla of the industry in the early 1990s, Intel had to learn to be a process technology leader and to develop systems whereby it could continue to improve process technology while accelerating its pace of product development.

Intel crafted a brilliant 3-DCE strategy that used product/process modularity to reduce significantly the complexity of the company's technical challenge: Throughout the 1990s, the company launched each new microprocessor generation on the "platform" of an old (line-width) process. Alternately, each new process generation was launched with an "old" product technology. For instance, Intel introduced its i486 chip on the one-micron process developed for the i386 chip, a process that had already been debugged. Following the success of this process, Intel created the .8-micron process, which was first tried on the now-proven i486 chip. Next, it launched the Pentium chip on the proven .8-micron process before moving it over to the new .6-micron process. Leveraging this system of alternating product and process launches, Intel created almost perfect modularity between product and process, a marriage that reduced dramatically the complexity of any given launch. Reducing the complexity of concurrent engineering has, of course, been one of the keys to Intel's success in its hyperfast-clockspeed industry.

When viewed through the lens of the third dimension, however, Intel's link between process and supply chain is much more integral. That is, process development goes hand in glove with supply chain development. Especially by the mid-1990s, when Intel needed to drive new process technologies rather than adapt technologies that had already been pretty much debugged by the DRAM manufacturers, Intel found itself nurturing start-up companies that were just developing the advanced technologies necessary for the next-generation processes Intel needed. As a result, Intel fostered integral development of new processes and new suppliers to support those processes.[28]

Chrysler

In chapter 4, we saw that Chrysler in the 1990s could be likened to Compaq in the 1980s. Through a modular product and supply chain strategy, each company managed to upset the advantages of much larger rivals and to trigger a chain reaction of events capable of altering dramatically the structure of the entire industry. In the case of Compaq and the fast-clockspeed computer industry, this series of events is already history. In the slower-clockspeed automobile sector, events are still unfolding before our eyes. In particular, the automobile is not as modular as the personal computer, and neither is the supply chain associated with the car industry.

Through the lens of 3-DCE, we can see both the strengths and the potential weaknesses of Chrysler's strategy more clearly: By out-sourcing the development and integration of numerous automotive subsystems, Chrysler cut dramatically the total time and cost required to develop and launch a new vehicle. The company has effectively exploited the opportunities from this approach, as described earlier. However, in executing this strategy of modularizing the product and the corresponding sectors of its supply chain, Chrysler seemingly sub-ordinated its relative emphasis on process development, somewhat to the detriment of overall vehicle system features such as reliability.[29]

Because Chrysler, in contrast to many of its competitors, could move so quickly from concept to car, the company enjoyed a high rat-ing with consumers on the most desirable designs and features. Such designs allowed Chrysler to charge premium prices with minimal rebating in the first several years of the 1990s. However, while earn-ing a premium on its designs, Chrysler perhaps lost some ground over customer dissatisfaction with the vehicles' reliability. These, of course, are features that cannot be outsourced to suppliers. Rather, they are inherent in the overall systems engineering of the vehicle.[30]

To build on its early-1990s recovery, perhaps Chrysler will have to reinvest some of its bounteous profits into deeper 3-D systems inte-gration skills, particularly in integrating the process development activities with the advantages the company has already gained through its system of product-supply chain modularity. This system is so well executed that it has been christened the "new American *keiretsu*,"[31] drawing an analogy to Toyota's effective use of outsourced subsystem development. Toyota's systems integration skills and core technology capabilities, however, are very deep. Toyota has outsourced manufacturing capacity, but rarely the fundamental knowledge, a topic discussed in chapter 9.[32]

With the acquisition by Daimler-Benz, Chrysler gains a partner with some of the deepest systems engineering skills in the automotive industry. In the best of all possible worlds, the new Daimler-Chrysler will excel at both the cost-reducing, speed-enhancing modularization of product and supply chain and the quality–enhancing process integration capabilities that provide the true test of a vehicle engineering team's capabilities.

Toyota

As we have seen, Toyota Motor Corporation brilliantly exploited its highly integral Nagoya/Toyota City supply chain in developing its famed lean production system. Furthermore, when Toyota began globalizing its production—to NUMMI in California and to Georgetown in Kentucky, for example—the gold standard that the company had established for quality production systems seemed to be exportable without a hitch.

However, globalizing the entire Toyota system of 3-DCE has not gone nearly as smoothly.[33] In their early launch experiences, Toyota's North American suppliers underperformed dramatically relative to Toyota's Japanese suppliers in the entire development process: in quality, cost cutting, and on-time development. These supply chain snafus delayed by as many as ten months the launch of Toyota's North American Camry and Avalon vehicles and raised the development costs by as much as 40 percent.[34] Furthermore, for some critical parts, Toyota took the unprecedented step of arranging for backup suppliers in Japan whose rush-shipment air freight costs to North America sometimes topped $1 million per month.[35] These problems resulted primarily from the relative inexperience of North American suppliers with the Toyota production engineering system, as well as the communication complexity of involving Toyota's Japanese and North American engineering organizations with a complex set of suppliers in both Japan and North America.[36]

Because the Toyota system is built on dense communication links across the entire supply network, adding more nodes for each development step exponentially increased the number of communication channels used. This added complexity of global 3-DCE has led to a more complex overall process. As mentioned, Toyota is investing in improved electronic media to bridge this communication bottleneck, but only time will tell whether Toyota will be the world-class benchmark in *global* 3-DCE the way its lean production system was for integral *local* 3-D concurrent engineering.

Boeing

The aircraft industry has long been one of the turtles of the manufacturing sector. Its development cycles are long; its product lives are long; its processes are long-lasting, as are its supply chain relationships. When a company such as Boeing makes a decision about a supplier or an airplane design, it has to live with that decision for years, if not decades. As a result, when Boeing develops a new airplane (something that only happens perhaps twice a decade), it tends to get representatives from each of product, process, and supply chain involved and talking with each other at a fairly early stage. This is how 3-DCE is supposed to work—at least in a slow-clockspeed world. I call this *static 3-DCE*.

In a fast-clockspeed world, the challenges are significantly more difficult. In such settings, firms need to practice *dynamic 3-DCE*. So what's the difference? In *dynamic 3-DCE*, the three-dimensional team tasked with developing the product, process, and supply chain for the current airplane project (or whatever product) not only needs to focus on the enormous complexity of the current project, but also must consider the impact of the decisions the team makes on the developers of future projects. In particular, how do these decisions affect the set of competencies the firm will have mastery over once the project is completed? What kind of dependencies on which other members of the value chain will result from the choices made on the current project?

These issues take us out of the realm of the theoretical and into that of practical applications. In the final four chapters of Part III, we will see how the theoretical notions of fruit fly industries, capability (supply) chains, and the fluctuation along the double helix between the vertical structure (with its reliance on integrated products) and the horizontal structure (which features modular products) can help companies make both short- and long-term business decisions.

9 ENRICHING THE GENE POOL

What to Make, What to Buy

If the fruit flies of business teach us one thing, it's to outsource capacity, not knowledge.

IN CHAPTER 5, I argued that supply chain design is the most important competency in the firm. Supply chain design consists of choosing *what work* to outsource to suppliers (that is, make versus buy), choosing *which suppliers* to use (that is, supplier selection), and negotiating the *contract*—both the legalities and the culture of the supply chain relationships. Among these three, the most important, and the focus of this chapter, is the competency of choosing which capabilities are worth developing and maintaining, and which may safely be outsourced—that is, the competency of deciding which capabilities to make and which to buy, which are core and which are peripheral.

It is tempting to think that *the* answer to the make versus buy issue exists and is simple. Adherents of the buy-anything-you-can theory match their voices against those of the make-everything-you-can school in a confusing din of debates. But neither extreme strategy, even when employed single-mindedly (no matter how carefully), can stand the test of time and the changing world of competition. The double helix model discussed in chapter 4 suggests one reason why: If companies and industries cycle between horizontal/modular and vertical/integral structures, then the best strategy for an individual company is not necessarily to strive for a condition of stability, but to learn to move fluidly even in the most turbulent waters.

Much has been written on the make versus buy decision. When is it better to own and operate all the suppliers yourself (vertical integration), and when to own nothing of the supply chain and try to control it by other means (virtual integration)? The simplest and perhaps oldest way of approaching these questions in a manufacturing setting is to compare cost per part if manufactured inside the company with the cost of outside manufacturing. Traditional cost accounting textbooks present this analysis in the context of "relevant costing."[1] Although simplistic, this type of analysis has the merit of illustrating clearly that from a purely economic viewpoint, neither the "make everything" nor the "buy everything" approach will always produce optimal results.

Economists, however, have developed a rich theory of vertical integration that takes into account a number of important factors to consider in deciding what to make or what to buy. These include the technological dependencies along a supply chain, market power exploitation for price discrimination, transaction costs among chain members, asset specificity (specialization) and the irreversibility of investments dedicated to specific chain relationships, incentives for the various members in the chain, and the allocation of decision rights in the chain.[2]

But these approaches are often difficult to apply in a decision-making context, particularly in the three-dimensional concurrent engineering setting introduced in chapter 8. In the present chapter, therefore, I discuss four viewpoints that enrich the make/buy decision framework in this new light.

First, in response to the insufficient depth of the make versus buy dichotomy for capturing the range of relationships observed in practice, I discuss how the integral versus modular supply chain concept presented in chapter 8 provides a much richer and more useful framework in which to consider the issues of supply chain design. Second, in response to the increasing clockspeeds faced by many industries, I propose a dynamic framework that highlights the role of technological and organizational change over the life of a supply chain relationship. This framework is based on an analogy between making out-sourcing decisions and sowing seeds that will grow and take shape as new, but not always predictable life forms. Third, in a classification scheme for supply chain dependency, I distinguish between dependence on a supplier for capacity (for example, to manufacture a certain fraction of a required demand for a product) and dependence for knowledge, where that dependence is deeper and perhaps more difficult to uproot. Fourth, I describe a conceptual decision framework for make versus buy decisions that attempts to capture those issues highlighted here.

The Effect of the Integral versus Modular Supply Chain on the Decision to Make or Buy

In 1968, an elite team of three engineers—Gordon Moore, Robert Noyce, and Andrew Grove—left Fairchild Semiconductor to start Intel in Mountain View, California. Three decades later, that start-up had become a household word ("Intel Inside") and a multibillion-dollar enterprise. Although Fairchild's key business was semiconductors and much of the promising new "silicon gate MOS technology" had been developed there, the company's most valuable assets just walked out the door and launched Intel's fortunes based on that technology.[3] Having decided to "make" a key technology within its own walls, the vertically integrated Fairchild Semiconductor was hardly able to reap full benefits from its apparently "strategic" position of having the silicon gate MOS technology internal to the corporation.

Consider also the case of Toyota and Denso, which have independent governance structures, yet work hand in glove on design and manufacturing problems on their many customer-supplier projects. By standard parlance, Toyota is "buying" from Denso, but the relationship looks very cozy, and the incentives seem fairly well aligned.[4] On the other hand, General Motors develops many automotive projects that involve subprojects between its North American Operations (NAO) organization and its components organization (Delphi). Several aspects of these relationships involve significant contention and often feel like relationships conducted at arm's length by parties whose incentives are not closely aligned. However, standard categories would label this a "make" relationship within General Motors.

The examples of very different supply chain relationships structured by General Motors and Toyota are helpful for illustrating why the categories in "make versus buy" or "vertical integration versus outsourcing" are inadequate: They do not account precisely for the complexity of relationships we observe in practice. Instead, I believe the categorization introduced in chapter 8—the integrality versus modularity of a supply chain—provides a much richer and more useful framework for examining the traditional "make versus buy" issues in supply chain design. That is, rather than using the categorization of vertically integrated or disintegrated, supply chain relationships can be categorized on a scale running from the highly integral to the highly modular, depending on the degree of proximity of the members in the chain along four dimensions: geographic, organizational, cultural, and electronic. In conjunction with assessments of the modularity of the product and process architectures, I believe this framework is very rich for providing strategic assessments of a make versus buy situation.

In the Fairchild Semiconductor example, the members of the organization had close geographic and cultural proximity. In addition, some aspects of its organizational proximity—close ownership and managerial control—were common among the defector team and the rest of the organization. However, the "Intel team" within Fairchild was sufficiently modular from the other work processes at the organization that the defectors were able to set up a new organizational home for their work with relative ease."[5]

In the automotive example, Denso shares close geographic and cultural proximity with Toyota, as well as some common ownership. In contrast, although GM-NAO and Delphi share common ownership, their management structures are separate and their organizational incentives are not tightly aligned. Both types of relationships have their pros and cons in the immediate present, of course, but as we will see in the next section, this is not always the case over the long term, especially within fast-clockspeed industries.

Dependency Dynamics

Think of the elements in the value chain as capabilities, each of which can be "planted" and nourished so that they grow, blossom, and perhaps in their full maturity inspire awe. Although they eventually decline and die, their adaptation, if successful, lives on in their offspring.

This section describes some of the dynamics of such capability development. It explores the interaction between decisions affecting the design of the chain (insourcing versus outsourcing, for instance) and the location and speed of capability development. Every time that an organization makes a sourcing decision, whether internal or external, it is planting a "capability seed" that has the potential to grow into a valuable and powerful organizational competency. A supplier's relationship with its customer helps determine whether the company will become more independent or more dependent with respect to the technology in question. In the case of work or products produced internally, we can speak of the dynamics of an *independence loop,* by which insourcing strengthens internal capabilities. As those capabilities become stronger, they in turn encourage further insourcing. In contrast, a *dependence loop* can be triggered by an outsourcing decision, which encourages suppliers to develop their capabilities, predisposing the customer to become dependent on those suppliers. These relationships are depicted schematically in figure 9.1.

The faster the clockspeed of the industry, the faster the seeds of capability will grow, if nourished. On the other hand, the faster the industry clockspeed, the less predictable the path of that growth and the form of the ultimate blossom. The sourcing decision determines in part the location of that seed and its subsequent growth—that is, whether it develops into a full competency. Once the seed begins to grow, the company that planted it may not always be able to control the growth. IBM, for instance, spent over $1 billion on its OS/2 operating system for personal computers, unsuccessfully trying to uproot the sprout that had grown from the DOS seed it had earlier sown at Microsoft.[6]

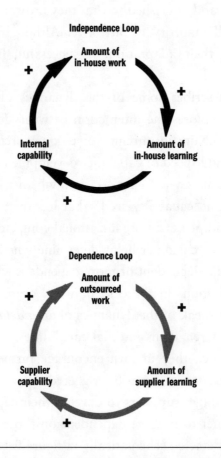

Figure 9.1. The Dynamics of Capability Sourcing and Capability Development

The Polaroid Corporation

As an illustration of the independence loop, consider the case of Polaroid's development of expertise in automated camera manufacturing and its relationship with Sony. In the early 1980s, hundreds of men and women bent over benches in a spacious and modern (but labor-intensive) electronics assembly plant, screwing and soldering Polaroid cameras together—camera after camera, day after day. The dollar was strong, and labor costs were high. Maintaining high quality was a constant challenge, given the high labor content of the process.

Polaroid managers decided they had to "automate, emigrate, or evaporate," as a contemporary slogan in manufacturing circles expressed the choice. Although steeped in scientific and technical knowledge about instant photography, Polaroid had little internal knowledge about robotics and automated assembly of consumer electronics products. Realizing that they would have to go outside for expertise, managers searched for a supplier that could expertly install automated assembly technology into Polaroid's camera operations. For a variety of reasons, Polaroid chose to partner with Sony, one of the top firms in the world at automated assembly of high-volume consumer electronics products.[7]

The two companies developed an extensive relationship. In the beginning, Sony provided robotics system hardware, software, applications engineering, tooling, design-for-manufacturability (DFM) advice—a complete turnkey package. Across several generations of systems, Polaroid engineers aggressively absorbed knowledge from Sony, eventually developing their internal capability in software development, DFM, applications engineering, tooling, and maintenance and improvement. Between 1985 and 1995, as illustrated in figure 9.2, both Polaroid and Sony increased significantly their knowledge of the robotics assembly of cameras. Polaroid used its increasing knowledge base to bring in-house more and more technical work over the generations of equipment used in its factory.

Within ten years, Polaroid was buying "plain vanilla" machines from Sony and doing the remaining work internally. The company developed an ability to launch rapidly its new lines of cameras and other products into the factory and to reconfigure and reuse a high proportion of the flexible automation, which it came to perceive as providing a strategic advantage in the marketplace.

By choosing to continue to insource as much of the knowledge work as possible in each succeeding generation, Polaroid developed an important technological capability that it initially had been forced to outsource because the company had inadequate internal knowledge. Meanwhile, the partnership enabled Sony to strengthen its own opportunities. Polaroid engineers would often stand up at conferences and vouch for the quality and value of the Sony equipment.

The Boeing Corporation

As an example of the dynamics of capability outsourcing and dependency, consider the case of Boeing, first discussed in chapter 1. By outsourcing to Japanese aerospace suppliers, Boeing planted the seeds of

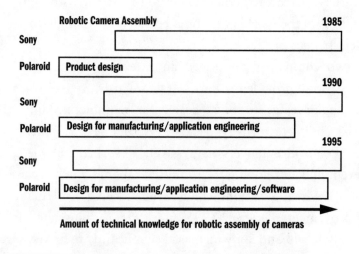

Figure 9.2. Polaroid's Capability Insourcing and Internal Development

various competencies that grew under their own power, eventually beyond the ability of Boeing to control them. As illustrated in figure 9.3, Boeing's subcontracts had a positive impact on the size and technological capabilities of the Japanese suppliers, which, in turn, increased Japanese industry autonomy and ultimately the ability of that industry to demand more critical work. In addition, the suppliers gained in their appeal as subcontractors, which, in turn, won them more contracts. On the U.S. side, fewer contracts resulted in a shrinking of size and capability, which, in turn, reduced the suppliers' attractiveness and encouraged Boeing to shift even more business away from them in subsequent contracts.

Once such a dynamic process is initiated, it can take on a life of its own and evolve far beyond the control of the initiator. In Boeing's case, this process has unfolded over a period of 25 years or more, far exceeding the duration of any individual Boeing employee's executive career. Furthermore, although the Boeing-Japan relationship has been fruitful for all the players involved, one must ask whether this relationship constricts Boeing as the company attempts to trade production for sales in the emerging markets of China and India, for

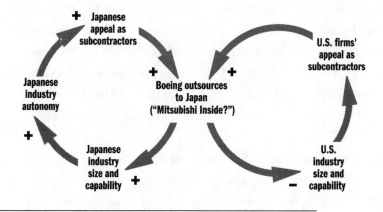

Figure 9.3. Boeing's Dependency Dynamics: Capability Outsourcing and Technological Dependency

example. To anticipate such possibilities, especially for slow-clockspeed industries, one must develop dynamic models and far-sighted incentive structures so that sourcing decisions will reflect the company's long-term interests.

The Dynamics of Core Competencies

A very simple diagram (figure 9.4) can be used to generalize this dynamic process and link three-dimensional concurrent engineering directly to core business strategy.[8] A company's existing capabilities constrain the set of projects that the enterprise can fruitfully under-take, but those capabilities also serve as the asset base upon which the company will build its next project. Project execution creates capabilities, which, in turn, permit launching successful projects. Every time a company makes a choice involving the development of a product, a process, or a supply chain relationship, that company is going to alter its set of capabilities. Thus, the set of capabilities within the organization influences the feasible set of product, process, or supply chain decisions available to the company at the next opportunity.

In a fast-clockspeed industry like consumer electronics, a company such as Dell or Sony launches new products on almost a monthly basis and thus has many opportunities to refine or modify its set of capabilities. However, since its competitors also have these frequent opportunities, the race for competitive advantage in capabilities plays itself out at a rapid pace. On the other end of the clockspeed spectrum, a company such as Boeing, Lockheed Martin, or Airbus has only a few opportunities *per decade* to launch a new project and adjust its set of capabilities.

Rather than looking upon core capabilities as immutable and undy-ing, we must see their duration as a function of the clockspeed for the entire industry or the relevant technology. Project selection and competency development go hand in glove. The goal is to concentrate on the elements of projects that maximize competitive advantage and assemble the chain accordingly.

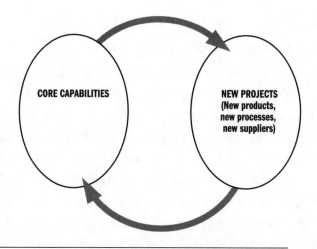

Figure 9.4. The Dynamic Interdependence of Capabilities and Projects for New Products, New Processes, and New Supply Chain Relationships[9]

Classes of Dependency

What are some of the reasons why a company seeks to outsource a process and leave the remainder to suppliers?[10] The classic reasons seem to be the following:

1. *Capability.* The company cannot make the item or easily acquire such a capability and must seek a supplier.

2. *Manufacturing competitiveness.* The supplier has lower costs or higher quality and can do the job faster, for what is presumably a directly substitutable item.

3. *Technology.* The supplier's version of the item is better for any of several possible reasons.

On the other hand, two important reasons for not seeking a supplier may be termed "strategic":[11]

1. *Competitive knowledge.* The item is crucial to the product's performance, or the skill in producing it has been judged basic to the company's technical memory.

2. *Customer visibility/market differentiation.* A company should make

what matters most to the customer or what differentiates the product in the marketplace; it should buy everything else.

This list can be condensed into two *categories of dependency:* dependency for *capacity* and dependency for *knowledge.*[12] In the dependent-for-capacity case, the company presumably could make the item in question and may indeed already do so, but for reasons of time, money, space, or management attention, it chooses to extend its capacity by means of a supplier. In the dependent-for-knowledge case, the company presumably needs the item but lacks the skill to make it; thus, it seeks an expert supplier to fill the gap. Between these two extremes lies a range of hybrid choices, but the extremes are useful for defining the issues. Table 9.1 illustrates the profound differences between Toyota's independence and dependence on certain suppliers relative to capacity and knowledge.

Table 9.1. Toyota's Sourcing and Strategy Choices

Toyota's sourcing and strategy choices	Independent for knowledge	Dependent for knowledge
Independent for capacity	ENGINES	RARE CASE
Dependent for capacity	TRANSMISSIONS	ELECTRONICS

Toyota designs, develops, and manufactures virtually 100 percent of the engines used in its vehicles. For its transmissions, Toyota designs all the products, but outsources the manufacture of 70 percent of the volume. Toyota depends heavily, however, on suppliers for design, development, and manufacture of its vehicle electronics systems.[13]

Toyota has often been recognized as an innovator and top performer in supply chain design and management as well as in using suppliers for "black-box" design.[14] The company seems to think strategically about which components and subsystems it retains inside, and which it outsources for capacity or design and development. Table 9.1 presents some examples of the variety of practice at Toyota. Two observations are notable: First, Toyota seems to vary its practice depending on the strategic role of the component or subsystem (for example, engines or transmissions); second, some of the decisions are based on historic judgments that may be reconsidered as circumstances change. For example, Toyota has historically relied heavily on Denso for the development and manufacture of electronic subsystems used in the vehicle. However, as electronics becomes more critical, both as a percentage of the total value of the vehicle and as an integrated element in both the design and the driver interface, Toyota seems to be moving toward developing internally a greater competency in electronics.[15]

Consider an example from the semiconductor industry. During much of the 1990s, Toshiba and Samsung, among others, manufactured DRAMs and bought manufacturing technology from Nikon. Among their purchases were photolithographic steppers, which, as discussed in chapter 5, sell for as much as $5 million apiece and are found by the dozen at both Toshiba and Samsung factories. The similarity, however, ends there. In terms of photolithography, Samsung is dependent on Nikon for both capacity and knowledge. Toshiba, while dependent on Nikon for capacity, is independent for knowledge by virtue of the "standing army" of photolithographic technologists the company employs.

What return does Toshiba get for its investment in this vast intellectual and technological capability? Perhaps Toshiba gets higher quality processes, faster volume ramp-ups, and a greater ability to judge the capabilities and technologies of its suppliers. However, to the extent that a less vertically integrated Samsung is nipping at Toshiba's heels in the DRAM market, the question arises how long Toshiba can afford to maintain its lithography capability. What advantage does it provide in terms of sales or profit advantage in its battle with the likes of Samsung? One possible answer was provided in chapter 5: Toshiba may have to choose between selling its knowledge to others (by going head-to-head against Nikon in stepper tools), or it may have to scale back its technological depth so it can compete on cost with Samsung.

A "Make versus Buy" Decision Analysis Matrix

The theory of make versus buy is complex because the issues are complex. There are no simple answers.[16] However, I believe that significant insight into the make versus buy issue can be gained from considering a four-dimensional matrix made up of four kinds of interdependencies:

- technological (integral versus modular)
- organizational (integral versus modular)
- intertemporal (clockspeed, cycling on the double helix)
- competitive (density of supplier base)

In the domain of technology, recall from chapter 8 the distinction between integral and modular product architectures. Product architectures determine the natural lines of decomposability into modular subsystems. Product decomposability is the artifact of technological interdependency that influences ease of outsourcing. In the realm of organizational interdependencies, consider the concepts introduced earlier in this chapter on dependence for knowledge and dependence for capacity. Finally, the double helix model of chapter 4 as well as the independence/dependence loops of this chapter describe intertemporal dependencies and the modeling of technological and organizational dynamics. Competitive interdependencies relate to how rich the supplier base is in a given capability. These four dimensions are introduced here in two stages.

First, let us examine the two-dimensional matrix of Fine and Whitney, as presented in figure 9.5:[17]

This matrix suggests how product architecture and outsourcing strategy interact. When a product has a modular architecture, it can

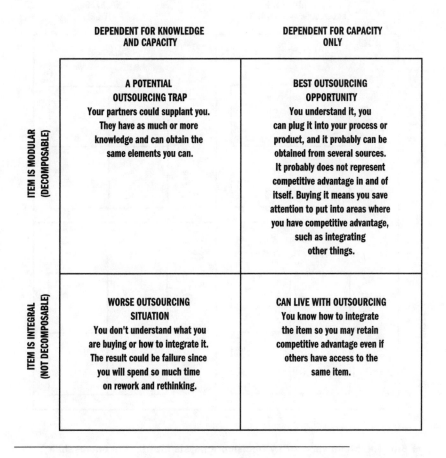

	DEPENDENT FOR KNOWLEDGE AND CAPACITY	DEPENDENT FOR CAPACITY ONLY
ITEM IS MODULAR (DECOMPOSABLE)	**A POTENTIAL OUTSOURCING TRAP** Your partners could supplant you. They have as much or more knowledge and can obtain the same elements you can.	**BEST OUTSOURCING OPPORTUNITY** You understand it, you can plug it into your process or product, and it probably can be obtained from several sources. It probably does not represent competitive advantage in and of itself. Buying it means you save attention to put into areas where you have competitive advantage, such as integrating other things.
ITEM IS INTEGRAL (NOT DECOMPOSABLE)	**WORSE OUTSOURCING SITUATION** You don't understand what you are buying or how to integrate it. The result could be failure since you will spend so much time on rework and rethinking.	**CAN LIVE WITH OUTSOURCING** You know how to integrate the item so you may retain competitive advantage even if others have access to the same item.

Figure 9.5. The Matrix of Organizational Dependency and Product Decomposability

typically be decomposed into subsystems (modules) that are relatively easy to outsource. If a company chooses to outsource both the manufacturing (dependent for capacity) and the design and development (dependent for knowledge) of such modular subsystems, the upper left quadrant of figure 9.5 suggests that such a decision might create the opportunity to be "held up" (that is, price gouged) by the supplier. Considering the upper left quadrant of figure 9.6, where clockspeed and supplier-industry concentration are also included, sharpens this

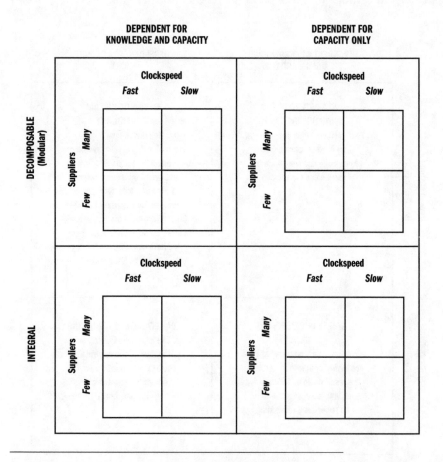

Figure 9.6. The Make versus Buy Decision Analysis Matrix: Decomposability, Dependency, Clockspeed, and Industry Competitiveness

intuition further. In particular, if the clockspeed is slow and the potential suppliers are numerous (for instance, windows and doors for houses or windshield wipers for cars), then outsourcing development and production may pose few strategic risks for the house builder or the car maker. Alternately, where clockspeeds are fast and potential suppliers are few (for instance, engine control systems for airplanes or cars), by outsourcing the modules the company may risk losing control of a key performance-determining subsystem.

For integral-architecture items, a similar reasoning applies. When suppliers are numerous and clockspeeds are slow, outsourcing poses fewer risks. However, since integral products are, by definition, difficult to decompose into subsystems, all outsourcing imposes challenges to maintain intensive communication and iteration among the various subsystem development teams. One early version of this model[18] was used by the North American Strategy Board of General Motors to classify every component of its vehicle systems by the degree of strategic importance and strategic outsourceability.

Toyota's 3-D Capability Development

Toyota is a master of capability development and utilization. Although it relies heavily on outsourcing, it also maintains world-class levels of expertise in all of the capabilities it deems critical in the chain. It executes very well a strategic make/buy policy on core capabilities complemented with continual capability upgrading in all three of the dimensions of product, process, and supply chain. Consider these experiences in process, product, and supply chain development that illustrate how Toyota continuously strengthens and deepens its capabilities.

Process development. In 1990, Toyota was heralded in *The Machine That Changed the World* as a lean producer par excellence, exceeding the manufacturing capabilities of every other automaker in the world.[19] The company could have easily rested on its laurels. But it didn't.

Not for a moment has Toyota stopped exploring and refining its production concepts and technology to anticipate and meet increasingly demanding requirements and competition.

Within half a decade, Toyota had launched four successive generations of its production process—the highly automated Tahara assembly plant in Toyota City, its Greenfield Kyushu plant in southern Japan, its widely heralded Motomachi plant renovation that, remarkably, added buffers to the system but improved productivity even more, and its Kentucky plant expansion in the United States.[20] As traced by Tokyo University Professor Takahiro Fujimoto, Toyota used each of its new plants to add to its continuous learning and improvement of the famed Toyota Production System.[21] Toyota has been both methodical and opportunistic in enhancing its production capabilities. Most important, the company seems to have been highly cognizant of the systematic process in which it was engaged.

Product development. Toyota's rapidly evolving product development process illustrates similar learning. In the early 1990s, Chrysler stunned its competitors with the astounding reductions in cost and time that it was able to squeeze out of the development and manufacturing process for its revolutionary Neon subcompact vehicle. The Japanese companies in particular, reeling from yen shock at the time, suffered a cold splash in the face. Their era of undisputed leadership in lean production seemingly had ended.

Toyota, however, wasted no time with hand wringing. In rapid succession, it introduced three major products—the redesigned Corolla, the all-new RAV4 mini sport-utility vehicle, and the redesigned Camry. Each of these vehicles set new standards for lean production, increasing the value to the customer. In an industry addicted to annual price increases, Toyota announced in 1996 a lower price for its newer, better Camry.

Capability chain development. Finally, consider the most subtle aspect of genetic engineering, capabilities-chain development. Some time ago, the *New York Times* reported the formation of a joint venture between a Toyota subsidiary and Texas Instruments to build a $1.5 billion semiconductor factory to make memory chips and automotive electronic components.[22] The article described Toyota's earlier moves into telecommunications and software and twice used the word "puzzling" to express the author's confusion over Toyota's strategy. To a corporate geneticist, those moves are anything but puzzling. The leading thinkers at Toyota seem to have studied the fruit flies, the fast-clockspeed electronics companies, and concluded that the auto industry may very well undergo the same structural shifts the electronics industry underwent during the last two decades. When this shift occurs, car companies may risk a fate similar to IBM's "Intel Inside" computers. Toyota, with the prescience afforded by the tools of three-dimensional concurrent engineering, is adjusting its capabilities-chain design strategy to position itself for the coming changes.

As Toyota is proving, managers have an enormous advantage over mere mortals: They have the power to design the genetic structure of their companies, to redesign it as often as necessary, and to accelerate the company's evolution, thereby enabling it to seize opportunity.

Because even Toyota cannot control everything through vertical integration, it must look to leverage along the chain and judicious selection of internal capabilities. As we have seen, every process, product, or service designed and manufactured in-house increases a company's intellectual inventory and its breadth of capabilities. Every piece an organization outsources provides the opportunity for a supplier to build capabilities. That's not to say that companies ought to shun outsourcing. But, as we saw, with the IBM PC, these decisions must be taken with careful consideration. Furthermore, even if one determines that certain key capabilities need to be outsourced, one needs to consider how contractual relationships with the supplier might be designed so as to retain for the company some of the control of those capabilities if they do indeed become significantly more valuable.

Returning to our original fruit fly, clearly IBM's decision to outsource key PC subsystems to Intel and Microsoft was a supply chain design decision with monumental consequences. Subsequent to this decision, IBM's market value fell by a staggering $90-plus billion as its domination of the computer industry screeched to a halt. However, even given the outsourcing decision, IBM had the opportunity, very early in the relationships, to own up to 30 percent of Intel's stock and 40 percent of Microsoft's stock. The company initially invested in Intel, purchasing 20 percent of its shares, but sold them (about a decade too early) at a profit of $625 million.[23] Taking full opportunity of the options to buy shares in these two companies would have netted IBM shareholders more than $100 billion, a missed second opportunity of striking proportions. Thus, we can conclude that outsourcing certain activities need not lead to disaster even if those outsourced activities turn out to be key levers in the value chain—provided the contractual relationship anticipates the opportunity.

The next chapter explores some of the tools for implementing 3-DCE; two additional examples of supply chain design and control are provided in chapter 11.

10 MOLECULAR MANIPULATION

The Engineer's Toolkit

To implement clockspeed concepts, you don't have to
blow up the organization and start over. You can
build on existing tools in the kit.

STIMULATED BY THE SUCCESS of superior Japanese manufacturing methods, many Western manufacturers in the 1980s worked overtime to benchmark remarkable companies such as Toyota and Sony. By the early 1990s, many had achieved a huge breakthrough in their understanding of competitive advantage through manufacturing. A large portion of the learning came under the heading of concurrent engineering (CE) or design for manufacturing (DFM). Managers realized that they could not achieve improved manufacturing performance solely, or even primarily, by concentrating on the factory; rather, they had to focus on concurrently designing the product and the manufacturing process— that is, designing the product for manufacturability.

Three-dimensional concurrent engineering (3-DCE) extends this concept from products and manufacturing to the concurrent design and development of capabilities chains. As discussed in chapter 8, product development, manufacturing, and supply chain management have traditionally been thought of as separate business processes. Some companies still think of them this way.

I recently attended a briefing by a senior executive of a Fortune 50 manufacturing company who stated that management had decreed that the corporation had four core business processes, among which were product development and supply chain management.

Such statements—and the implicit thinking about strategy that goes with them—make me uneasy. By declaring each a "core business process," management appears to have decided to separate product development and supply chain development. As I have argued in this book, however, 3-D concurrent engineering should be treated, both conceptually and operationally, as a *single, integrated capability,* rather than as three separate functions, one each for products, processes, and capabilities.

I am also convinced that supply chain design and development ought to be thought of as a *meta*-core competency—the competency of passing judgment on and choosing all other competencies and the strategies for competency development. This approach represents a radical rethinking of supply chain development and its role in business strategy. Furthermore, most managers realize that implementing new ideas into existing business processes can prove to be exceedingly challenging. The good news is that the implementation of clockspeed and 3-DCE ideas does not require radical surgery in organizational processes. This news should come as a relief for the many who have reengineered and been reengineered by managers who insist they must blow up their existing organizations in order to create necessary change.[1]

Instead of such a radical solution, even as an antidote to it, I advocate leveraging one basic organizational methodology, variously referred to as concurrent engineering, the product development process, design-build teams, or integrated product teams (IPTs), as the core of the implementation process for three-dimensional concurrent engineering.

The Product Development Process

Especially over the past decade, as clockspeeds in many industries have revved up, many more managers are recognizing the strategic importance of a firm's product development processes. In many industries, product development is the lifeblood of the company. Substantial investment in streamlining and shortening both the product's development time and its time-to-market has taken precedence over many other programs. Competitors with short development cycles and fast industry clockspeeds make a company's survival dependent on its ability to develop products and services rapidly.

As a rule of thumb, many managers assume that as much as 80 percent of life-cycle system design and manufacturing costs are fixed by decisions made during the product development process.[2] This decision making occurs often within the first 20 percent of the design-and-manufacturing life cycle of the product. Furthermore, the eventual product's quality, reliability, serviceability, and overall value as perceived by the customer are also determined at this early stage.

No wonder firms have increased their investment in better product development processes! A good portion of this investment has been directed toward concurrent engineering methods,[3] and their application in the context of the product development process.

In their book *Product Design and Development*, Karl Ulrich and Steven Eppinger present an enlightening table that illustrates the extreme range of complexity in developing manufactured products—from a Stanley Tools power screwdriver, which requires a development team (both internal and external) of about six people and a development budget of about $300,000, to a Boeing 777 aircraft, which requires tens of thousands of people and a budget approaching $6 billion.[4] Obviously, the organizational tools to be deployed in the screwdriver project would be hopelessly inadequate for developing a jet airplane, whereas the methods employed for the airplane would be hopelessly clumsy and bureaucratic for the screwdriver project. Steven Eppinger, Daniel Whitney, and their MIT students distinguish between what they call "product development in the small" and "product development in the large" to recognize the vast differences between projects such as the Stanley Works screwdriver and the Boeing aircraft.[5]

Where does one draw the line between small and large? If you can get the entire development team (including supply chain members) in a room frequently enough to manage the entire project in a face-to-face manner, then you are in the "small" situation. In contrast, if the team size and distance require communication with layers of organization or heavy use of interactive technology (for example, e-mail and videoconferencing), then you are in the "large" situation.

Most of the formal tools for managing product development projects are relevant conceptually for both small and large teams. However, small-team management can be much more informal about how the structures are used. The discussion in this chapter focuses primarily on "product development in the large," with occasional comments referring to the application to the far simpler case of "small" projects.

Tools for Product Development Management

For "product development in the large," the complexity of the project often exceeds the analytical capability of any single available tool or perspective. We have all heard the story about the blind men touching various parts of an elephant and trying to make inferences as to what the thing might be. One touches a foot; another, a tusk; another a trunk: Each one, isolated from the others, is mystified about the identity of the whole, until they confer over how the separate pieces produce a solution to the puzzle.

"Product development in the large" requires a similar effort, plus a set of tools, or "lenses," that afford multiple viewing angles from which to gain an appreciation of the entity in all its complexity. A number of tools from multiple perspectives exist for two-dimensional concurrent engineering to support this process, including the various perspectives defined by DFM, project scheduling, design structure, process bottleneck, and customer requirements.

The development process for large products such as automobiles and airplanes is extremely complex. No single tool exists, at present, to address comprehensively the intricacies involved in an automobile development project, for example. Rather, a suite of tools is required. A car development project has to design a product, a process, and a supply chain with staggering complexity: production volumes of up to 1,000 per day, each vehicle comprising over 10,000 parts furnished by thousands of suppliers arrayed in multiple tiers, and production processes utilizing scores of different manufacturing processes and tens of thousands of workers. Managers of "product development in the large" face the challenge of the blind men touching various parts of the elephant: Each has an intimate familiarity with the part or process immediately at hand, but it is very tough to put all the details together in a comprehensive whole.

In this chapter, I describe a number of the tools and perspectives that are productively employed for piecing together the elephant. I describe them both as they currently exist and as they may be extended to focus on supply chain issues and therefore three-dimensional concurrent engineering. In what follows, I will examine five "lenses" to help see the elephant in its totality:

• design for manufacturability (DFM)

• project scheduling

• design structure

• process bottlenecks

• customer requirements

Each of these tools is rich in supporting the management of product development, but will render an incomplete picture if you try to use it alone. The chapter closes with additional suggestions for managing product development and 3-DCE from the vantage point of the combined power of these perspectives.

Design for Manufacturability (DFM)

Much of the benchmarking efforts in the 1980s yielded a near-consensus among American manufacturers that design for manufacturing and its twin, concurrent engineering of product and process, were far superior to throwing the product designs "over the wall." You can come up with the greatest design imaginable for a new product or service, but if you merely throw it over the wall to your production team, they may not have the skills or resources to actually manufacture it. It's hard to imagine anyone ever intentionally creating a dysfunctional process and tossing products over the wall, but it's not atypical for successful companies to grow so rapidly that they do not keep a close eye out for their transition from product development "in the small" to that "in the large."

In a small company, everyone on the product and process development team can meet regularly in the same room. "Can we manufacture this product?" is a question that team members could raise informally, and they could thrash through many of the production issues in an afternoon. As the company grows and expands its production lines, product and process developers move to different departments, different buildings, even different continents. Geographical distance is one challenge to overcome, but more important is the need for more formal approaches to reconcile design-for-product performance with the realities of manufacturability.

In the 1980s, Boothroyd and Dewhurst became well known for their design-for-assembly (DFA) tools for systematically analyzing manufacturability issues in assembly processes.[6] Their work provided "design rules" to help product designers avoid creating designs that were too difficult to build or assemble. In addition, they provided analytic tools to estimate how much it would cost to design and assemble a new product. Later, Ulrich and others pointed out that product development managers needed to assess both assembly and fabrication, as well as both costs and lead time.[7] While researchers added other considerations to the mix, such as designing products that could be upgraded and easily serviced, Boothroyd and Dewhurst broke new ground in design for assembly or manufacturing. The tools they developed have helped managers better understand product development "in the large."

Lee and Billington go beyond this classical approach to DFM, adding supply chain issues into design for postponed customization. They describe a case at the Hewlett-Packard Company (HP), which serves as an excellent example of how the design for supply chain cost can be integrated into concurrent engineering.[8] For the European market HP manufactured printers designed with a modular power supply unit that could be customized once customers specified what kind of power supply they needed. This customization design not only reduced HP's inventory costs for that line of printers but also dramatically improved customer service, since customers no longer had to wait as long to receive a printer with a special power unit.

Similarly, in the semiconductor industry, Intel has begun to work aggressively with its equipment suppliers to encourage design for maintainability and serviceability.[9] Depending on the circumstances, Intel may service the product, or the work may be done by the original equipment manufacturer or by a third party. This example suggests other ways that supply chain design can interact with product and process design.

Project Scheduling

Probably the most commonly used tool in product development management today is the project scheduling activity chart, known in some circles as PERT (Project Evaluation Review Technique) or CPM (Critical Path Method) or sometimes as PERT/CPM.[10] This tool arrays graphically and sequentially all of the activities required for a project's completion with data on expected completion time and precedence: What activities must precede other activities to develop a "critical path" for the project? The path one follows through these activities is "critical" in that any delay along the path will delay the entire project. Many product development managers use this tool as their primary lever for managing and controlling the project's schedule.

Typically, when a supplier has an essential role, its activity is represented in both the manufacturer's model and its own complex CPM model. What the customer actually sees, however, is only a single activity for the supplier's completed contribution. The supplier's failure to meet the project manager's schedule may come as a rude shock to the customer who has not planned for such a contingency. Toyota, for example, had such a problem with a number of its North American suppliers during the product development and launch process for the 1997 Camry.[11] Late in the program, Toyota received the bad news that suppliers could not meet the schedule requirements. As a result, the automaker had to move into emergency mode and have the items shipped from Japanese suppliers—at a much greater cost. The "map" represented by the CPM model traces the route from point X to point Y, but it doesn't always tell you how to get around the places where the road has fallen down the mountainside.

By taking the supplier's map, one that shows every activity in the production process, and incorporating it into the customer's map, you can avoid many of the risks and delays inherent in any supply chain. This view into the supplier's production can help you monitor those processes more closely and gain some control over the supplier's ability to fulfill promises. In the case of Toyota, the automaker went a step further and developed a software domain where the technical development work of a supplier in North America could be observed and tightly integrated with the development work of the Toyota engineers in Japan, in effect substituting electronic proximity for geographic proximity in the supply chain.

This is not micromanaging. It is good business practice that takes advantage of information technology that increases our knowledge of and participation in those items essential to our own product development. We should note, however, that such assessments of a supplier's process capability to meet schedule are often possible when the customer is dependent on the supplier only for capacity, but less so if that customer is dependent for knowledge as well.[12]

Design Structure

The design structure perspective has been championed and refined by MIT professor Steven Eppinger, who, with students and colleagues, has built a suite of tools around the design structure matrix (DSM), a diagramming tool for capturing the structure of projects that require many tasks.[13] To construct a DSM, you arrange tasks in a square array that permits task relations to be recorded at various intersections in the diagram. Unlike the Critical Path Method, the matrix can capture iteration, the need to revisit designs and decisions as new information becomes available. The DSM is especially good at highlighting project tasks that are tightly coupled—for example, designing and refining components for a highly integral product design.

Figure 10.1 illustrates the basic DSM tool with a simple example.[14] The process proceeds in two steps, represented respectively by the matrices on the left and right side. The first step is to list all the major activities required in the product development process along both the top and the left side. In the figure, these activities are represented by the letters *A* through *L*. For each row, an × is placed in all columns

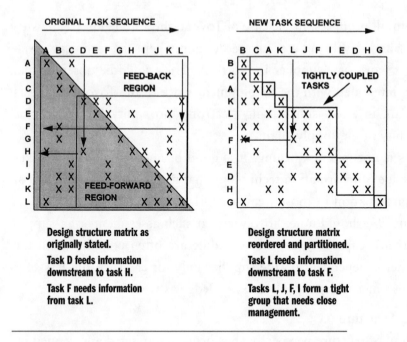

ORIGINAL TASK SEQUENCE

NEW TASK SEQUENCE

Design structure matrix as originally stated.

Task D feeds information downstream to task H.

Task F needs information from task L.

Design structure matrix reordered and partitioned.

Task L feeds information downstream to task F.

Tasks L, J, F, I form a tight group that needs close management.

Figure 10.1. Design Structure Matrix for Representing Complex Design Tasks and Seeking a More Efficient Design Process[17]

that have an activity that produces information required for the completion of the activity in that row. On the left side of the matrix, for example, activity E requires information from itself as well as from activities F, H, and K before it can be completed. Gathering information for a large project presents a challenging task, which many organizations are not prepared for, as we have found in several studies of development projects for industrial products.[15]

The DSM matrix also recognizes that some activities are likely to be interdependent. For example, in an airplane development project, the engine specifications are likely to be dependent on the passenger capacity, whereas the passenger capacity will, in turn, be dependent on the available engine power. Such an interdependency is represented in the DSM by having each of these activities receive an × in the row of the other. Once this data is collected for all activities, the activities are resequenced by the DSM ordering algorithm,[16] and the activities are ordered in the most managerially useful sequence.

The resequenced matrix is shown on the right side of figure 10.1. Because activity B has no predecessors, it should be undertaken first, then followed by activity C, which has only B as a predecessor. After C, activities A and K may be undertaken simultaneously and independently. After activities A and K are completed, activities L, J, F, and I should be undertaken simultaneously in a highly interactive, concurrent, and iterative manner. The grouping in a single box tells us that these four activities are highly interdependent. High levels of interactive communication are likely to be needed for completion of this set of activities.

An × appearing high in the upper right corner of the resequenced matrix (in row A, column H, for example) indicates that iteration back to the beginning is required fairly late in the process. You might think of a situation as representing one very large box such as the one containing L, J, F, and I, but often it is impractical and defeats the purpose of deconstructing the project to treat every activity from A to H in the right-hand matrix as one large concurrent subproject. Rather, when such instances occur, they represent the need to revisit decision A, in this case to confirm the absence of a major problem. For example, in an automobile development project, suppose A represents the target value for total mass of the vehicle, a design parameter chosen early in the project. Late in the project return to A to check, once all the other components have been developed, that the target mass has, in fact, not been exceeded.

When General Motors developed the Oldsmobile Aurora, one of a new generation of luxury cars in the company's fleet, the engineers determined fairly late in the process that the car (as initially developed) was too heavy to give the performance they desired. However, the solution to this problem this late in the project was not to go over every component, shaving off an ounce here, a pound there. Because the problem occurred very late in the Aurora project, engineers did not revisit each item. Rather, they returned immediately to activity "A," assessed the problem, and made one major change: They manufactured the hood out of aluminum rather than steel, thereby shaving many pounds off the design in one (not inexpensive) decision.

This may seem a simplistic example with an "obvious" solution. However, in an actual development project "in the large," a useful DSM has hundreds of activities. Identifying when iteration is most useful, when activities should be done in sequence or in parallel, and when overlapping activities are usefully grouped into one, tightly coupled, concurrent subproject is virtually impossible without a design structure matrix.

As Steven Eppinger, Daniel Whitney, and their students at MIT have demonstrated repeatedly, DSMs can be used successfully in industries ranging from automobiles to semiconductors, for both product development and concurrent product and process development projects.[18] To extend the DSM tool to supply chain development is not conceptually difficult, but it does demand the same kind of effort required in building a DSM for a product development project. In particular, for suppliers whose contributions are critical to the project under consideration, you should expand the DSM to include those suppliers' activities as though they were seamlessly a part of your overall project. Once you complete your analysis (that is, you compute the matrix on the right side of figure 10.1), the degree, timing, and type of interaction required with each supplier become all the more evident. If a supplier's activities bunch up in a box like that of activities L, J, F, and I in figure 10.1, then that supplier can work fairly independently once the necessary preceding activities have been completed. If, however, one supplier's activities are tightly intertwined with those of your project or those of another supplier, you will be able to see this logjam at a glance. At that point, you can begin to coordinate the activities of the suppliers in order to avoid as much of the jam as possible. If you see a high degree of inter-dependence, you may want to rethink whether outsourcing such an integral subproject continues to make sense.

Process Bottlenecks

The critical path method and the design structure matrix are designed for and applied primarily to the analysis of a single engineering proj-ect. Often, each project within a company is managed by its own project manager, not infrequently a *heavyweight* project manager, as suggested by the lean production paradigm,[19] who may have a great deal of autonomy in managing his or her project, using tools such as CPM and DSM. In such cases, however, there are often resources in the firm that must be shared across multiple projects. For example, in a semiconductor design house, the prototype manufacturing facility is often shared across all the design projects. In an automotive company, the clay model shop, where models of the concept vehicles are made, is typically shared by the designers in various divisions, each of which is working on its own projects.

The process bottleneck perspective, explored in work by research teams at MIT and Stanford,[20] reconceptualizes the product develop-ment function as analogous to a factory for product development. Instead of focusing on the activities and relationships within the CPM or DSM model for each project, the process bottleneck approach focuses on the resources to be used by all the projects. These resources collectively represent the firm's product development factory. Applying the concepts from Goldratt's "theory of constraints," which states that all factories have a bottleneck (or "constraint") resource,[21] one then looks for the constraint resources in the company's product development "factory."

In the product development context, when multiple projects com-pete for bottleneck resources, each must wait in queue for its turn to access the constraint capacity. Managing these queues and the relative demand versus supply of capacity at them typically has an enormous impact on the development time of the individual projects. In one study at Polaroid, for example, individual projects under the direction of several project managers working separately were often completed many months, or even years, later than scheduled in the CPM models.[22] Our analysis, using the process bottleneck perspective, concluded that these models had ignored in their calculations the large chunks of time that projects waited for an opportunity to be serviced by the scarce bottleneck resources. Once top management realized that someone in the organization below the level of CEO needed to "own the process" of assessing the capacity levels of various product development resources, the knowledge was available to reduce project completion times significantly.

As important as this insight and accompanying analysis is, its power can be increased by applying it to an integrated 3-DCE framework. In many development projects, supplier contributions can be the bottlenecks. These suppliers serve a large number of projects, sometimes more than one from the same customer. Adding key suppliers as resources in the model and, for those who may be bottlenecks, then managing them as carefully as internal bottlenecks are managed, can have a huge impact on total project time and performance.

In a research project at General Motors, we analyzed one of the key bottlenecks for the entire vehicle development process: the provision of stamping dies, large steel tools that provide the shape for all stamped metal body parts.[23] Within die development at GM, outsourcing was allowed (by union contract) only if the internal die development capacity was utilized at 100 percent. Individual vehicle program managers typically found that external suppliers provided dies much faster than the internal shop, but managers were not generally allowed to go outside to other sources. Meanwhile, since the corporate directives loaded the internal capabilities to full capacity, the throughput and delivery times were very high because of the long queues that occurred in the internal operation. By including the supplier capacity in a three-dimensional analysis, we were able to demonstrate how the combined internal and supplier capability could explain and eventually improve performance.

Customer Requirements

To be successful, all product development projects need a heavy dose of external reality. Any product whose development does not capture the "voice of the customer" begins life with a huge, frequently fatal handicap. Although this principle seems obvious, many engineering organizations with product development responsibility get so excited about their whiz-bang science and technology that they often neglect to confirm with their intended customers what features and attributes are actually viewed as desirable and worth paying for.

The best-known tool for the customer requirements perspective in product development is Quality Function Deployment (QFD),[24] another import from Japan that came to the West during the great wave of immigration of Japanese management thinking in the 1980s. One of its early proponents and exponents in the United States was Don Clausing of Xerox, later at MIT.[25] QFD offers a tool called the "house of quality," a name derived from the analytical diagram that resembles a box with a slant roof. It offers a high-level overview of a range of issues in customer-driven product development, including identification of key product features, relation of these features to perceived customer requirements, identification of product technologies for their delivery, and assessment of competing products.

Two related tools, concept engineering and key characteristics, have grown out of the QFD and customer requirements perspective to add more depth to the house-of-quality approach for integrating formally and systematically the voice of the customer into the product development process.

Concept Engineering

Concept engineering[26] is a structured process, with supporting decision aids, for developing product concepts by a product development team.[27] The process alternates between the level of thought (reflection) and the level of experience (data) in a way that allows participants to understand what is important to the customer, why it is important, how it will be measured, and how it will be addressed in the product concept. As presented in figure 10.2, concept engineering has five stages, each with three steps.[28]

Stage 1: Understanding the Customer's Environment

In stage 1, the team develops empathy for the customer in the actual use environment of the product or service. Images of the customer's use environment are selected and analyzed with a KJ diagram.[29] This "Image KJ" visually and verbally links the product concept to the customer's real world and provides the product development team members a common map to help visualize the customer's environment to help with the product concept decisions.

Stage 2: Converting Understanding into Requirements

Stage 2 distills a small set of well-understood, carefully articulated, critical requirements for the customer. The customer's language, often laden with subjective wording, is converted into an objective, fact-oriented requirement statement better suited for use in downstream development activities. A small set of the vital few requirements, taken from the useful many, is selected. The relationships among them are then analyzed.

Stage 3: Operationalizing What Has Been Learned

In stage 3, the team validates the customer's key requirements, operationally defined in measurable terms, and displays them so that the relationships among requirements, metrics, and customer feedback are easily seen.

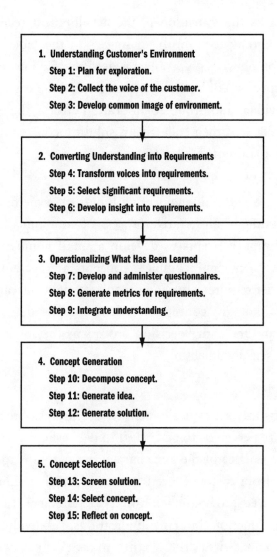

Figure 10.2. The 5 Stages and 15 Steps of Concept Engineering

Stage 4: Concept Generation

This stage marks the transition in the development team's thinking from the "requirement or problem space" to the "idea or solution space." The complex design problem is decomposed into subproblems based on perspectives of both the customers and the design engineers. Through individual and group collaboration efforts, the team creates first individually, and then collectively, solution concepts from which the final design concept will be developed.

Stage 5: Concept Selection

The final stage of concept engineering builds on a method known as "concept selection,"[30] an iterative process of combining and improving initial solution concepts to develop a small number of superior concepts. The "surviving" complete concepts are evaluated in detail against customer requirements and organizational constraints in order to select the dominant concept(s). When completed, an audit trail exists for tracing the entire decision process as the concept engineering process is self-documenting.

Key Characteristics

Key characteristics[31] are typically defined as features of the product or process that are perceived to be critical to delivering value to the final customer. The essence of the key characteristics tool is to flow down requirements, from customer needs to manufacturing requirements to support those needs, to manufacturability requirements to support the manufacturing function. In many applications, subdividing these into product key characteristics (PKCs), manufacturing key characteristics (MKCs), and assembly key characteristics (AKCs) has proved to be useful.[32] PKCs are associated with the important properties of the product that create customer satisfaction. MKCs are associated with the manufacturing processes that create the detail level PKCs. AKCs are those features required to support assembly (or manufacturability) of the product. Figure 10.3 illustrates how product, manufacturing, and assembly are related.[33]

At the far left of the diagram is the final product delivered to the customer, including those PKCs or features he or she desires. MKCs are the features of the manufacturing system that are required to deliver the PKCs from the factory to the product. Thus MKCs flow from the PKCs. On the right side of figure 10.3 are the AKCs, those features that support assembly and manufacturability of the product.

MKCs support the manufacturing organization's delivery of special product features. For example, if a customer wants a disk drive in her laptop PC that holds ten gigabytes of data (the PKC), then certain manufacturing tolerances (MKCs) must be achieved in the disk-making technology to make such a product feasible. AKCs, on the other hand, are features directed toward design for assembly. For example, if the disk drive has features that allow it to snap-fit directly

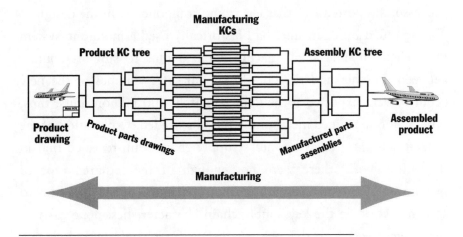

Figure 10.3. The Relationship among Product, Manufacturing, and Assembly: Key Characteristics

into the laptop frame, assembly is less costly and less prone to defects than it would be if the design relied on screws for the assembly process.

The key characteristics approach supports a range of decisions within the product and process development process, including feature choice, detailed product design, and equipment choice. The 3-DCE approach pushes firms to extend this tool to include supplier key characteristics (SKCs) by flowing the requirements outside of the customer's firm into the value chain. The key characteristics tool can be used to help identify key features on supplied subsystems, key capabilities in suppliers' factories, and key components from the suppliers' supply chains.

For example, consider what happened to a product design at Intel when the company included supply chain issues in a 3-DCE effort. As Intel has worked to add more functionality to its products, the company has planned expansion of the features of the key product from a stand-alone microprocessor to a circuit board with a mounted microprocessor supported by other electronic components. In the design of the expanded product, Intel had historically used a mounting system that relied on nine small machined metal pins to support contact between the chip and the board. Annual sales volumes of the new product were expected to be approximately 100 million units; thus, 900 million machined metal pins would be needed. Exploration of the capacity characteristics by Intel's supply chain team revealed that in the entire world there were not enough of the required type of machine tools for making 900 million machined pins![34] Needless to say, this work on the key supply chain characteristics, done early in the design process so that the product features could be redesigned, prevented what could have been a disaster for one of Intel's key product launches.

The Growing Importance of CE Tools

Many of these product development management tools do not have household names. Historically they have been part of engineering project managers' purview, not that of general business unit managers. Let me suggest three reasons, however, why *all* managers need to become more familiar with this toolkit.

1. The increasing clockspeeds in our economy are forcing firms to launch products more frequently. As a result, a larger fraction of the total work in the firm is project work.[35] In effect, then, the business manager becomes a project manager or an overseer of project managers for a larger fraction of his or her job and career. The premium paid for project management skills and tools is thus likely to increase.

2. Those faster clockspeeds are also forcing companies to compress their product development cycles. One important strategy for cycle compression is to perform historically sequential activities in parallel. Concurrent engineering accomplishes this goal. Thus, more companies are finding that concurrency is a necessity and that more managers will have to learn concurrent engineering tools.

3. When one comes to view supply chain design as the competency of choosing all other competencies, then supply chain design becomes the purview of senior management. However, once one understands the inseparability among supply chain architecture, process architecture, and product architecture, greater communication between senior strategists and project managers becomes essential. As a result, all will need to understand the tools of product development management in order to have a common language with which to discuss issues and solve problems related to the product, process, and supply chain architectures.

To illustrate the use of these tools in more detail, the next chapter cites two actual cases, both moving at fast clockspeeds within their industries. Both the Patient Monitoring Division of Hewlett-Packard's Medical Products Group and Teledesic's project for launching a constellation of hundreds of satellites to provide an "Internet in the sky" demonstrate the power of concurrent engineering to develop capabilities, not at the expense of profits, but actually in ways that enhance profits.

11 GENETIC ENGINEERING IN A FAST-CLOCKSPEED WORLD

Building Capabilities through Dynamic
3-D Concurrent Engineering

The ultimate competency is the ability to create and manage new capabilities while growing profits and adjusting to ever-faster clockspeeds.

HAVING DESCRIBED BOTH THE THEORY AND the tools of three-dimensional concurrent engineering, I offer in this chapter two cases to illustrate how a 3-DCE analysis can guide managers in making complex decisions in a fast-clockspeed world. The Patient Monitoring Division (PMD) of Hewlett-Packard's Medical Products Group, headquartered in Andover, Massachusetts, exemplifies how the clockspeed and 3-DCE frameworks, together with the make/buy models of chapter 9, can help managers design an appropriate strategy in response to a shift along the double helix from integral to modular. In the second example, we see how a project team at Teledesic employed 3-DCE to support development in its ambitious plan to launch an "Internet-in-the-sky," a plan to create a constellation of 288 satellites that will ultimately provide Internet access from any point on the globe. In both cases, the fast or increasing clockspeeds mandate the use of *dynamic* 3-D analysis: Current decisions not only must be coherent across the three dimensions, they must also anticipate the changes in store for later generations of decisions makers.

Hewlett-Packard's Patient Monitoring Division

The Medical Products Group of the Hewlett-Packard Company (HP) provides clinical measurement and information solutions, as well as services and support, for the health-care industry.[1] In fiscal year 1996, the group employed 5,300 people worldwide and had revenues of $1.4 billion. Within this group, the Patient Monitoring Division (PMD) offers a variety of products that collect and process patient data in acute care settings, particularly in hospitals. These products include sensors and monitors, clinical information systems, and information management tools, which enable people and machines to monitor and analyze signals from patients—in an acute care setting or in some other location. For example, using a central station, a nurse might identify something unusual about a patient's heart rhythm, or the tool itself would sound an alarm if there were some abnormality. The nurse, then, would contact a cardiologist, who could access the data on a computer display in his or her office, make a diagnosis, and prescribe a treatment.

The Patient Monitoring Industry

Historically, the patient monitoring industry has been rather slow moving and conservative. Major customers—for example, clinicians, physicians, and hospital administrators—are unwilling to risk patients' lives on unproved technologies. In addition, patient monitoring systems represent a major capital investment and have to remain in use for up to ten years or longer. On the other hand, because the technology level is high and continually changing, the systems tend to have very short product life cycles; indeed, some components within PMD's products may themselves have life cycles of fewer than six months. Furthermore, because HP's medical information management tools are largely computational, the company can enjoy much faster increases in capability with minimal product redesign by using industry standard computation and data handling hardware.

PMD's customer base comprises both independent hospitals and conglomerates that may own many clinics and hospitals. Because many independents often do not have sophisticated information technology support staff, they are more likely to need and be willing to pay for HP's full-service approach to medical systems delivery. Many conglomerates, however, have information technology departments for managing every aspect of hardware and software within their facilities. Such capabilities give these companies significant bargaining power against HP. These larger institutions are driving a shift toward modularity in patient data management products because they are less willing to pay for components they do not need or integration they prefer to do themselves.

The supply chain for patient data management products has three major segments: customizing the hardware, integrating the software, and configuring and testing it. Customizing hardware consists of installing proprietary hardware extensions, such as the proprietary network card, as well as doing some modification of the hardware itself (for example, removing a PC's speaker volume control). Integrating the software involves loading the operating system, specialized hardware drivers, and the application software in a generic form. In the configuration stage, PMD customizes the software for the customer's specific applications, enabling the options that the customer has purchased, and testing the configured system to ensure that it is functioning properly.

All three links are interdependent. Not only are they sequentially dependent, but they have special technical requirements that make it difficult to source the hardware or configure systems to a customer's specifications. And if the standard hardware exhibits even slight variations, the proprietary hardware and software may not function properly. Before the management of this supply chain can be outsourced, the integration and test processes must be made more tolerant to hardware variation and more simple and self-contained.

HP's information management tools are not easy to build with industry standard hardware. Because these instruments must function in life-and-death situations, it is critical that the software perform without flaw all the time. The reputations of both health-care providers and Hewlett-Packard cannot afford a malfunction of one of these tools in an acute care setting. Known for its high-quality products and manufacturing, Hewlett-Packard's PMD must be as concerned about having somebody else's product "inside" as any company that decides to resort to outsourcing.

Complicating the picture is the fact that PMD is a small user of computing hardware, compared to giants such as Compaq and Dell. In fact, PMD's volume never exceeds 10 percent of its primary hardware supplier's total. Thus, it has limited clout to control the hardware it receives. Although suppliers are often willing to help when problems arise, they will not freeze hardware configurations for PMD's benefit at the volumes PMD requires.

Finally, there is the bundling problem. Throughout the 1990s most medical monitoring systems have been sold for a single price as a *bundled* package: hardware, software, and services. PMD has used bundling to offer its monitoring software fully integrated into hardware, and fully customized and configured to the customer's specifications. Another division provides installation services (bundled into the sales price), completing a turnkey solution for HP's customers.

Bundling offers several advantages over separate sales arrangements: It gives a company like HP complete control of the product and the implementation of the design, in accordance with Good Manufacturing Practices. Many customers, unable or unwilling to integrate the solution on their own, prefer everything from soup to nuts with a single price: They receive the system, the software, delivery, an invoice, and an installation team. What's more, HP uses its reputation as a great single-source vendor as a core competitive advantage for PMD.

HP will probably continue to provide turnkey solutions to at least some of its customers for a long time to come. And some of those systems can be built from unbundled, modular components. However, the unbundling of medical software solutions seems an inevitable consequence of market forces along the double helix. Those forces will eventually force PMD to offer unbundled software solutions. Customers will be able to purchase software only or combinations of software and hardware and services as they see fit. A number of forces are contributing to this change:[2]

- Savvy customers know that they can source and install standard hardware more cheaply than can HP's field organization.

- Once customers can easily identify the hardware components and price them out themselves, the value perceived in the bundle may be reduced below HP's delivered cost, so the software will need to be priced separately. Some customers will demand that they be allowed to integrate and install software themselves, on their own hardware.

- To the extent that providing a turnkey solution is HP's competitive advantage, competitors can diminish that advantage by shifting customer expectations toward unbundled products, provided that their prices and quality are at least as good as HP's. Competitors may be able to increase perceived value by offering exactly the components that customers want at better prices.

Once the hardware and the execution of integration processes become commodities, the future dominant capabilities in the patient data monitoring industry will be robust software development and integration process development. PMD will eventually find itself in a modular industry, and it should attempt to control the most important capabilities within it. Exactly when customers will demand the ability to buy software only is not clear, but experts at HP's marketing and product development department suggest the change will occur within five years at most.[3] However, PMD must begin the process of preparing for life in a modular world.

Because of the different market segments, PMD will have to offer both bundled turnkey solutions and unbundled software in the future. The eventual unbundling of software from hardware will necessitate several changes within PMD. Because HP will not be part of the integration and installation processes in all cases, PMD must begin to develop simplified processes and procedures for building its products so that at installation time HP's specialized expertise is no longer required.

Product Competence

Most important, HP must be sure that the final product works and performs adequately to ensure the patient's safety. In an unbundled environment, HP has less direct control over the integration of its products, and liability risks will increase for instances in which processes are not performed properly. HP will require a way to control that liability in carefully written contracts, "idiot-proof" tests for product quality which are easily executed and assessed, and methods for auditing customer use of the system.

For its part, PMD must maintain some process and some product competencies with regard to its tools for managing patient information, but only those that add unique value; others should be considered for outsourcing. Product competence is likely to be in the design of the product, not in its assembly.

PMD's hardware must be reliable and fast, able to handle the load placed on it by the software and the people who use it. By using industry standard hardware, PMD is eliminating the value in hardware competence, and hardware is increasingly becoming a commodity.

PMD's software, however, has to perform an ever-increasing variety of functions without fail. To avoid putting patients at risk, the software must not overload the hardware, yet it must recognize when it has done so (or failed in some other way). New data analysis algorithms and new features for users are the primary sales drivers of these products. That is why the software is the primary product competence. This was not the case a couple of product generations back, but PMD made the decision that designing new hardware was not the most efficient way to get functionality to the market.

Process Competence

Process competence resides in a provider's execution capabilities and in the design of its demand fulfillment processes. HP's process competence in patient data management tools lies in manufacturing, testing, delivery, and installation processes. However, HP's unique and non-outsourceable process skills reside in the development of these processes and in customer management.

As a leader in the medical products industry, HP Medical must have process development and control as core competencies. PMD's relationship with the supervising regulatory agency—in this case, the Food and Drug Administration (FDA)—relies on that control. If we remove process control and customer order management processes from the picture, the remainder of the integration processes are arguably non-core; they are also becoming commodity processes.

Because the delivery processes currently performed by HP will be performed in the future by customers or by third-party providers, either within or outside HP Medical, PMD will not have complete control over the execution of the processes it designs. Therefore, those processes must be more robust in order to provide similar value. Products will no doubt cost more, but it is not a cost that customers will want to pay. To stay competitive, then, HP must depend on its ability to design implementation processes whose increase in cost is less than the perceived increased value customers see in the unbundled software product. This perceived increase in value is likely to be small, particularly if multiple competitors are offering unbundled software products; thus, low-cost HP process development capability is crucial to its leadership position in the patient data management market.

Selection of Core Competencies

If we apply the matrix of outsourcing and decomposability concept to HP (see figure 9.5), we immediately recognize a problem with the outsourcing that PMD has already undertaken: PMD has voluntarily become dependent for hardware capacity and partially dependent for knowledge for its industry standard hardware. While PMD's engineers understand hardware very well, they have chosen not to maintain a deep skill set in the computational heart of the hardware they buy; that is, they could not themselves design the hardware they use. To the extent that the product is still integral, they would be in the "worst outsourcing situation"; if it is modular, they still would be in a "potential trap."

However, as PMD has decided to build products with industry-standard hardware, it has also driven the hardware portion of the product toward modularity. It is working to make the hardware entirely interchangeable within a limited set of product specifications. In reference to figure 9.5, PMD is moving out of the lower left quadrant and into the upper left as it reduces its software's dependence on its hardware. Pointing to further disintegration, the decision model says that the upper left quadrant is not much better than the lower left, but in PMD's case it can be considered a safe haven. Safety comes through being a small part of a big commodity market.

If we add the number of suppliers to dependence and modularity in the matrix (see figure 9.6), we see that dependence on an industry is less dangerous than dependence on a single supplier. Computer hardware is becoming a commodity industry in which many players offer substantially the same product. As long as the software works on many hardware products, PMD is less susceptible to holdup because of its ability to change suppliers. This condition makes the robustness of software to hardware variation a strategic sourcing issue, one that overshadows the current cost considerations.

Hardware manufacture, software development, integration, delivery, and customer management are very different links in the capability chain. If HP becomes dependent for knowledge on a critical piece of the capability chain, the decision model implies that HP can expect to lose its position in the market if and when the owner of the critical piece exercises its newfound strength. PMD already outsources hardware manufacture, and the risk is controlled. If the division maintains control over software development and customer management, it can control the risks in outsourcing integration and delivery. If HP outsources its software development indiscriminately, then it is reasonable to expect that eventually the designers of the critical software components could go into the medical information management business for themselves.

If PMD retains all of its hardware sourcing capabilities in-house, it will have a large investment in technical skills on the hardware platform currently in use. There will be a number of technical applications built for software load and integration that rely on the current generation of components. As the best architecture for the product changes, HP may be reluctant to scrap that investment to stay on the cutting edge.

PMD also has management structures, metrics, and processes established to manage a hardware handling business. These systems will not serve PMD as well when it must ship unbundled, software-only products. Customer-oriented metrics will clearly shift, for example, toward ease of installation and use, less toward delivered cost. If PMD defines itself primarily based on its hardware handling capabilities, it may find itself in a software world, without the nimbleness it needs to address customer needs.

Implications for PMD

Because PMD needs to focus on only the most important capabilities for the future and because the smallest future value will lie in hardware handling, PMD should retain control over the software product competence (including competence in maximizing robustness) and process development, while outsourcing hardware assembly and integration. This strategy will allow PMD to focus resources where value will be most concentrated.

One could reasonably argue, however, that since PMD has a significant lead over its competitors in product and process technology, perhaps PMD should leave the product and market intact while it is still achieving high margins on its products. After all, the market moves fairly slowly, and PMD should have time to get to the next product paradigm before it is forced to. Why should PMD hasten the demise of a profitable structure?

The response to this argument depends on one's view of the clockspeed in medical monitoring. If one believes that product life cycles will continue to be up to ten years, then the only response is one of long-term strategy and an appeal to PMD's vision, which would suggest that advancing the industry and the quality of patient monitoring in general is good independent of short-term profits. Many others believe, however, that the move to industry-standard hardware will increase the clockspeed in patient data management products. In this environment, PMD's best chance to stay on top of the industry is by being first to market with fully unbundled solutions. Furthermore, HP should begin the process well before the market demands unbundled solutions. The transition will take time, particularly if PMD follows a conservative transition plan. Also, there is a strong synergy between readiness for outsourcing and readiness for unbundling software and hardware.

To proceed, HP must eliminate the dependence of its software on its hardware. HP must also develop implementation processes that can be performed by any partner. In the extreme case of a software-only product, that partner will be a customer over whom HP will have very limited control.

These technical requirements to offer unbundled solutions are the same as those to outsource the hardware handling for a bundled solution. By moving to outsource hardware handling, PMD can develop the competencies it needs for a future that includes software-only products. Outsourcing can be considered to include the first steps toward unbundling the software products from the hardware. HP will thereby enhance its competencies in developing robust software and installation processes.

By taking on a project to outsource hardware handling, PMD can exercise and develop those important skills before it is forced to demonstrate them directly to customers. Taking advantage of this head start over its competition, PMD can leverage commodity hardware (for knowledge and capacity) and mass integration services (for capacity only) to cut costs and increase the pressure on its competition.

Given that PMD will offer unbundled software to some of its customers, it must offer the best perceived value per process to all of its customers. When customers ask PMD to perform hardware sourcing and integration, those services must be provided at minimum cost. By focusing on robust software development and integration processes, while relying on outside suppliers for hardware handling, PMD can maintain its market leadership and deliver at the lowest cost possible.

Teledesic

In 1990, two of Seattle's wealthiest entrepreneurs—Craig McCaw, who built and then sold to AT&T a nationwide cellular telephone system, and Bill Gates, CEO of Microsoft—decided to launch a venture to provide what they call the "Internet-in-the-sky."[4] The concept is to deploy a constellation of 288 low-Earth-orbit (LEO) satellites (plus a few dozen spares) that will dot the planet's atmosphere at an altitude of 850 miles and enable Internet access and telecommunications services from ground or sea locations anywhere on the globe. The goal is to provide "Internet-like" flexibility and "fiber-like" quality of service but without the fiber-optic tether.[5] Because all travelers want seamless access to communications networks regardless of their location and because more than half of the world's population does not have access to a wire-based telecommunications system,[6] Teledesic planners hope that the market for their service will be vast.

The project is ambitious. Teledesic hopes to have the entire system up and running on a budget of about $9 billion for design, product development, manufacturing, and launch of the satellites and ground stations. For satellite production, this goal represents a huge leap in expected performance: cost levels of $10 million to $20 million per "bird" and a lean production system that delivers one minivan-sized satellite per day for the better part of a year.[7] In contrast, Motorola's LEO Iridium project spent approximately $47 million per satellite, and a typical high-orbit geostationary communications satellite costs between $125 million and $175 million[8] and has a production cycle that can span 18 months to three years or more—in a craft production mode.[9]

These larger satellites fly much higher—about 22,000 miles up—and, with a much smaller contingent, they can provide coverage for the entire planet. But their greater distance from the earth causes transmission delays, which are intolerable to impatient voice and data users in today's fast-clockspeed world.

The Teledesic program is defined by challenging functional, cost, and schedule requirements. Functionally, the satellites have to withstand the stresses of an orbital launch and then perform flawlessly for ten years. (How many computer hardware systems do you know of that haven't had a service visit in *ten years?*) Service visits are not feasible, nor can these birds fly down out of orbit for a tune-up and then back up again into space. In geostationary satellites, $150 million or so can buy a lot of redundancy. But with Teledesic's ambitious targets, business as usual with redundant designs is not an option. The cost and schedule constraints on this project have sharp teeth—a novelty and a shock for the satellite engineers on the project.

The Teledesic project illustrates a wide range of issues in three-dimensional concurrent engineering and strategic supply chain design. Each satellite is a complex manufactured system comprising optical systems, wire harnesses, a metal and graphite fiber composite body that has extreme survivability requirements, a power system with solar cells and batteries that must power both a propulsion system with thrusters and the on-board telecommunications computers, and on and on.

So how do you design one of these complex systems? If you really plan to build only one, the answer is relatively easy: You build a highly integral design where all the subsystems are tightly coupled. But if you are creating a design for which a high-volume (by aerospace standards) production line and supply chain are to be assembled, the problem gets a bit sticky. Indeed, satellites have historically been thought of as quite integral—the subsystems are highly interconnected and interdependent. As Thomas Haines puts it:

> If the engineers designing Teledesic's computer network decide they need to send more data through each satellite, that means more capacity to send signals. To get more capacity, they need more power on each satellite. To get more power, they need a larger solar array—the giant panel that captures energy from the sun and transfers it to on-board batteries. Adding a larger solar array increases the satellite's total weight. A heavier satellite costs more to launch. If it gets too heavy, it may mean getting another rocket to launch it. That may mean launching it in California, say, instead of Russia, or vice versa.[10]

One path to fast production is modularity in design and assembly. If each subsystem can be built and tested independently, then much work can proceed in parallel. But could Teledesic engineers come up with a modular design that meets all the requirements and develop a modular supply chain to build it?

In the spring of 1997, seven years into the project, Teledesic (with all of its 100 employees) sold a 10 percent share for $100 million to another Seattle neighbor: the Boeing Company, with 200,000 employees.[11] For Boeing, space represents the next great flight frontier. The company's composite and antenna strengths, combined with its acquisitions of Rockwell's Rocketdyne, Space Shuttle, and GPS expertise and McDonald-Douglas's launch capacity, create the potential for a space systems juggernaut. As in Boeing's traditional businesses, natural scale economies make space systems a market with only a few large competitors because of the immense cost and scope of launching a major satellite system.

For Boeing, this seemed a opportunity made in (and for) heaven. As the ferocity of competition in commercial aircraft continued to heat up with Airbus, Boeing needed a new venue perhaps. Commercial satellites build on Boeing's strengths in aerospace and enable the company to participate in the telecommunications markets that will reduce the world's needs for jet transport. Boeing might also develop capabilities that would make it the world's low-cost producer of a complex commodity likely to experience a huge increase in business as the world demands more bandwidth and greater connectivity in the coming decades.

Three-Dimensional Design: The Struggle between Flow-Time and Weight

In the fall of 1997, Boeing and Teledesic decided to use the 3-DCE framework as the high-level model for managing satellite, process, and supply chain development. Managers felt that the culture of military satellite development, from which many of the engineering team had come, needed a strong dose of cost-and-schedule awareness, which the 3-DCE framework could provide.

One critical test of the team's 3-D process methodology occurred over the issue of how modular the Teledesic satellite design should be. One of the difficult production requirements is short overall material flow-time. By shortening the flow-time for all assemblies, managers reduce system inventories and shorten the time-to-launch. Thus, production flow-time has a strong impact on the overall program cost and scheduling. Because the launch dates need to be negotiated far in advance, production flow-time needs to be solidified. To reduce the overall material flow, managers divided the satellite into several large pieces and contracted with suppliers to produce those sections in parallel. This strategy led to a requirement for a modular design: a satellite that could be physically broken up and assigned to separate suppliers.

Once these pieces are assembled on the ground, the satellites become extremely heavy objects that have to be launched into space. Multiplied 288 times, the launch requires an enormous amount of energy, for which few suppliers in the world have such capabilities. An aggressive launch cost, which required that each launch vehicle carry several satellites, put tight constraints on satellite weight and volume.

The weight constraint was the program's most challenging restriction for some time, leading to an aggressive redesign effort to get the most satellite into the lightest package possible. Because joints that attach modules require excess material, the baseline design was reduced from several to two modules. The design group claimed that it still met the modular requirement because the satellite could, indeed, be divided into two modules and assembled in parallel, although with a much longer flow-time than the original design specified.

In a traditional production process, this decision would have been thrown over the wall to the production engineers. Because the goal for a modular design would have been captured in the manufacturing plan rather than in the higher level requirements document, the decision to compromise modularity for weight might have happened without a full consideration of all the issues. Even if managers recognized the conflict, they might well have allowed the weight restriction to take precedence.

In the requirement-centric 3-DCE process, however, both the modularity requirement and the weight requirement were linked back to program costs. As such, the team rigorously assessed the trade-off curve of weight versus flow-time and arrived at a compromise—across product, process, and supply chain boundaries—that all agreed was closer to a global optimum.

At the strategic supply chain level, issues are no less complex. Although Teledesic may have the most ambitious offering of Internet-in-the-sky, that does not guarantee a positive return on the $9 billion invested. One glance at the complex MICE chain (see figure 2.1) suggests that the transmission field will be crowded with players and technologies. As a result, Teledesic needs to use its supply chain decisions to generate revenue as well as satellites.

On the revenue side, the company needs governmental approval from every jurisdiction from which it wishes to offer service to its traveling or stationary customers. More business might flow from the nations of Russia and China if they are suppliers in the launch process. In production, Matra Marconi Space, the joint venture between the General Electric Company of Great Britain and Lagardere of France, will also participate in the project.[12]

On the technical side, Motorola joined the project as an equity partner in early 1998 (about $750 million in exchange for 26 percent),[13] bringing its expertise from the Iridium project. At the same time, this move served to consolidate Motorola's efforts with Teledesic instead of creating a situation whereby each company would offer a competing system, which had been in the works.[14]

Teledesic plans to grow little beyond its 100 employees. Rather, it intends to develop supply chain design as its core competency and to create a telecommunications giant through strategic partnerships. Of course, this path has its risks. If the system ends up as essentially having "Boeing and Motorola Inside," then Teledesic may find itself on the outside looking in. Given the technological clockspeeds involved in this industry, the system Teledesic buys is bound to be obsolete shortly after its launch. If Boeing and Motorola can go on to do the next generation, they may not need Teledesic. On the other hand, if Teledesic keeps a firm hold on the chain relationships with all the regulators and international partners, then each party may have significant value to bring to the project for generations to come.

This brief description of the Teledesic project, as well as that of Hewlett-Packard's Patient Monitoring Division, indicates just how intricate a three-dimension concurrent engineering analysis can become. In the case of HP-PMD, we get a front-row seat into supply chain design as an industry begins to turn along the helix—from vertical/integral to horizontal/modular. HP, as the old leader, faces tougher choices than does a new entrant because it must voluntarily dismantle its old—and profitable—competencies, lest a brutal competitor arrive there first. The key choices involve identification of risk and reward along the capability chain that is anticipated once the transition to horizontal/modular is complete—for how long, nobody knows. Profit and quality are in severe conflict—in a product that deals in human life one heartbeat at a time.[15]

Teledesic is about classic engineering—in three dimensions. Here we see the pull between the vital weight-saving properties of integral designs in conflict with severe cost and time-to-market requirements that favor modular designs.[16] At a higher level, we see the strategic levers of value chain partnerships manipulated judiciously so that Teledesic can navigate the needs of creating a winning team without making the team independent of its convener.

Above all, these analyses illustrate that careful assessment of industry dynamics and consideration of engineering in three dimensions enables rational choices in dynamic, uncertain environments.

In the final chapter of this section, I return to the computer industry, one of the fastest clockspeed industries around, where empires come and go with startling rapidity. In particular, I examine, through the lenses of clockspeed analysis and three-dimensional concurrent engineering, Compaq's recent acquisitions of Tandem and Digital. The Compaq story is enlightening for what it tells us about its managers' attempts to gaze ahead in time, catch a glimpse of the future with the double helix, and build their strategy based on projections of industry structure and opportunity.

12 BACK TO THE FRUIT FLIES

Evolutionary Pressures Spawn New Hybrids

Evolutionary processes create a constant stream of new competitors, the close observation of which can yield new insights. The faster the clockspeed, the richer the lesson book.

IN A POPULAR MOVIE OF THE 1980S, Christopher Lloyd, playing an eccentric inventor of a time-travel machine, exclaims to Michael J. Fox, his protégé, that in order to save the world they have to go "Back to the future!" Outside the realm of science fiction, we have no time-travel machines. To my knowledge, no one has even perfected a forward-looking crystal ball either.

Lacking the ability to see into the future, we are left to make do with learning from case studies of the past to help us peer into the future. This necessity brings us management scientists "back to the fruit flies."

As I argued in Part I of this book, the fruit flies of business give us the opportunity to watch industrial evolution in fast-forward speed. Like the biologist seeking to unravel the laws of nature, the business geneticist has the opportunity to observe economic principles that might otherwise remain invisible. In this quest for the discernible, the personal computer industry has served steadfastly as a subject in our test tube. Before synthesizing the methodology of this book in the second half of this chapter, let's first return to the PC industry laboratory to see what's evolving.

In Part I, we observed that IBM's 3-DCE decisions on its first personal computer laid the groundwork for Intel and Microsoft to create brand-name technological subsystems that computer buyers came to see as more important than the venerable name of the system designer, IBM. The resulting modularization of the product and supply chain architectures enabled first Compaq, then Dell, to launch and direct their strategies for making and selling IBM "clones."

Compaq's leap into the industry marked a turn on the double helix—from integral product and supply chain to modular product and supply chain—whereby fortunes were made and lost with the new structure. The most startling fortune of them all was made by Bill Gates, the wily and relentless conqueror of the software platform for virtually all of computerdom.

But nature, seemingly, abhors a monopolist. Not only do they tend toward corruptive use of their power, but monopolists also attract jealous entrepreneurs who will use all possible means, economic and political, to break the lock-in and spread the wealth around—to themselves and others. Furthermore, in a fast-clockspeed industry, the forces of the double helix work at warp speed, rendering temporary the advantage of even the most ensconced industrial titan.

As we observed in chapter 4, the computer industry, after modularizing in the image of Compaq, Intel, and Microsoft, came under pressure from the upstream victors, Intel and Microsoft, to pivot once again, back to an integral structure with the lion's share of the profits—and control of the industry's standards—falling to the Wintel partners.

But survivalists among the fruit flies don't stay still: They seek to evolve rather than expire. After vanquishing IBM and reaching the top of the charts in PC sales, Compaq hardly had time to celebrate before it was being hounded by Wintel upstream and by Dell nipping at its heels. Let's look at the chase in more detail.

In his book on business ecosystems,[1] James Moore recounts the intense, but short-lived battle in 1994–1995 between Compaq and Intel at the time of the transition from Intel's i486 machines to its new and powerful Pentium processor. Wrestling for more control of the chain, Compaq wanted to convince the computer buyer that the name on the microprocessor was not the primary designator of value. The company experimented with other processor vendors in an attempt to offer lower prices to its customers and ease the grip that Intel had on Compaq's supply chain.

Intel, of course, had other plans. Its hyperaggressive "Intel Inside" marketing campaign was designed to convince the computer-buying public that there was nothing to a computer other than the micro-processor.[2] The battle was fierce, but short. Forced to pledge fealty to Intel, Compaq leaders gritted their teeth and accelerated their growth by promoting and embracing advanced Intel processors. The vertical competition went dormant—for a time.

Compaq merely waited for another opportunity to strike. That opportunity came in the fall of 1997, when the company launched a new industry segment, the "sub-$1,000 PC," built around lower-priced microprocessors made by Intel competitors Cyrix and AMD. Sales growth in the PC industry had slowed, and Compaq had a hunch that it could reignite growth if it fueled a market segment for which the PC had been too expensive.

Compaq's new strategy paid off in spades. In the spring of 1997, Intel had been forecasting that the principal price point for PCs would be $2,000 for as far into the future as the company could see.[3] Within a year, however, Intel managers had completely revamped their strat-egy, having launched a new, low-cost microprocessor product line to supply the sub-$1,000 PC market, which had become the fastest growing segment in the industry. Intel's previously gravity-defying stock price dropped 20 percent in an up market after some analysts concluded that Intel's profit margins would never be the same.

One way to look at Intel's change in fortunes is that the clockspeed of its principal product slowed while the company was still geared for a fast pace. Throughout the early history of the PC, increasingly complex software applications (often Microsoft's) drove customers to demand ever more powerful microprocessors. However, after the industry had upgraded in the mid-1990s in response to the greater demands of the ubiquitous Windows 95, no new power-hungry "killer applications" hit the industry in the ensuing years. Intel meanwhile had perfected the cadence of frequent introductions of increasingly more powerful chips and fast ramp-ups, but was caught off guard when the market did not gobble up all that power nearly so voraciously as it once had. Indeed, many consumers opted to save money on non-Intel machines.

In fact, customers still wanted more performance for their PCs, but the Internet revolution had caused the bottleneck on performance to shift—from the box to the network. Upgrading one's modem became more important to the customer than having the fastest microprocessor.

With the business computing environment also shifting its focus to networks, the PC itself began to lose its place as the driving engine of sales. With the increased complexity and connectivity of networks, customers began to seek suppliers who could integrate hardware and software. Increasingly, service quality and availability became a key sales driver.

For such an environment, the acquisition by Compaq of Tandem in 1997 and DEC in 1998 makes sense.[4] If the complexity of networks makes them a more integral system, integrating the organizations can be a logical response. DEC's service organization, comprising 25,000 highly skilled (and very scarce) professionals, can address customer needs in the PC, workstation, and server markets, on both UNIX and Windows NT platforms. This open-architecture capability complements Compaq's manufacturing ability and presence in PCs, servers, and PC workstations.

Compaq's acquisition potentially increases its advantage relative to

Dell in that Compaq can offer either stand-alone PCs or a turnkey network with ongoing service. When the system architecture is integral, but a customer buys components from disparate suppliers, then assigning responsibility for problems can be extremely difficult. In such cases, customers often prefer a full-system supplier.

By virtue of scale and a now trusted brand name, Compaq can continue to offer its customers non-Intel machines, keeping the pressure on microprocessor prices. Compaq even gains some potential leverage with Microsoft since it can offer networks that run on either Windows NT or UNIX.

To understand the leverage gained by Compaq, consider the series of announcements made in June 1998 by Intel, Compaq, and Microsoft.[5] Intel told customers and analysts that its highly promoted 64-bit microprocessor, nicknamed "Merced," would be delayed by six months. In response, Compaq announced that it would use its newly acquired DEC "Alpha" chip to provide customers with 64-bit processors, thereby gaining a potential lead on Intel's chip and Intel's customers (Compaq's competitors) who planned to wait for Merced. In response, Microsoft seemingly threw all its weight into the Intel camp—to the disadvantage of Compaq, one of Microsoft's largest customers—and announced that it would delay release of its 64-bit version of Windows NT, an operating system for running high-capacity network servers, until the Merced version was also ready. Microsoft thereby denied an opportunity for Compaq/DEC to get another leg up on Microsoft's long-time partner Intel.

But Microsoft's move encourages Compaq/DEC, long-time close allies of Microsoft, to sell more Alpha-with-UNIX 64-bit systems, possibly undercutting Microsoft's efforts to have 64-bit Windows NT drive UNIX out of the corporate server market. So Compaq's acquisition of DEC gives it the opportunity to push aggressively against Wintel (and its loyal customer Dell), which captured a huge fraction of industry profits and market value in the 1990s.

In this fruit fly we see one company that is convinced that the industry is rounding the double helix again and does not want to be left behind. Of course, Compaq could guess wrong. Perhaps the technology of PCs, servers, and networks will remain sufficiently modular that individual PC sellers (such as Dell) and service sellers (such as EDS) will continue to thrive and will gain a flexibility advantage that comes with successful modularity. The double helix can help us understand the industry dynamics, but it cannot predict them precisely.

Methodology Synthesis for Clockspeed-based Strategy

I conclude this chapter and Part III of the book with a synthesis of the methodology inherent in the preceding chapters. First, to reiterate the message of this book, supply chain design is the meta-core competency for organizations. It is the competency of choosing all other competencies. This assertion arises from the observation that all advantage is temporary and that high-leverage control points in industrial capability chains shift over time, with a frequency dependent on the underlying clockspeeds.

It follows that the only lasting competency is the ability to continuously assess industrial and technological dynamics and build capability chains that exploit current opportunities and anticipate future ones. Among capabilities, this competency of selecting all others *is not to be outsourced!*

To employ outside help in assessing capability chain design choices and industry dynamics is certainly reasonable, but I believe that making those final decisions is so central to a company's viability that to outsource one's own thinking is to relinquish one's responsibilities for the core of executive decision making. In short, *thinking* is a core capability not to be outsourced. And the faster the clockspeed, the more frequent is the need to think and rethink.

This thinking consists of one's own strategic analysis of capability chains and clockspeeds within the chains, one's own industry analysis (assisted by the double helix), one's own market and technological forecasting, and one's own capability chain design and development (with the aid of 3-DCE). Think of the process as having four key steps, as summarized in Table 12.1:

Table 12.1. Summary Methodology for Clockspeed-based Strategy

	Action	Discussed in Chapter(s)	Examples
Step 1	Benchmark the fruit flies of fast-clockspeed industries	1, 2, 3, 4, 5, 11, 12	Intel Microsoft Compaq Dell Information-entertainment
Step 2	Understand, map, and assess your supply chain	5, 6, 7	Chrysler Dell Merck
Three chain maps: • Organization • Technology • Capability			AlliedSignal
Step 3	Apply clockspeed analysis (dynamic chain analysis) • Double helix • Chain clockspeed analysis • Dependency loops	4, 7, 9, 11, 12	Defense aerospace Information-entertainment Polaroid/Sony Boeing Hewlett-Packard

Step 4	Exploit and execute	8, 9, 10,	Hewlett-Packard
	3-DCE and competency	11, 12	Teledesic
	development dynamics		Compaq/DEC
	• 3-D architecture		
	• Make/buy		
	• Tools for product development and concurrent engineering		

Following the example of the biologists, step 1 in the methodology benchmarks the fruit flies, as illustrated in a variety of settings in chapters 1, 2, 3, 4, 5, 11, and 12. Observing the dynamics of fast-clockspeed industries enables you to discover patterns of evolution more quickly and apply them more readily to fit their particular situations. In addition, given the acceleration of clockspeeds almost everywhere, the fruit flies provide a glimpse of what future life may be like for a wide variety of industries.

In step 2 (the focus of Part II of the book), you work to comprehend the complexities and dynamic forces within your industry and create maps of your organization's supply chain—all the way downstream to the final customer and all the way upstream to knowledge creation and mineral extraction. As chapter 7 argues, these maps should take into account at least three views of the chain: those of the organization, of technologies, and of the network of capabilities. Drawing the chain from all three viewpoints is extremely challenging, but often managers discover important links, just as the managers at Chrysler found when they visited the casting clay supplier several tiers removed from their principal operations. In addition, the two laws of supply chain dynamics (chapter 6) will help you determine the magnitude and frequency of the dynamic forces you can expect, both in patterns of demand and in clockspeeds.

Step 3 applies the clockspeed concept to the chain maps of step 2. Understanding the clockspeeds in your environment is critical. The double helix (chapter 4) decodes the rates and directions of change in industry structures—from vertical/integral to horizontal/modular and back—proving an indispensable guide in making decisions about how best to invest in the capability chain. The dependency loop models of chapter 9 can help you assess the likely impacts of sourcing decisions on future corporate interdependencies. They help one anticipate what traps and opportunities may result from insourcing and outsourcing decisions. Finally, the clockspeed analysis of the chain maps, illustrated for defense aircraft and information-entertainment at the end of chapter 7, provides a tool to support strategic assessment of capability ownership or outsourcing along the entire chain.

In step 4, you begin to execute the capability development process through the use of three-dimensional concurrent engineering (3-DCE). Analysis of product, process, and supply chain architectures enables you to sharpen your analysis of a strategy for outsourcing certain components if necessary. Using the make/buy decision analysis matrix of chapter 9, you can begin to align architectures across the three dimensions of products, processes, and industry. You can then begin implementing your decisions within the framework of existing concurrent engineering tools (chapter 10), provided that strategic thinking authority is integrated within the concurrent engineering processes.

This book seeks to provide a new lens for strategic business analysis—the lens of industry clockspeeds. Although I am certain that many of the specific case studies of fast-clockspeed firms and industries that appear here will be obsolete long before the pages of this book yellow, I am hopeful that the general principles might outlive a few generations of *Drosophila*, at least. Without a doubt, however, ideas in management (as in all other fields) will continue to evolve, driven in part by the rates of evolution their subjects embody, whether those subjects are tiny insects or gargantuan corporations.

These evolutionary processes are likely to affect public sector organizations as well as the private sector ones that have been the purview of this book. In the epilogue that follows, I explore some implications of the clockspeed concept for the public sector, sampling from the domains of governmental, educational, and religious institutions.

WHEN FRUIT FLIES INHERIT THE EARTH

The Clockspeeds of Public Institutions and Humans

Social systems and public institutions have clockspeeds too.

THIS EPILOGUE SPECULATES on how to apply the clockspeed concept to nonbusiness sectors of global activity—in contrast to the hypercompetitive industries discussed throughout the book. In particular, I look first at national economic systems, comparing the *keiretsu* system that helped bring Japan to great economic heights in the 1980s to what we might call the American "Silicon Valley model" in the 1990s. Next I look at universities, a traditionally slow-clockspeed sector, and observe that their main activities—education and research as information commodities—may see their organizational clockspeeds driven to dizzying rates. Last, I offer some thoughts about the clockspeeds of moral and religious systems, the relative stability of which may prove to be exactly what human beings need in order to balance their sense of time's rapid passing.

The Genetics of Regions

In pure market-based economies, as in biological ecosystems, there is no place to hide from the pressures and terrors of evolutionary processes. Uncompetitive

225

firms and practices are swept away as superior approaches win customers and markets. In capitalist societies, social systems are designed in part to foster the healthy aspects of these processes of competition-driven evolution and to take some of the sharp edges off the harsher sides. Policy makers, in democratic nations at least, attempt to steer their way between these rocky shoals, hoping for relative stability and some degree of equity, accompanied by economic growth and prosperity.

Thus, nations engage in industrial policies in part because they don't want to leave local outcomes solely to the forces of competitive dynamics. Two strategies are prevalent: first, the attempt to control or dull the dynamic forces of competition; second, the attempt to harness or guide those forces. Inevitably, the first strategy is doomed to fail, although enough power can always slow the clock for a time until it springs forward with a snap. The second strategy is much more promising in theory but notoriously difficult to sustain because policy makers need to hone many of the same skills used in capability chain analysis and design that have been discussed throughout this book. They also need to know when to leave well-enough alone.

Nations must come to appreciate the capability chains that are relevant to the well-being of their populaces. They have to understand the technologies and competitive dynamics such as the double helix, and they need to have the same modeling and forecasting skills as many business organizations are developing. National policies come down to making choices for investments through subsidies, regulations, tax policies, and so forth, in capabilities such as education (for instance, teaching math and science versus safe sex), infrastructure (for example, new asphalt highways versus fiber optics), and social welfare (for example, investment in better health care or better prisons). Nations, like corporations, must anticipate windows of opportunity and invest accordingly. Fortune most often smiles on the prepared and the prescient.

Even within a governmental strategy of trying to guide rather than blunt competitive forces within a capitalist economy, different systems are possible. In the 1980s we witnessed the global ascendancy of Japanese manufacturing companies in industry after industry. American and European corporate leaders watched, scratching their heads and wondering how they could compete with the huge *keiretsu* structures fueled by capital that was available at much lower rates than in the West.[1]

David Friedman and Richard Samuels, writing near the peak of this industrial trend, capture a part of the Japanese mind-set at the time, contrasting it with that in the United States:[2]

> Japan, we believe, values industries differently than does America . . . [and it is convinced] that industries have importance beyond the goods they produce. Acting on this belief, the Japanese are driven to procure or develop skills and knowledge that they may lack for their domestic economy so that non-production benefits—especially learning and diffusion—can be realized at home. Industrial policy in Japan is guided by the effort to maintain the nation's knowledge and technology base rather than to produce a specific product to which a domestic firm might affix a nameplate. . . . The U.S., in contrast, does not value industries in this way . . . leading to wholesale capacity losses, or even domestic skill displacement from the American economy that Japan would never tolerate. . . . As we have seen in the aircraft industry, Japan is willing to pay (and pay dearly) for the same technical knowledge that the U.S. is willing to transfer abroad because it values the ancillary industrial results of that knowledge as much, or more than, the ability to make specific goods.

This characterization makes it sound very much as if the Japanese people, as a national collective, were thinking and acting in ways consistent with the approach that I advocate in this book for business organizations. That is, Japanese corporate and government planners thought strategically about industrial dynamics and capability chains, using their assessments to direct technology investment choices.

This strategy seemed fantastically successful in the 1980s but was followed by an almost equally fantastic failure in the 1990s, resulting in nearly a decade of economic stagnation after almost 40 years of continuous, robust growth. What changed? I do not want to understate the complexities and subtleties of these events, for which many have offered explanations, but I do believe that the lens provided by a clockspeed analysis can sharpen our perception.

Japanese planners targeted certain postwar industries—steel, automobiles, and electronics-based products, to name the predominant ones—which flourished in a period characterized by vertical/integral structures. A significant portion of the Japanese economy shaped itself around the *keiretsu,* the model for this kind of organizational relationships. Adopting a strategic outlook, which Friedman and Samuels describe above, the economy thrived far beyond the expectations of most observers. Japan joined the rich countries' club in the postwar period, and was one of very few nations to do so.

Other sectors of the Japanese economy—finance, retailing, and distribution—were also structured vertically and protected from international competition at a time when many world-class performers were moving to horizontal/modular structures. Accordingly, Japanese planners learned only half of the important lessons: They mastered vertical/integral structures, but were protected from the lessons of both the importance of horizontal/modular structures and of their proper cultivation.

In the 1990s, globalization and clockspeed acceleration hit the Japanese economy hard. Some of the industries the Japanese had mastered—electronics and telecommunications, for example—accelerated along the double helix to horizontal/modular. At about the same time, international political forces pushed Japan to open up some of its less competitive sectors that were unprepared to compete with the horizontal/modular structures from the West. As a result, the Japanese economy stagnated, in bewilderment as to how to adapt.

Of course, faster clockspeeds and the double helix imply that vertical structures will play an important role as well. But I do not believe that a set of assets—human, physical, and organizational—can sit out half the double helix and expect to catch it when it comes around again to vertical/integral. Rather, the horizontal/modular periods offer opportunities to break down outmoded structures and relationships, so that the next round of vertical/integral can look much different from the old. The Wintel vertical/integral structure led by Intel and Microsoft in the 1990s looked dramatically different from that of IBM in the 1970s. Similarly, vertical structures in MICE in the 1990s—those of Disney, Time-Warner, and the News Corporation, for instance— look very different from that of RCA/NBC in the 1950s and 1960s.

To help clarify this explanation, contrast the *keiretsu* structure with that of Silicon Valley, the horizontal/modular high-tech mecca in California with an extraordinary high population of fruit flies. In communities of *Drosophila* (the *real* fruit flies, those studied by biologists), individual members are short-lived. Yet their short lives need not lead one to the judgment that the species is unsuccessful in ecological and evolutionary competition. In contrast, the fast clockspeed gives the species many opportunities to adapt rapidly to change. Rather that assessing the success of the species by the life span of a single member, we can judge that species by the efficiency with which it passes its genetic material along to the next generation and its ability to adapt that genetic material to new circumstances.

In Silicon Valley, the lives of many firms are short. However, the precious genetic material of those firms—the human capital and the financial capital—is recycled with great efficiency from fruit fly to fruit fly. Silicon Valley has very efficient capital markets. In fact, the term "venture capital" was invented there, coined by Arthur Rock, financier to Intel and a slew of other Silicon Valley start-ups over the past 30 years.[3] Venture capitalists take their profit from one venture and plow it back into the next, recycling the genetic material from firm to firm. The labor markets in "the Valley" are no less prodigious. Project managers and engineers live nomadic lives, moving from Fairchild to Intel to Cyrix or from Hewlett-Packard to Apple to Sun, without any stigma or apologies. Again, the genetic material is recycled efficiently.

This fluidity of human and financial capital lies at the heart of evolution in a fast-clockspeed world. Although situated in the modular world of Silicon Valley, the Intel juggernaut of the 1990s could be characterized only as a vertical/integral giant in semiconductors—performing design, product development, process development, manufacturing, and packaging. But Intel's employees and venture capitalists are not locked into the vertical/integral model. They can comfortably and rapidly move on to other ventures when the opportunity is right.

Thus, Silicon Valley seems to be a model colony of fruit flies, certainly the best example seen in the 1990s. The model has two critical features for industrial development in a fast-clockspeed world: first, the ability to recycle genetic material rapidly and efficiently; second, the ability to configure that material either vertically or horizontally, on demand. Lest we sing the praises of this model too long or too loudly, it is worthwhile to recall that because all advantage is temporary, the faster the clockspeed, the more tenuous the hold.

We conclude that regional industrial structures—from Japan's economy to California's—can exhibit similar characteristics of integrality and modularity that we saw in individual organizations. Furthermore, these regional structures seem to exhibit some of the double helix dynamics we saw at the organizational level. Industrial planners at the governmental level, therefore, those tasked with overseeing the welfare of nations and states, can also learn from the fruit flies and the dynamic structures they demonstrate.

One example where this shift has begun occurs in the U.S. defense aerospace industry. That industry was hit by a double shock in the early 1990s—the "peace dividend" from the fall of the communism and a resolve in Washington to reduce dramatically the budget deficits of the Reagan and Bush administrations. These twin shocks led, in part, to the creation of the "Lean Aerospace Initiative" at MIT by the U.S. Air Force and a score of its top suppliers.[4] That initiative has grown to include a large collection of government, industry, and academic leaders who are undertaking research and experiments in search of principles for redesign of the defense industrial sector and its supply chains. Interestingly, the program began by benchmarking fruit flies. In this case, the U.S. automotive industry was viewed as a suitable fruit fly, and much effort went into understanding the dynamics of the restructuring that was chronicled in *The Machine That Changed the World*, the 1990 MIT report on research into automotive industry practices and industrial dynamics.[5]

The Pace of Universities

Another area of the public sector that might benefit from a clockspeed analysis is the domain of education—in particular, universities. Universities evolve slowly; they are in a historically slow-clockspeed industry. Whereas nine out of ten of the Fortune 500 companies of 1900 are long gone (GE being the notable exception), the preeminence of the Ivy League schools has remained pretty much untouched for a century or more. Perhaps the turnover is slow because of the tenure system. Or, maybe it is the relatively stable technology of teaching—a nineteenth-century professor would feel quite at home with the chalk-and-blackboard technology in the vast majority of university classrooms today.[6] In contrast, a nineteenth-century factory manager would be lost in a modern factory, such as one at Intel, Dell, or Boeing.

In the 1990s, the technology of computers and communications may finally be the impetus to ratchet up university clockspeeds and send them rocketing out of the nineteenth century. The possibility of fast-clockspeed change on university campuses raises a large number of questions. Take my home institution, the Massachusetts Institute of Technology, for example. Since we can now project the image of MIT's world-class professors—still in front of their blackboards—to virtually any spot on the globe, will our students still need to come to campus? For that matter, will the faculty still need to come to campus? Once they gain fame from the worldwide stage, will they even need an MIT affiliation anymore? What will MIT provide other than certification of excellence for an increasingly entrepreneurial faculty? Because technology permits inexpensive storage, retrieval, and projection of every lecture, will any professor ever have to give the same lecture twice? Will this capability free up more time for research or trigger price competition and downsizing for improved labor productivity?

Management education may be on the leading edge of discovering just how much impact the changes in information and communications technology will have on the university education industry at large. Since management education is purchased on the basis of return on investment, with minimal consideration given to geographic location or the sentimentality of alumni loyalty, it is more likely than the humanities or the sciences to be subjected to the forces that drove the fate of the top Fortune 500 companies of yesteryear. (No doubt, the sciences and humanities do feel those pressures increasing, but perhaps not quite so quickly as management education, probably the fastest-clockspeed component of the university's teaching enterprises.)

If the clockspeed of business schools is being driven up by increased rates of innovation in information technologies and by increased competition, where ought they look for insights on how to respond? One answer is to seek analogs in other fast-clockspeed industries, that is, to benchmark industrial fruit flies, the speedsters of industrial evolution.

Consider the electronics industry for example. The major American prewar producers of radios became the postwar giants of black-and-white televisions, and they gave over low-profit-margin radios to the decimated, but rebuilding, Japanese. When color television arrived, the low-profit black-and-white TVs were offloaded to Japan as well. As color TVs matured, the now capable Japanese companies got to do first the manual assembly and then the higher-technology automated circuit board assembly as the television industry entered the solid-state era. By 1970, their domination of TV technology positioned the Japanese to displace RCA, the company that had invented and launched color TV almost single-handedly. Who could then be surprised when the next hot technologies reached the marketplace? Ampex lost out to Sony in camcorders, and RCA stumbled with its video-disc system so that JVC got to set the VCR standards. The consumer electronics game was over for a generation of American companies, not to be reborn until the explosion of the personal computer, almost two decades later.

Can management education learn anything from its own industry case studies? Business schools have been riding the cash cow of mass-production MBA programs for over twenty years now. Perhaps they are the black-and-white TVs of that industry. If so, executive education is probably the color TV of the future. It has higher margins and a larger potential market. If this is the case, perhaps management schools have little to worry about. They can just take the mass-produced MBA courses, repackage them into smaller executive-education modules, and sell them at a higher margin to the executive masses.

But what if the change is more complex? Will the same mass-marketing and mass-production model work for this customer and product class? What if the key to executive education is electronic transmission of education, a delivery mode that could eventually undermine the economic feasibility for anyone to take a two-year hiatus from earning a salary in order to get an MBA? How does the faculty perform quality assurance in this kind of world, not to mention marketing, product development, production, delivery, and supply chain management? What if learning how to do executive education is not just repackaging, but the core of knowledge development that will be the foundation for the next transformation in education yet unseen? Could some major business schools completely miss out on the next transition to the camcorders and VCRs of *their* industry?

And what if the customers come in the form of corporations rather than individuals, each wanting a customized product? Are schools equipped to respond if every customer demands a product development process and project manager for that process? Furthermore, how many customers will source education "Toyota-style" with long-term partnerships? And how many will follow the pattern of General Motors with short contracts to the low-cost, high-quality bidder?

I don't pretend to know the answers to these questions. I believe, however, that the frameworks may be useful in this area of the public sector in thinking about how to respond to accelerated clockspeeds in information technology.

Legal and Moral Absolutes in a Fast-Clockspeed World

As discussed above, actors in the noncommercial sectors of life—government policy and education, as examples—have sometimes seen much slower clockspeeds than the commercial domain witnesses. Often they are governed by rules (for example, tenure[7]) that were created in much slower clockspeed times, both to the benefit and the detriment of human well-being in the fast-clockspeed times of the recent past.

Consider the United States Constitution, for example. That venerable document states that presidential elections should occur every four years, that presidential candidates must be at least 35 years of age, and that a minority of 41 senators can filibuster on the Senate floor for as long as they want to. When the prescient Founding Fathers penned those directives, the average life span of an American citizen was well under 50 years and a message took almost a week to cross the Atlantic.

Now a president can get a message or a missile to a billion people around the world in minutes, millions of voters can be polled on any issue in less time than the U.S. Senate can conduct a roll-call vote, and a 35-year-old is no longer an elder statesman. However, the earth still takes 365 days to go around the sun, a human fetus still requires nine months for gestation, and once every seven days still seems about the right interval for taking a day of rest. Given the changes in the relative clockspeeds in different aspects of our lives, how frequently ought we ask whether the time constants in the Constitution are still the right ones?

As the clockspeeds in the commercial sector increase, one might wonder whether a slow pace in the public sector is a curse or a blessing. Consider that the U.S. regulations on corporate average fuel economy (CAFE) were set separately for cars and trucks at a time when trucks were primarily commercial vehicles. In the late 1990s, almost half of all new vehicle purchases in the U.S. are vehicles classified as trucks, the vast majority of which have much lower fuel economy than the cars they are replacing. Essentially, the clockspeed in the auto industry market has far exceeded those of the regulatory processes overseeing it.[8]

Or consider the regulation of pornography or violence on the Internet and other electronic media. Even the staunchest free-speech advocates do not condone the seduction and entrapment of children by pedophiles. Yet technology has outstripped society's ability to regulate such activities while allowing the social and economic benefits of the Internet.

In a related vein, governmental authorities, perhaps for good and bad, have less control over their economies in a world where trillions of dollars of financial transactions are closed daily across an almost seamless international economy. A national government may decide that the best interests of its populace are served by certain financial policies. However, if currency traders disagree, such policies can be unraveled in a matter of hours—or even minutes. The clockspeed of financial decision-making by the markets far exceeds that of the governmental policy makers, giving the faceless traders a strong upper hand in many policy matters.

Yet the slow responses of some of our social institutions may be just the right complement to a fast-paced commercial world. Consider, for example, the religious institutions around the world. The Catholic Church has been headquartered in the Vatican for almost two millennia, the Hebrew bible and oral law are even older, and the passions and practices of millions of people are influenced by the writings of prophets and leaders from many centuries ago.

These observations lead one to ask whether, despite (and perhaps because of) the extreme clockspeed acceleration in our technological and commercial lives, the human soul needs some complementary sources of stability. Increasingly, if stability is no longer to be found in our business institutions, our slow-clockspeed social institutions may take on added importance to reduce the vertigo from conducting commerce at light speed.

In addition, it may be that our moral compasses are particularly in need of such stability in the face of rapid technological change. The moral laws laid down in ancient times, for example, may become a more important anchor at a time when parents feel increasingly helpless in shielding their children from the ever-accessible channels of "entertainment" provided in living color from the MICE chain or when business executives or public servants feel that survival in a fast-clockspeed economy almost seems to require cutting corners—of either moral or legal principles.

But this topic, the role of societal absolutes in a world of dizzying clockspeeds, must await another book.

MEASURING CLOCKSPEEDS

ALTHOUGH INTUITIVELY appealing and strategically valuable at a conceptual level, the *measurement* of clockspeed is fraught with complexity at all levels, from the technology, to the firm, and ultimately to the entire industry. Let me draw an analogy to measuring cost—seemingly the simplest of objects in a modern business organization.

It turns out that measuring cost is not such a simple matter. Consider the question in a manufacturing firm, for example, "How much does it cost us to make this product?" A sophisticated cost accountant will reply cagily, "Why do you want to know?" before daring to offer a number. Why is this?

The reason is that the answer will differ depending on what decisions will be based on the number. If the data is used to compute income for a taxing authority, one number might be reported. If it is to be used to decide on product pricing, another number might be offered. If the decision is whether to make or buy the product, or whether to invest in new equipment to manufacture the product, or how to compensate the manager of the factory producing the product, yet other numbers might be provided.

The underlying principle is that of *relevant cost*. One must first ask which components of cost are *relevant* for the decision at hand, then calculate the relevant cost for that decision. A cost number is meaningless without the context of the decision maker who will use the cost number. In fact, one leading accounting thinker, Professor Robert Kaplan of Harvard, even went as far as to suggest that companies should have multiple cost accounting systems to handle this complexity.[1]

Measuring clockspeed is similarly complex. Furthermore, we don't have the luxury of decades of experience with clockspeed measurement practices to report on at this time. Clockspeed measurement is in its infancy. Consider an industry such as automobiles. One could measure product clockspeed as the frequency of change in a given model (for example, Honda introduces a new Accord sedan every four years), the frequency of changes in dominant designs (internal combustion engine or frameless body or front-wheel drive), or the frequency of changes in options packages (many times within a model design). Similarly, for process technology, one can measure by rate of introduction of dominant process/organization paradigm (mass production, lean production), by age of factory and equipment, or by introduction of some new process technology in one area of the factory. And, for organization clockspeed, one can assess the intervals between CEO transitions, organization restructurings, ownership changes, and the like.

Mindful of these caveats, I have attempted to begin developing quantitative measures of clockspeed along the dimension of product, process, and organization. To begin this endeavor, I have polled management and technical people asking for their assessments of appropriate measures and rankings in industries with which they are familiar.[2] Note that this does not represent systematic research, but is, I hope, sufficiently suggestive that it will stimulate such research.[3] The results from this process are presented in the table on the following page.

Table A.1. Measuring Clockspeed—Sample Industries

Industry	Product Tech Clockspeed	Process Tech Clockspeed	Organization Clockspeed
FAST-CLOCKSPEED INDUSTRIES			
Personal computers	< 6 months	2–4 years	2–4 years
Computer-aided software engineering	6 months	2–4 years	2–4 years
Toys and games	< one year	5–15 years	5–15 years
Athletic footwear	< one year	5–15 years	5–15 years
Semiconductors	1–2 years	2–3 years	3–10 years
Cosmetics	2–3 years	5–10 years	10–20 years
MEDIUM-CLOCKSPEED INDUSTRIES			
Bicycles	4–6 years	10–15 years	20–25 years
Automobiles	4–6 years	4–6 years	10–15 years
Computer operating systems	5–10 years	5–10 years	5–10 years
Agriculture	3–8 years	5–10 years	8–10 years
Fast food	3–8 years	25–50 years	5–25 years
Beer brewing	4–6 years	400 years	2–3 years
Airlines	5–7 years	25 years (hardware) 2–3 years (software)	< 5 years
Machine tools	6–10 years	6–10 years	10–15 years
Pharmaceuticals	7–15 years	10–20 years	5–10 years
SLOW-CLOCKSPEED INDUSTRIES			
Aircraft (commercial)	10–20 years	5–30 years	20–30 years
Tobacco	1–2 years	20–30 years	20–30 years
Steel	20–40 years	10–20 years	50–100 years
Aircraft (military)	20–30 years	5–30 years	2–3 years
Shipbuilding	25–35 years	5–30 years	10–30 years
Petrochemicals	10–20 years	20–40 years	20–40 years
Paper	10–20 years	20–40 years	20–40 years
Electricity	100 years	25–50 years	50–75 years
Diamond mining	Centuries	20–30 years	50–100 years

Two further complexities of measuring clockspeed must also be addressed. First, aside from measuring an industry's average clockspeed, one must also consider its variance. In the electronics industry, both the semiconductor and the circuit board industries are reasonably fast clockspeed, but microprocessor development has followed a low variance path as predicted by Moore's law, whereas circuit boards were slow-moving until the advent of surface mount technology, which represented a burst of improvement in the technology.[4] Second, industry clockspeed may not be stationary in all (or any) industries. In particular, life cycle effects may exist. One could imagine an industry pattern wherein early bursts of technological discovery generate a fast pace, which slows down as the industry matures. As industry maturity causes the slowing of product clockspeed, process technology may then be the most fruitful arena for rapid technological development.[5] Alternately, a slow-moving industry could be hit with an innovation or an increased level of competition that drives the clockspeed up. As mentioned in chapter 2, the change in the clockspeed in the automotive industry during the 1970s and 1980s, following the entry of Japanese competitors into North America, vividly illustrates this phenomenon.

Notes

Acknowledgments

1. Although commonly attributed to Sir Isaac Newton, the rich history and subtle interpretation of this quotation is provided brilliantly by Robert K. Merton, *On the Shoulders of Giants: A Shandean Postscript* (New York: Free Press, 1965). Although the phrase now carries much depth of meaning, readers should probably not attempt to read into my usage any more subtlety than borrowing the phrase to acknowledge the great intellectual debts I owe as well as acknowledging that there is not much new under the sun.

2. Speaking of giants, I would be remiss if I did not mention Harvard Business School Professors Kim Clark and Clay Christiansen, as well as the heritage they received from Bob Hayes, Steve Wheelwright, and Wick Skinner. Clark's project with Taka Fujimoto on automotive product development (see footnote 4 in chapter 8) was the exemplar for me when I began this research project in 1990. Also Christiansen mentions in the opening of his book based on disk drive industry research (see footnote 2 in chapter 4), that Clark, his advisor, had rationalized examining disk drives based on a fruit fly analogy. Independently, I hit upon the same idea.

3. Edward Hallowell and John Ratey, *Driven to Distraction: Coping with Attention Deficit Disorder from Childhood through Adulthood* (New York: Pantheon Books, 1994).

Chapter 1

1. Natalie Angier, "Scientist at Work: Christiane Nusslein-Volhard: 'The Lady of the Flies' Dives into a New Pond," *New York Times*, December 5, 1995, p. C1.

2. Thomas Ginsburg, "Gene 'Breakthrough' Awarded Nobel: Two Americans and a German Win," *San Jose Mercury News*, October 9, 1995, p. 1A.

3. Peter A. Lawrence, *The Making of a Fly: The Genetics of Animal Design* (Cambridge: Blackwell Science Ltd., 1992), p. ix.

4. Ibid., p. xii.

5. Malcolm Gladwell, "The New Age of Man," *The New Yorker,* September 30, 1996, p. 57.

6. Michael Hammer and James Champy, *Reengineering the Corporation: A Manifesto for Business Revolution* (New York: HarperBusiness, 1993).

7. Michele M. Mlynarczyk, "Improving Synergy in Multi-Site Microprocessor Manufacturing: An Analysis of a Copy Exactly Approach," unpublished thesis, Massachusetts Institute of Technology, Leaders for Manufacturing Program, Cambridge, Mass., June 1995. See also Dan Gillmor, "Curb on Tweaking Made Intel Strong," *San Jose Mercury News,* August 18, 1997, p. 1E.

8. Kurt Andersen, "Auteur Gridlock," *The New Yorker,* December 8, 1997, p. 35.

9. Ibid.

10. Philip Shenon, "Jet Makers Preparing Bids for a Rich Pentagon Prize," *Wall Street Journal,* March 11, 1996, p. 1.

11. Jim Womack, Daniel Jones, and Daniel Roos, *The Machine That Changed the World* (New York: Rawson Associates, 1990).

12. This information is based on interviews with Toyota executives conducted by Daniel Whitney, Nitin Joglekar, and Sharon Novak of the Massachusetts Institute of Technology, Cambridge, Mass., June 1994. See also Andrew Pollack, "Move by Toyota Reported into Japanese Chip Market," *New York Times*, August 8, 1996, p. D8.

13. See chapter 7 in Richard J. Samuels, *Rich Nation, Strong Army: National Security and the Technological Transformation of Japan* (Ithaca: Cornell University Press, 1994).

14. I primarily use the term "supply chain" to mean the entire chain or network of organizations, technologies, and capabilities that provide some good or service to a final customer. I elaborate on these three levels in chapter 7. I typically use the term "supply chain" equivalently with "value chain" or "value network" or "supply network." I also like the term "value web," used by Adam M. Brandenburger and Barry J. Nalebuff, *Co-Opetition* (New York: Doubleday and Company, 1996).

15. Although some authors have tried to distinguish between the terms "competencies" and "capabilities," my reading of the business strategy literature is that they are used interchangeably for the most part, a practice continued here. The concept of core competencies was popu-

larized by C. K. Prahalad and Gary Hamel, "The Core Competence of the Corporation," *Harvard Business Review* (May–June 1990): 79–91. An earlier reference on the concept is Birger Wernerfelt, "A Resource-Based View of the Firm," *Strategic Management Journal 5*, no. 2 (1984): 171–80. For a discussion of the concept within the strategy literature, see Arnoldo C. Hax and Nicolas S. Majluf, *The Strategy Concept and Process* (Upper Saddle River, N.J.: Prentice Hall, 1996).

16. Hammer and Champy, pp. 77–79.

CHAPTER 2

1. These dimensions to measuring clockspeed were first mentioned in Charles Fine, "Industry Clockspeed and Competency Chain Design," *Proceedings of the 1996 Manufacturing and Service Operations Management Conference*, Dartmouth College, Hanover, N.H., June 24–25, 1996, pp. 140–43. This paper may be downloaded from http://www.clockspeed.com.

2. Kurt Andersen, "Auteur Gridlock," *The New Yorker,* December 8, 1997, p. 35.

3. Steve Lohr, "Leashes Get Shorter for Executives," *New York Times*, July 18, 1997, p. C1.

4. Haim Mendelson and Ravindran R. Pillai, "Industry Clockspeed: Measurement and Operational Implications," *Manufacturing and Service Operations Management* (forthcoming, 1999).

5. "Boeing vs. Airbus," *The Economist*, July 26, 1997, pp. 59–61.

6. "Deflating the Jumbo," *The Economist*, January 25, 1997, pp. 58–59.

7. For more on this theme, see "Biography of a Killer Technology: Optoelectronics Drives Industrial Growth with the Speed of Light," by Charles Fine and Lionel Kimerling, Special Report for the Optoelectronics Industry Development Association, June 1997. This paper may be downloaded from http://www.clockspeed.com.

8. "The Comeback of Cable TV," *Fortune*, July 7, 1997, p. 27.

9. "There's No Business Like Show Business," *Fortune,* June 22, 1998, pp. 86–104.

10. See the exposition of killer technologies in Fine and Kimerling. Also

note that Moore's law, named for Gordon Moore, one of the co-founders of Intel, quantifies the exponential growth of semiconductor capability states that semiconductor performance/price will double every eighteen months, yielding $2^{(10/1.5)}$ or about a hundredfold per decade.

11. The image and theory of creative destruction, clearly a close cousin to fast-clockspeed evolution, is taken from Joseph Schumpeter, *Capitalism, Socialism, and Democracy* (New York: Harper and Row, 1975).

12. This is Moore's law again; see footnote 10 above.

13. Fine and Kimerling.

CHAPTER 3

1. See Monroe Strickberger, *Evolution* (Boston: Jones and Bartlett Series in Life Sciences, 1990), p. 440.

2. Pankaj Ghemawat, *Commitment: The Dynamic of Strategy* (New York: Free Press, 1991).

3. For more on temporary advantage, see Shona L. Brown and Kathleen M. Eisenhardt, *Competing on the Edge: Strategy as Structured Chaos* (Boston: Harvard Business School Press, 1998).

4. For a more complete argument on the benefits of sustainable architectural advantages, see Charles Ferguson and Charles Morris, *Computer Wars* (New York: Times Books, 1993).

5. This account is based on research by Rebecca Henderson, professor of strategic management at the Massachusetts Institute of Technology, Sloan School of Management. A version of this work appears in Rebecca Henderson and Kim Clark, "Architectural Innovation: The Reconfiguration of Existing Product Technologies and the Failure of Established Firms," *Administrative Science Quarterly* 35 (1990): 9–30.

6. This account relies upon and borrows liberally from Brian Black, "Eastman Kodak: A Slow-Clockspeed Player in a Fast-Clockspeed Technology?" unpublished paper, Course 15.769, Massachusetts Institute of Technology, Cambridge, Mass., 1998. See also "A Dark Kodak Moment," *Business Week,* August 4, 1997, pp. 30–32.

7. Elizabeth Brayer, *George Eastman: A Biography* (Baltimore: Johns Hopkins University Press, 1996), pp. 236, 480.

8. Steve Ditlea, "Fisher Labors to Get Kodak off the Treadmill," *Upside* 7, no. 12 (December 1995): 62–75.

9. Black, p. 2.

10. "A Dark Kodak Moment," *Business Week,* August 4, 1997, pp. 30–32.

11. Ibid.

12. Phillippe Kahn, quoted by Jiri Weiss in "Computer Hell," *Stanford Magazine,* September–October 1997, p. 86.

13. Randall Stross, "Mr. Gates Builds His Brain Trust," *Fortune,* December 8, 1997, pp. 84–100.

14. This analysis of the QWERTY keyboard relies heavily on Paul A. David, "Clio and the Economics of QWERTY," *American Economic Review* 75, no. 2 (1985): 332–337; and Brian Arthur, "Competing Technologies, Increasing Returns, and Lock-in by Historical Events," *Economic Journal* 99 (March 1989): 116–31. I have also relied on the discussion of this topic in Paul Krugman, *Peddling Prosperity* (New York: W. W. Norton and Company, 1994).

15. David, p. 332.

16. Krugman, p. 223.

17. See http://www.urbanlegends.com/misc/railroad_gauge.html.

18. See http://www.spikesys.com/Trains/st_gauge.html. See also Achsah Nesmith, "A Long, Arduous March toward Standardization," *Smithsonian* 15 (March 1985): 176ff. Nesmith confirms the standardization set at 4 feet 8.5 inches and details the changing of over 11,000 miles of track from Virginia to Texas in 1886 so that it would conform to the standard gauge observed by the Pennsylvania Railroad and others in the North.

CHAPTER 4

1. James D. Watson, *The Double Helix: A Personal Account of the Discovery of the Structure of DNA* (New York: Atheneum, 1968), p. 197.

2. The double helix model portrayed here is adapted from Charles Fine and Daniel Whitney, "Is the Make/Buy Decision Process a Core Competence?" working paper, Massachusetts Institute of Technology, Cambridge, Mass. The model arose from our discussions over a semi-

nar on "Technology Supply Chains" in the fall of 1995 at the MIT Sloan School. Other observers have noted some of the same evolutionary forces. See, for example, James Moore, *The Death of Competition* (New York: HarperCollins, 1996); Clayton Christiansen, "The Drivers of Vertical Disintegration," Harvard Business School working paper, October 8, 1994, which was followed by *The Innovator's Dilemma: When New Technologies Cause Great Firms to Fail* (Boston: Harvard Business School Press, 1997); Richard Langlois and Paul Robertson, *Firms, Markets, and Economic Change: A Dynamic Theory of Business Institutions* (New York: Routledge, 1995); and Joseph Farrell, Hunter Monroe, and Garth Saloner, "The Vertical Organization of Industry: Systems Competition vs. Component Competition," *Journal of Economics and Management Strategy* 7, no. 2 (1998): 143–82. See also the evolutionary model in chapter 11 of Carliss Baldwin and Kim Clark, *Design Rules: The Power of Modularity* (Cambridge, Mass.: MIT Press, 1999).

3. This figure is adapted from Andrew S. Grove, *Only the Paranoid Survive* (New York: Currency Doubleday, 1996), p. 40.

4. For a thoughtful treatment of modularity, see Carliss Baldwin and Kim Clark, *Design Rules: The Power of Modularity* (Cambridge, Mass.: MIT Press, 1999). Baldwin and Clark argue convincingly that the IBM 360 mainframe and its followers had highly modular architectures relative to their predecessors. However, since (as Baldwin and Clark discuss) IBM chose to control all of the subsystem technologies internal to the firm, the effect was to improve the efficiency with which IBM could upgrade its products, but not to open up the architecture to competing suppliers in any real sense. My use of the term "modular" is therefore consistent with what Baldwin and Clark might call "modular and open."

5. This figure is adapted from Grove, p. 42.

6. Baldwin and Clark, chapter 1.

7. Grove, p. 52.

8. See Nitindra Joglekar, "The Technology Treadmill: Managing Product Performance and Production Ramp-Up in Fast-Paced Industries," unpublished dissertation, Massachusetts Institute of Technology, Sloan School of Management, Cambridge, Mass., 1996.

9. The dynamic forces of the double helix are described more rigorously in a modeling framework in Charles Fine, Mila Getmansky, Paulo Goncalves, and Nelson Repenning, "Industry and Product Structure

Dynamics: From Integration to Disintegration and Back," working paper, Massachusetts Institute of Technology, Sloan School, Cambridge, Mass., 1998.

10. The double helix diagram is adapted from Fine and Whitney, "Is the Make/Buy Decision Process a Core Competency?" This paper may be downloaded from http://www.clockspeed.com.

11. This subsection on the bicycle industry is based primarily on Judith Crown and Glenn Coleman, *No Hands: The Rise and Fall of the Schwinn Bicycle Company* (New York: Henry Holt and Company, 1996). See also Robert A. Smith, *A Social History of the Bicycle: Its Early Life and Times in America* (New York: American Heritage Press, 1972); Andrew Ritchie, *King of the Road: An Illustrated History of Cycling* (London: Wildwood House, 1975).

12. The Schwinn Company history related here is from Crown and Coleman.

13. Ibid., p. 19.

14. Ibid., p. 23.

15. Ibid., p. 31.

16. Ibid., pp. 33–34.

17. Ibid., p. 34.

18. Ibid., p. 35.

19. Ibid., pp. 1–2.

20. Ibid., p. 2.

21. Ibid., p. 3.

22. Ibid., chapter 24.

23. This subsection and the next are based on a term paper written in 1995 by Todd Barrett (MIT-LFM '96), Dan Crocker, and Steve Muir (MIT-LFM '97) for Charles Fine of the MIT Sloan School of Management's Technology Supply Chain course, 15.795. The paper was subsequently modified by the first two authors under Professor Fine's supervision for a teaching case entitled "Grip Shift: Just a Shooting Star?" published by MIT's Leaders for Manufacturing Program. Some proprietary data may have been disguised.

24. Judith Crown and Glenn Coleman, "Owners' Goal: To Get Schwinn Back in Shape," *Crain's Chicago Business,* October 11, 1993, p. 59.

25. Ibid.

26. Pamela Baldinger, "Hot Wheels: Shenzhen China Bicycle Company," *The China Business Review,* May 1993, p. 52.

27. "Intel's Insider Plugs into Future. Grove Sees Gap in Interactive Programming," *Advertising Age*, Crain Communications, Inc., November 15, 1993.

28. Andrew Pollack, "Move by Toyota Reported into Japanese Chip Market," *New York Times,* August 8, 1996, p. C8.

29. Interestingly, the success of the "Intel Inside" campaign rested far more on marketing than on technology. Through advertising, Intel was able to convince millions of computer buyers that when they go to a computer store, the key feature to seek out is that "Intel Inside" logo. Yet, the microprocessor of a computer is not, in any way, an experiential good: Customers can neither see nor touch that computer chip. Most users could not tell whether an Intel chip was inside the box they purchased if it were not for the logo on the outside.

CHAPTER 5

1. "Michael Dell Rocks," *Fortune*, May 11, 1998, pp. 59–70.

2. Michael E. Porter, *Competitive Strategy* (New York: Free Press, 1980). Porter's "five forces" model suggests assessing one's competitive position by examining the power of buyers and suppliers, as well as the rivalry among competitors, opportunities for new entrants, and availability of substitute products (p. 4).

3. Stuart Smith, "Capitalizing on Clockspeed in the Direct Business Model," paper presented at "Creating and Managing Corporate Technology Supply Chains: Value Chain Design in the Age of Temporary Advantage," symposium at the Massachusetts Institute of Technology, Cambridge, Mass., May 12–13, 1998.

4. Ibid.

5. Ibid.

6. This diagram was developed by Nitin Joglekar, "A System Dynamics Model for Benchmarking the Effectiveness of 'Made-to-Order' Decisions against 'Made-to-Stock' Alternatives," unpublished paper, Massachusetts Institute of Technology, Cambridge, Mass., 1998.

7. "The Sad Saga of Silicon Graphics," *Business Week*, August 4, 1997, pp. 66–72.

8. Ibid.

9. Personal communication from Alberto Moel, an MIT undergraduate who worked in Toshiba's advanced lithography lab for several years.

10. Gary Pisano and Sharon Rossi, "Eli Lilly and Company: The Flexible Facility Decision (1993)," Harvard Business School case services, Boston, Mass., April 21, 1994.

11. Gary P. Pisano, *The Development Factory: Unlocking the Potential of Process Innovation* (Boston: Harvard Business School Press, 1987), p. 54.

12. Ibid., p. 56.

13. This section borrows liberally from Seth Taylor's account of the biotechnology industry and its technology. See his "Wheel of Fortune: The Evolution of a Drug Discovery Platform through Strategic Alliances and Acquisitions," unpublished thesis, Massachusetts Institute of Technology, Sloan Management of Technology Program, Cambridge, Mass., 1997.

14. W. W. Powell et al., "Interorganizational Collaboration and the Locus of Innovation: Networks of Learning in Biotechnology," *Administrative Science Quarterly* 41, no. 1 (1996): 116–45.

15. Ibid.

16. Michael L. Tushman and Philip Anderson, *Managing Strategic Innovation and Change: A Collection of Readings* (New York: Oxford University Press, 1997).

17. This framework is from Seth Taylor (see note 13 above).

18. Taylor, p. 34.

19. "A Survey of the Pharmaceutical Industry," *The Economist*, February 21, 1998, special insert, pp. 1–18.

20. Taylor, p. 43.

21. Ibid., p.44.

22. G. Poste, "Managing Discontinuities in Healthcare Markets and Technology: Creativity, Cash and Competition," *Vital Speeches of the Day* 63, no. 10 (1977): 309–13.

23. Taylor, p. 46.

24. Ibid, p. 47.

25. M. Ward, "Europharmas Increase Stakes in U.S. Biotechs," *Bio/Technology* 14 (1996): 21–22.

26. "Mercky Waters," *The Economist*, May 24, 1997, p. 60. As of May 1998, Merck's market capitalization had grown to $140 billion.

27. Ibid., pp. 59–60.

28. Ibid., p. 59.

29. Ibid.

30. *The Economist* reported that Ed Skolnick, Merck's head of research, "is sometimes scathing about the standards of research at other big firms. Roche's protease inhibitor for AIDS, which does not seem to work as well as other pills in the same family, he calls 'a disservice to the world.'" See "Mercky Waters," p. 60.

31. "Wintel" is often used as an abbreviation for the Microsoft Windows-plus-Intel technology combination that has held so much power in the personal computer industry.

CHAPTER 6

1. See, for example, Hau Lee and Shu Ming Ng, eds., *Global Supply Chain and Technology Management* (Miami: Production and Operations Management Society, 1998); Ram Ganeshan, Michael Magazine, and Sridhar Tayur, eds., *Quantitative Models for Supply Chain Management* (Amsterdam: Kluwer Publishers, forthcoming).

2. See, for example, Jay W. Forrester, "Industrial Dynamics: A Major Breakthrough for Decision Makers," *Harvard Business Review* 36, no. 4 (1958): 37–66; idem, *Industrial Dynamics* (Cambridge, Mass.: Productivity Press, 1961); John Sterman, "Modeling Managerial Behavior: Misperceptions of Feedback in a Dynamic Decision Making Experiment," *Management Science* 35, no. 3 (1989): 321–39; John Sterman, "Misperceptions of Feedback in Dynamic Decision Making," *Organizational Behavior and Human Decision Processes* 43 (1989): 301–35; Peter Senge, *The Fifth Discipline* (New York: Doubleday, 1990), chapter 3; Hau Lee, V. Padmanabhan, and Seungjin Whang, "Information Distortion in a Supply Chain: The Bullwhip Effect," *Management Science* 43, no. 4 (April, 1997): 546–58; Robert Kallenberg, "Analysis of Business Cycles in the U.S. Machine Tool Industry Using the System Dynamics Method," unpublished thesis, Rheinische-Westfaelische Techische Hochschule Aachen, Aachen, Germany, 1994.

3. This "law" of clockspeed amplification might be better termed a "hypothesis," which is a candidate for a law. Much more research, both theoretical and empirical, will be required before it is as well understood as the law of volatility amplification. Some of this initial research is in Nitindra Joglekar and Charles Fine, "Decomposition of Clockspeed within Technology Supply Chains," working paper, Massachusetts Institute of Technology, Cambridge, Mass., 1998. This paper may be downloaded from http://www.clockspeed.com.

4. See, for example, Kim Clark and Takahiro Fujimoto, *Product Development Performance* (Boston: Harvard Business School Press, 1991).

5. Adapted from Edward Anderson, Charles Fine, and Geoffrey Parker, "Upstream Volatility in the Supply Chain: The Machine Tool Industry as a Case Study," working paper, Massachusetts Institute of Technology, Cambridge, Mass., 1996. This paper can be downloaded from http://www.clockspeed.com.

6. See the references in note 2 of this chapter.

7. See, for example, chapter 1 and Appendix E in Michael Dertouzos et al., *Made in America* (Cambridge, Mass.: MIT Press, 1989); Max Holland, *When the Machine Stopped* (Boston: Harvard Business School Press, 1989).

8. Richard Kegg, personal interview, Cincinnati, Ohio, June 1993.

9. Edward G. Anderson and Charles H. Fine, "Business Cycles and Productivity in Capital Equipment Supply," chapter 13 in Ganeshan, Magazine, and Tayur. This paper can be downloaded from http://www.clockspeed.com.

10. See, for example, Charles Fine and Lionel Kimerling, "Biography of a Killer Technology." This paper may be downloaded from http://www.clockspeed.com.

11. For more on Sematech, see chapter 2 of Helmut Willkie et al., *Benevolent Conspiracies: The Role of Enabling Technologies in Reframing the Welfare of Nations, The Case of SDI, Sematech and Eureka* (Berlin: Walter De Gruyter Inc., 1995).

12. I am indebted to Lance Mansfield, a 1998 MIT-LFM graduate, for his elucidation of Amazon.com's supply chain design strategy.

13. David Plotnikoff, "Cyber Sellers Nab Browsers before They Know It," *San Jose Mercury News*, May 17, 1998, p. 1E.

14. "Amazon's a Good Read," Cable News Network, Financial News on the Web, April 27, 1998.

15. Anthony Bianco, "Virtual Bookstores Start to Get Real," *Business Week*, October 27, 1997, pp. 146–48.

16. Donald Trott, analyst for Brown Brothers Harriman, New York, as quoted in "Online Book Wars Rev Up," Cable News Network, Financial News on the Web, May 21, 1998.

CHAPTER 7

1. This anecdote was related by Barry Price, Chrysler's executive director of platform supply at the symposium "Creating and Managing Corporate Technology Supply Chains," Massachusetts Institute of Technology, Cambridge, Mass., May 10–11, 1995.

2. This account borrows heavily from Christopher Mastro, "Manufacturing Policy in a Slow-Clockspeed Industry," unpublished paper, Massachusetts Institute of Technology, Cambridge, Mass., 1998; idem, "Using Six Sigma to Optimize a Continuous Chemical Process at AlliedSignal, Inc.," unpublished thesis, Massachusetts Institute of Technology (Leaders for Manufacturing), 1998.

3. R. J. Palmer, "Polyamides (Plastics)," *Encyclopedia of Chemical Technology*, 4th ed. (New York: Wiley, 1997), 19: 559–84.

4. This case is based on the field work of Richard Keiser while he was an M.S. student in MIT's Technology and Policy Program, and on Richard Keiser and Charles Fine, "Technology Supply Chains in the Defense Aerospace Industry: Lockheed Martin Tactical Aircraft Systems," unpublished paper, Massachusetts Institute of Technology, Cambridge, Mass., 1997.

5. Jeff Cole, Andy Pasztor, and Thomas Ricks, "The Sky, the Limit: Do Lean Times Mean Fighting Machines Will Be Built for Less?" *Wall Street Journal*, November 18, 1996, pp. A1, A7.

6. Randy Bollig, director of corporate capital acquisition, Intel Corporation, presentation at the Massachusetts Institute of Technology, Cambridge, Mass., January 21, 1998.

7. I am grateful to Dan Whitney for emphasizing this point.

8. "There's No Business Like Show Business," *Fortune*, June 22, 1998, pp. 86–104.

CHAPTER 8

1. Parts of this chapter were developed in conjunction with my Wharton colleague Morris Cohen and appear in our joint paper, "Architectures in 3-D: Concurrent Product, Process, and Supply Chain Development," working paper, Massachusetts Institute of Technology, Cambridge, Mass., 1998. This paper may be downloaded from http://www.clock-speed.com.

2. Richard S. Rosenbloom and Michael A. Cusumano, "Technological Pioneering and Competitive Advantage: The Birth of the VCR Industry," *California Management Review* 29, no. 4 (Summer 1987): 62.

3. Ibid., pp. 51–76.

4. Kim Clark and Takahiro Fujimoto.

5. Ibid.

6. Michael Dertouzos, Richard Lester, and Robert Solow, *Made in America* (Cambridge, Mass.: MIT Press, 1989).

7. Womack, Jones, and Roos.

8. See, for example, James Nevins and Daniel Whitney, *Concurrent Design of Products and Processes: A Strategy for the Next Generation in Manufacturing* (New York: McGraw-Hill, 1989); K. Ulrich and S. Eppinger, *Product Design and Development* (New York: McGraw-Hill, 1994); Mitchell Fleischer and Jeffrey Liker, *Concurrent Engineering Effectiveness* (Cincinnati: Hanser Gardner Publications, 1997).

9. For the most part, these principles are well described by Nevins and Whitney, *Concurrent Design of Products and Processes*, and by Ulrich and Eppinger, *Product Design and Development*.

10. For evidence on the first assertion, see Clark and Fujimoto. For evidence on the second, see David Ellison, Kim Clark, Takahiro Fujimoto, and Young-Suk Hyun, "Product Development Performance in the Auto Industry: 1990s Update," working paper 95–066, Harvard Business School, 1995.

11. Karl Ulrich, "The Role of Product Architecture in the Manufacturing Firm," *Research Policy* 24 (1995): 419–40.

12. Ibid.

13. This example is given by Ulrich.

14. For a thorough discussion of the theory and application of product architecture, see Timothy W. Cunningham, "Chains of Function Delivery: A Role for Product Architecture in Concept Design," unpublished dissertation, Department of Mechanical Engineering, Massachusetts Institute of Technology, Cambridge, Mass., 1998; Timothy W. Cunningham and Daniel E. Whitney, "The Chain Metrics Method for Identifying Integration Risk during Concept Design," working paper, Massachusetts Institute of Technology, Center for Technology Policy and Industrial Development, Cambridge, Mass., 1998.

15. I am grateful to Dan Whitney for emphasizing this point to me.

16. See, for example, Sharon Novak, "Sourcing by Design: Product Architecture and the Supply Chain," working paper, Massachusetts Institute of Technology, Cambridge, Mass., 1998. This paper presents data from the auto industry to suggest that supply chain integration is a significant variable in explaining performance in the auto industry, whereas traditional vertical integration is not significant.

17. To my knowledge, these dimensions of supply chain proximity are first mentioned in Charles Fine, George Gilboy, Kenneth Oye, and Geoffrey Parker, "The Role of Proximity in Automotive Technology Supply Chain Development: An Introductory Essay," working paper, Massachusetts Institute of Technology, Cambridge, Mass., May 1995. The paper is available at http:/www.clockspeed.com.

18. Jared Judson, "Integrating Supplier Designed Components into a Semi-automatic Product Development Environment," Massachusetts Institute of Technology, LFM Master's Thesis, 1998; idem, "Assessing a New Product Development Process Using 3-Dimensional Concurrent Engineering," term paper for Course 15.769, Massachusetts Institute of Technology, Cambridge, Mass., 1998.

19. Christopher Couch, "Power in the Chain," working paper, Massachusetts Institute of Technology, Sloan School, Cambridge, Mass., October, 1997.

20. Womack et al.

21. Christopher Couch, "Power in the Chain."

22. Italy's garment manufacturing industry has been studied extensively by business academicians, including Michael Porter, *The Competitive Advantage of Nations* (New York: Free Press, 1990); Michael Piore and Charles Sabel, *The Second Industrial Divide* (New York: Basic Books,

1984); and Richard Locke, *Remaking the Italian Economy: Local Politics and Industrial Change in Contemporary Italy* (Ithaca: Cornell University Press, 1995).

23. Cunningham, "Chains of Function Delivery."

24. Novak.

25. Janice Hammond and Ananth Raman, Sport Obermeyer, Ltd., Case Study #N9-695-022, (Boston: Harvard Business School Publishing, 1994); Marshall Fisher et al., "Making Supply Meet Demand in an Uncertain World," *Harvard Business Review* 72 (May–June 1994): 83–93.

26. Robert H. Hayes and Roger Schmenner, "How Should You Organize Manufacturing?" *Harvard Business Review* 56 (January–February 1978): 105–18.

27. Sean Osborne, "Product Development Cycle Time Characterization through Modeling of Process Iteration," unpublished thesis, Massachusetts Institute of Technology (LFM Program), Cambridge, Mass., 1993.

28. I am indebted to Randy Bollig, Intel's director of corporate capital acquisition, for these insights into Intel's supplier development system.

29. "Reliability of Used Cars," *Consumer Reports*, April, 1998, p. 74.

30. Daniel Whitney, "Identifying Integration Risk during Concept Design," presentation to the MIT Symposium on Technology Supply Chains, May 13, 1998. Whitney observed vividly that integral characteristics, like vehicle reliability and NVH (noise, vibration, and harshness), cannot be outsourced to a relibility or NVH supplier. None exist.

31. Jeffrey Dyer, "How Chrysler Created an American Keiretsu," *Harvard Business Review* 74, no. 4 (1996): 42–56.

32. Charles Fine and Daniel Whitney, "Is the Make/Buy Decision Process a Core Competence?"

33. Christopher Couch, "Power in the Chain." This case example and the associated data and references are taken from this paper.

34. Ibid., p. 18.

35. Ibid.

36. Ibid., pp. 37–40.

CHAPTER 9

1. See, for example, discussions of break-even analysis in Charles Horngren, George Foster, and Srikant Datar, *Cost Accounting: A Managerial Emphasis*, 9th ed. (Upper Saddle River, N.J.: Prentice Hall, 1997), pp. 390–92.

2. For coverage of these approaches, see Richard Schmalensee and Robert Willig, *Handbook of Industrial Organization* (Amsterdam: North Holland, 1988); Jean Tirole, *The Theory of Industrial Organization* (Cambridge, Mass.: MIT Press, 1988); Oliver E. Williamson, *The Economic Institutions of Capitalism: Firms, Markets, Relational Contracting* (New York: Free Press, 1985).

3. Tim Jackson, *Inside Intel* (New York: Dutton, 1997), chapters 1 and 2.

4. Takahiro Fujimoto, "The Origin and Evolution of the 'Black Box Parts' Practice in the Japanese Auto Industry," working paper, Tokyo University Faculty of Economics, 1994.

5. In the language of economics, there were no "specific assets" at Fairchild that could not be duplicated in the new Intel organization. Oliver Williamson, among others, has championed the concept of "asset specificity," which has become prominent in the literature on vertical integration. See his *Economic Institutions of Capitalism*. In Williamson's terminology, the knowledge assets in the heads of the Noyce-Moore-Grove team were not specific to Fairchild. Those assets were transportable and highly usable in another organization.

6. Microsoft's first operating system for the IBM PC was named DOS for "Disk Operating System."

7. This example is based in part on Mark E. Friedberg, "A Computer-Based Technical and Economic Model for Choosing Automated Assembly Parts Presentation Equipment," unpublished thesis, Massachusetts Institute of Technology, Leaders for Manufacturing Program, Cambridge, Mass., 1990; and Jeffrey T. Gray, "Valuation of Investments in Manufacturing Technology," unpublished thesis, Massachusetts Institute of Technology, Leaders for Manufacturing Program, Cambridge, Mass., 1994.

8. For material on the development and exposition of the concept of core competencies, see Prahalad and Hamel, "The Core Competence of the Corporation." See also Gary Hamel and C. K. Prahalad, *Competing for the Future* (Boston: Harvard Business School Press, 1994).

9. This diagram was adapted from Dorothy Leonard-Barton, *Wellsprings of Knowledge* (Boston: Harvard Business School Press, 1995).

10. This section relies heavily on Fine and Whitney, "Is the Make/Buy Decision Process a Core Competence?" This paper may be downloaded from http://www.clockspeed.com.

11. Ravi Venkatesan, "Strategic Sourcing: To Make or Not to Make," *Harvard Business Review* 70, no. 6 (November–December 1992): 101.

12. This distinction between dependence for capacity and dependence for knowledge grew out of discussions with Daniel Whitney and Geoffrey Parker at MIT.

13. Satoshi Nakagawa, "Developing Core Technologies for Automotive Components," a paper presented at the symposium "Creating and Managing Corporate Technology Supply Chains," Massachusetts Institute of Technology, Cambridge, Mass., May 10–11, 1995.

14. Fujimoto, "The Origin and Evolution of the 'Black Box Parts' Practice in the Japanese Auto Industry."

15. Interviews by MIT researchers Daniel Whitney, Sharon Novak, and Nitin Joglekar, Toyota City, May 1994.

16. This matrix is an extension of an earlier model in Charles Fine and Daniel Whitney, "Is the Make vs. Buy Decision Process a Core Competence?"

17. Ibid.

18. Paul M. Gutwald, "A Strategic Sourcing Model for Concurrent Product, Process, and Supply-chain Design," unpublished thesis, Massachusetts Institute of Technology (Sloan School of Management), Cambridge, Mass., May 1996.

19. Womack, Jones, and Roos, *The Machine That Changed the World.*

20. Takahiro Fujimoto, "Reinterpreting the Resource Capability View of the Firm: A Case of the Development-Production Systems of the Japanese Auto Makers," working paper, Tokyo University Faculty of Economics, 1994.

21. Ibid.

22. Andrew Pollack, "Move by Toyota Reported into Japanese Chip Market," *New York Times*, August 8, 1996, p. D8.

23. Alfred Chandler, "The Computer Industry—The First Fifty Years," in David Yoffie, ed., *Competing in the Age of Digital Convergence* (Boston: Harvard Business School Press, 1998).

CHAPTER 10

1. In the words of the chief proponents of reengineering: Managers "must abandon the organizational and operational principles and procedures they are now using and create entirely new ones." See Michael Hammer and James Champy, *Reengineering the Corporation: A Manifesto for Business Revolution* (New York: HarperBusiness, 1993), p. 1.

2. Nevins and Whitney.

3. See, for example, Mitchell Fleischer and Jeffrey Liker, *Concurrent Engineering Effectiveness* (Cincinnati: Hanser Gardner Publications, 1997).

4. Karl T. Ulrich and Steven D. Eppinger, *Product Design and Development* (New York: McGraw-Hill, 1994), p. 6.

5. Steven Eppinger et al., "A Model-Based Method for Organizing Tasks in Product Development," *Research in Engineering Design*, no. 6 (1994): 1–13.

6. Geoffrey Boothroyd and Peter Dewhurst, *Product Design for Assembly* (Wakefield, R.I.: Boothroyd Dewhurst, Inc., 1989); Geoffrey Boothroyd, Peter Dewhurst, and W. A. Knight, *Product Design for Manufacturing* (New York: Marcel Dekker, 1994).

7. Karl Ulrich, David Sartorius, Scott Pearson, and Mark Jakiela, "Including the Value of Time in Design-for-Manufacturing Decision-Making," *Management Science* 39, no. 4 (1993): 429–47.

8. Hau L. Lee and Corey Billington, "Designing Products and Processes for Postponement," in *Management of Design: Engineering and Management Perspectives*, ed. S. Dasu and C. Eastman (Boston: Kluwer Academic Publishers, 1994), pp. 105–22.

9. Morris Cohen and Teck Ho, "Design for Service and Life Cycle Performance: Spares Consumption Reduction and Design for Serviceability," working research agenda, Wharton School, University of Pennsylvania, May 8, 1998.

10. See, for example, F. K. Levy, G. L. Thompson, and J. D. Weist, "The ABCs of the Critical Path Method," *Harvard Business Review* (September–October 1963): 98–108.

11. Chris Couch, "Power in the Chain."

12. I am grateful to Dan Whitney for making this point.

13. Robert P. Smith and Steven D. Eppinger, "Identifying Controlling

Features of Engineering Design Iteration," *Management Science* 43, no. 3 (1997): 276–93; Thomas Pimmler and Steven D. Eppinger, "Integration Analysis of Product Decompositions," *Design Engineering* 68 (1994); V. Krishnan, S. D. Eppinger, and D. E. Whitney, "Accelerating Product Development by the Exchange of Preliminary Information," *ASME Journal of Mechanical Design* (December 1995); V. Krishnan, S. D. Eppinger, and D. E. Whitney, "A Model-Based Framework for Overlapping Product Development Activities," *Management Science* 43, no. 4 (1997): 437–51; V. Krishnan, S. D. Eppinger, and D. E. Whitney, "Simplifying Iterations in Cross-Functional Design Decision Making," *ASME Journal of Mechanical Design* (December 1997).

14. This example comes from "Design Structure Matrix Tutorial," Daniel Whitney, Massachusetts Institute of Technology, Center for Technology Policy and Industrial Development, Cambridge, Mass., 1997.

15. See, for example, Thomas Black, Charles Fine, and Emanuel Sachs, "A Method for Systems Design Using Precedence Relationships: An Application to Automotive Brake Systems," working paper #3208-90-MS; Thomas A. Black, "A Systems Design Approach to Automotive Brake Design" unpublished thesis, Massachusetts Institute of Technology, Leaders for Manufacturing Program, Cambridge, Mass., June 1990.

16. Steven Eppinger, et al., "A Model-Based Method for Organizing Tasks in Product Development," *Research in Engineering Design*, 1994, No. 6, pp. 1–13.

17. From Daniel Whitney, "Design Structure Matrix Tutorial," Center for Technology Policy and Industrial Development, Massachusetts Institute of Technology, Cambridge, Mass., 1997.

18. See references in footnote 13.

19. James Womack, Daniel Jones, and Daniel Roos, *The Machine That Changed the World*; see also Kim Clark and Takahiro Fujimoto, *Product Development Performance* (Boston: Harvard Business School Press, 1991).

20. See Robert J. Alexander, "Scheduling and Resource Allocation Methodologies for Fast Product Development in a Multi-Product Environment," unpublished thesis, Massachusetts Institute of Technology, Leaders for Manufacturing Program, Cambridge, Mass., June 1991; Brian Kelly, "Use of a Simulation Game and Queuing Model to Achieve Shorter Lead Times in Stamping Die Development,"

unpublished thesis, Massachusetts Institute of Technology, Leaders for Manufacturing Program, Cambridge, Mass., May 1996; P. S. Adler, A. Mandelbaum, V. Nguyen, and E. Schwerer, "From Project to Process Management: An Empirically Based Framework for Analyzing Product Development Time," *Management Science* 41, no. 3 (March, 1995): 458–84.; idem, "Getting the Most out of Your Product Development Process," *Harvard Business Review* (March–April 1996): 134–52.

21. Eliyahu Goldratt and Jeff Cox, *The Goal* (Croton-on-Hudson, N.Y.: North River Press, 1984); and Eliyahu Goldratt, *Theory of Constraints* (Croton-on-Hudson, N.Y.: North River Press, 1990).

22. Alexander, "Scheduling and Resource Allocation Methodologies."

23. Kelly, "Use of a Simulation Game and Queueing Model."

24. John Hauser and Don Clausing, "The House of Quality," *Harvard Business Review* 66, no. 3 (1988): 63–73.

25. Ibid. See also Donald Clausing, *Total Quality Development: A Step-by-Step Guide to World-Class Concurrent Engineering* (New York: ASME Press, 1994).

26. See Gary Burchill and Diane Shen, "Concept Engineering: The Key to Operationally Defining Your Customer's Requirements" (Cambridge, Mass.: Center for Quality Management, 1992); Gary Burchill, "Concept Engineering: An Investigation of TIME vs. MARKET Orientation in Product Concept Development," unpublished doctoral thesis, Massachusetts Institute of Technology, Cambridge, Mass., 1993; Gary Burchill, "Concept Engineering: A Complete Product-Concept Decision-Support Process," *Design Management Journal* (Fall 1993): 78–85. See also Gary Burchill and Charles Fine, "Time Versus Market Orientation in Product Concept Development: Empirically-based Theory Generation," *Management Science* 43, no. 4 (April 1997): 465–78.

27. Ulrich and Eppinger provide a similar model in *Product Design and Development*.

28. More complete documentation is available from the Center for Quality Management at (617) 873–8950 or at http://www.cqm.com.

29. KJ diagrams structure detailed language (versus numerical) data into more general conclusions using semantic and abstraction guidelines. They are one of a family of tools invented by Jiro Kawakita and known as the KJ method. See Jiro Kawakita, *The Original KJ Method* (Tokyo: Kawakita Research Institute, 1991).

30. Stuart Pugh, *Total Design* (Workingham, England: Addison-Wesley, 1990); see also idem, "Concept Selection: A Method That Works," International Conference on Engineering Design, Rome, Italy, 1981.

31. For detailed references, see Don Lee, Anna Thornton, and Timothy Cunningham, "Key Characteristics for Agile Product Development and Manufacturing," Agility Forum Fourth Annual Conference Proceedings, March 1995; Don Lee and Anna Thornton, "The Identification and Use of Key Characteristics in the Product Development Process," ASME Eighth Design Theory and Methodology Conference, August 1996; Timothy Cunningham, Don Lee, Ramakrishnan Mantripragada, Anna Thornton, and Daniel Whitney, "Definition, Analysis, and Planning of a Flexible Assembly System," proceedings of the Japan/United States Symposium on Flexible Automation, ASME, June 1996.

32. Lee and Thornton, "The Identification and Use of Key Characteristics."

33. Ibid.

34. This anecdote was related to me by Randy Bollig, director of Corporate Capital Equipment at Intel, July 17, 1997.

35. Geoffrey Parker, "*Contracting for Employee and Supplier Capability Development,*" unpublished dissertation, Massachusetts Institute of Technology, Cambridge, Mass., 1998. Parker discusses the evolution of the economy to more project work and the implications of that change for supply chain relationships.

CHAPTER 11

1. This case study is an abridged version of Jay Burkholder, "The Effect of Industry Dynamics on Supply Chain Strategy for Patient Data Management Products," unpublished paper, course 15.769, Massachusetts Institute of Technology, Cambridge, Mass., 1998.

2. HP in fact started the trend toward unbundled software by leading the patient data monitoring industry in the use of standard hardware. By building systems on industry-standard hardware, leveraging technological advances, and cutting costs, HP increased its advantage; but it was also modularizing the product, shifting the product's value away from the particular hardware provided toward the software itself. Once the industry follows HP's lead, customers will value the system purely by the software and will in many cases be unwilling to pay PMD for anything but the software.

3. This estimate is based on interviews of HP personnel conducted by Burkholder.

4. This Teledesic case study is based primarily on Lance Mansfield, "Teledesic: A Product, Process, and Supply Chain Design Methodology," unpublished thesis, Massachusetts Institute of Technology, Leaders for Manufacturing Program, Cambridge, Mass., May 1998. Jim Miller of Teledesic and Mark Ellis of the Boeing Company contributed greatly to my understanding of the project as well. I have also relied on Lance Mansfield, Doug Bohn, and Doug Fong, "Boeing's Teledesic Project: Dynamic 3-D in Action," unpublished paper, Massachusetts Institute of Technology, Course 15.769, Cambridge, Mass., 1998. See also Thomas Haines, "Teledesic: A Dare on a Deadline," *Seattle Times*, December 7, 1997, pp. A1, A5–6; Seth Schiesel, "Motorola Joins 'Internet in Sky' Project," *New York Times*, May 22, 1998, p. C1.

5. Mansfield, "Teledesic: A Product, Process, and Supply Chain Design Methodology," p. 5.

6. Haines, p. A1.

7. This information is taken from the Teledesic website http://www.teledesic.com/overview/fastfact.html.

8. Mansfield, p. 11.

9. Haines, p. A5.

10. Ibid.

11. Ibid., p. A1.

12. Schiesel, p. C1.

13. Ibid.

14. Ibid.

15. I am indebted to Dan Whitney for this synthesis and imagery (personal communication).

16. Ibid.

CHAPTER 12

1. James F. Moore, *The Death of Competition* (New York: HarperBusiness, 1996), p. 226.

2. Andrew S. Grove, *Only the Paranoid Survive* (New York: Currency Doubleday, 1996), p. 18.

3. In an address to all of Intel's suppliers at Intel Supplier Day in San Francisco in March 1997, Gerry Parker, executive vice president of Intel, provided the consensus Intel forecast that the principal price point for the PC would continue at $2,000 for the foreseeable future.

4. This analysis relies heavily on and borrows from Celia Dieterich, Michelle Eggert, Greg Gunn, Brent Johnson, Nick Purzer, and Chris Schechter, "The Future of Compaq: Analysis Using the Double Helix and 3-D Concurrent Engineering Models," unpublished paper for Course 15.769, Massachusetts Institute of Technology, Cambridge, Mass., 1998 (my course on clockspeed and 3-D concurrent engineering). I have also relied on Todd Cooper, Tina Cortesi, Julie Endress, Charlene Johnson, and Randall Pinkett, "Intel and the Fragmentation of the PC Market," unpublished paper for Course 15.769, Massachusetts Institute of Technology, Cambridge, Mass., 1998. All the authors are 1998 graduates of MIT's Leaders for Manufacturing Program. In addition, discussions with Nitin Joglekar about his doctoral dissertation work, "The Technology Treadmill: Managing Product Performance and Production Ramp-Up in Fast-Paced Industries," Masachusetts Institute of Technology, Cambridge, Mass., Sloan School, 1996, have been most helpful in understanding recent dynamics in the PC industry.

5. Hiawatha Bray and Joann Muller, "Intel's Struggles Boost Alpha Chip: Delay of Merced Gives Digital Chance to Gain Market Share," *Boston Globe,* June 3, 1998, pp. C1, C6.

EPILOGUE

1. For an excellent treatment of this period, see Michael Dertouzos, Richard Lester, and Robert Solow, *Made in America: Regaining the Productive Edge* (Cambridge, Mass.: MIT Press, 1989).

2. David Friedman and Richard Samuels, "How to Succeed Without Really Flying: The Japanese Aircraft Industry and Japan's Technology Ideology," in *Regionalism and Rivalry: Japan and the U.S. in Pacific Asia,* ed. M. Kahler and J. Frankel (Chicago: University of Chicago Press 1993).

3. Tim Jackson, *Inside Intel* (New York: Dutton, 1997), p. 22.

4. Stanley Weiss, Earll Murman, and Daniel Roos, "The Air Force and Industry Think Lean," *Aerospace America*, May 1996.

5. James Womack, Daniel Jones, and Daniel Roos, *The Machine That Changed the World*.

6. I am indebted to my MIT colleague Lester Thurow for making this point to me.

7. Lifetime tenure slows down employee turnover, potentially putting a brake on organizational renewal in universities. However, my observation of tenure at MIT is that it creates hundreds of entrepreneurs and a very flat organization structure. Each entrepreneur can follow his or her own vision with little interference from hierarchical bureaucracies. On balance, this makes universities very vibrant, despite the occasional "deadwood" that is difficult to eliminate.

8. I am indebted to my MIT colleague Dan Roos for making this point to me.

APPENDIX

1. Robert Kaplan, "One Cost System Isn't Enough," *Harvard Business Review* (January–February 1988): 61–66.

2. I am especially grateful to the MIT Leaders for Manufacturing class of 1998 and other students in my course 15.769 (Spring 1998), Massachusetts Institute of Technology, Cambridge, Mass., for contributing their experience to this data.

3. I believe the best systematic research to date in measuring clockspeeds is the Stanford study by Haim Mendelson and Ravindran R. Pillai, "Industry Clockspeed: Measurement and Operational Implications," in *Manufacturing and Service Operations Management* (forthcoming). See also Geoffrey Parker, *Contracting for Employee and Supplier Capability Development*, unpublished dissertation, Massachusetts Institute of Technology, Sloan School, Cambridge, Mass., June 1998.

4. Timothy J. Sturgeon, "*Turnkey Production Networks for Electronics Manufacturing: Industry Organization, Economic Development, and the Rise of the Global Supplier*," unpublished dissertation, Department of Geography, Berkeley, Calif., University of California, 1998.

5. This is the essence of the concepts behind the well-known technology maturity curves in James Utterback and William Abernathy, "A Dynamic Model of Product and Process Innovation," *Omega* 13, no. 6 (1975): 639–56.

INDEX